A DAILY DEVOTIONAL

PRISCILLA DOREMUS

Copyright © 2021 Priscilla Doremus
All rights reserved.

SEVEN BEARS
PUBLISHING

ISBN: 978-1-7361474-2-9 (paperback)
       978-1-7361474-4-3 (hardback)
       978-1-7361474-3-6 (epub)

Scripture quotations are taken from the *Holy Bible*, New Living Translation, copyright ©1996, 2004, 2007 by Tyndale House Foundation. Used by permission of Tyndale House Publishers, Inc., Carol Stream, Illinois 60188. All rights reserved.

DEDICATION

This book is dedicated to you, the reader.
May God bless you as you seek to focus your life on Him.

"So we don't look at the troubles we can see now; rather, we fix our gaze on things that cannot be seen. For the things we see now will soon be gone, but the things we cannot see will last forever."
—*2 Corinthians 4:18*

JANUARY 1

New Lives For Old

"For we died and were buried with Christ by baptism. And just as Christ was raised from the dead by the glorious power of the Father, now we also may live new lives." —Romans 6:4

After packing away the Christmas tree, the lights and other festive goodies, it seems as though there is always a closet or two beckoning to be cleaned out and cleared of unwanted clutter. I never look forward to the task, but know that if I ignore it, the masses behind the closed door will only become harder to conceal and more difficult to clean in the future.

This particular post-Christmas season was no different. It was the same closet as before, the giant one that we like to call "the hidden room" at our house. I couldn't understand how it had gotten so cluttered and filled with junk so quickly! It seemed as though I had just cleaned it out yesterday. Yet, there it was. And, there was no denying the mess that I had created by shoving things away, not dealing with them, and just expecting them to magically disappear—out of sight, out of mind.

Do you have sins in your life that are like that? They seem to be the same ones you've struggled with before. And yet, you often simply close the door on them—hoping they will be hidden and magically disappear.

Just like behind the closet door, our sinful behavior doesn't magically disappear, and it isn't as hidden as we like to think (Can't you see the sock sticking out underneath the door?). The *Holy Bible* says, *"I am watching them closely, and I see every sin. They cannot hope to hide from me"* (Jeremiah 16:17).

I don't always enjoy the process of cleaning out the closet, but I always love the result. The *Holy Bible* says, *"Finally, I confessed all my sins to you and stopped trying to hide my guilt. I said to myself, 'I will confess my rebellion to the Lord.' And you forgave me! All my guilt is gone"* (Psalm 32:5).

This prayer I will pray for you in the coming year, that you will hide God's Word in the closet of your heart, rather than sin. *"I have hidden your word in my heart, that I might not sin against you"* (Psalm 119:11).

May you have the best year you've ever had in your life.

JANUARY 2

Stubborn Stains

"Blessed are those who fear to do wrong, but the stubborn are headed for serious trouble."
—Proverbs 28:14

Do you have a stubborn streak? Romans 2:5 tells us, *"But because you are stubborn and refuse to turn from your sin, you are storing up terrible punishment for yourself. For a day of anger is coming, when God's righteous judgment will be revealed."*

When King Saul turned away from God and refused to follow His plan, the prophet, Samuel, was sent with this message for him, *"Rebellion is as sinful as witchcraft, and stubbornness as bad as worshiping idols. So because you have rejected the command of the Lord, he has rejected you as king"* (I Samuel 15:23).

God's Word reminds us repeatedly that in order to walk in God's favor, we must be obedient to Him. We must yield our will to His.

There is no place for stubbornness in a yielded life. A stubborn heart will prevent us from experiencing God's best. A life bent on sin and having one's own way will end in defeat and destruction.

Proverbs 28:14 tells us, *"Blessed are those who fear to do wrong, but the stubborn are headed for serious trouble."*

Ask God to reveal any areas of stubborn sin in your life. Then, ask Him to help you yield those areas to Him.

May you repent, and may God become master over any area of rebellion that may be invading or controlling your life today.

JANUARY 3

Real Repentance

"For the kind of sorrow God wants us to experience leads us away from sin and results in salvation. There's no regret for that kind of sorrow. But worldly sorrow, which lacks repentance, results in spiritual death." —2 Corinthians 7:10

Repentance. It's not enough to feel bad when we do something wrong. When the bad feeling wears off, we're right back into our sin. That's worldly sorrow. That's the kind of sorrow that leads to death. Why? Because that kind of sorrow doesn't bring about change in our lives.

Godly sorrow is different. Godly sorrow changes us. It says, "I'm not going to do this anymore." Godly sorrow holds no regret, but is joyful about the change that God has wrought in our lives. It is overwhelmed by the goodness of God, and it is focused on Him and only Him.

Real repentance is a turning away from sin. It is a decision to stop sinning. As Jesus said, *"Go and sin no more"* (John 8:11).

Do you *really* long to be close to Christ? Then, dwell on His goodness, repent of your sin, and make it a priority to put Him first in every area of your life.

JANUARY 4

Boundless Generosity

"I am not commanding you, but I want to test the sincerity of your love by comparing it with the earnestness of others. For you know the grace of our Lord Jesus Christ, that though he was rich, yet for your sake he became poor, so that you through his poverty might become rich."
—2 Corinthians 8:8-9

The example of generosity set by Christ is matchless. Anything and everything we give in return doesn't come close to comparing.

Yet, Paul challenges the Church at Corinth to finish what they've started in the way of generous giving, and he reminds them that it is much more blessed to give than to receive. He reminds us that we cannot outgive God.

Malachi 3:10 tells us, *"'Bring the whole tithe into the storehouse, that there may be food in my house. Test me in this,' says the Lord Almighty, 'and see if I will not throw open the floodgates of heaven and pour out so much blessing that there will not be room enough to store it.'"*

When we honor God and are generous in giving—not just with money—He will bless us.

My father tells the story of my grandfather who owned a gas station, which he kept open on Sundays back in the early 1950s in South Carolina. Grand-Daddy claimed he had to stay open on Sundays to make ends meet. My father put a challenge to Grand-Daddy, that if he closed on Sundays and didn't make enough money, my father would make up the difference out of his own pocket. Grand-Daddy accepted the challenge.

By the end of the month, Grand-Daddy had made more money than in any month before. He never opened on Sunday again.

May you put our generous God to the test. He will never let you down.

JANUARY 5

Perfect Gifts

"Every good and perfect gift is from above, coming down from the Father of the heavenly lights, who does not change like shifting shadows. He chose to give us birth through the word of truth, that we might be a kind of firstfruits of all he created." —James 1:17-18

Perfect gifts . . . I remember tagging along with my father as he made hospital visits one evening when I was a teenager. We walked into one particular room in which the church member we had come to see was not there, but was having tests run. Daddy stopped to write a note letting the man know he had come by when a gentleman in the next bed said, "Sir, if you are a pastor, would you pray with me?"

Daddy said, "yes," and began to ask the man why he was there, and if he had a personal relationship with Christ. The man told him why he was there, and said that he didn't believe he had any relationship with Christ. My father very simply explained the plan of salvation while holding the man's hand.

I watched the man as he humbly focused on every word. Tears streamed down his face as he looked up and said, "I never knew it was so simple." Then, he prayed to receive Jesus Christ as his personal Savior.

The perfect gift.

A few days later, my father returned to visit the church member, but this time, the bed next to his was empty. When he inquired as to the man's whereabouts, he learned that the man had passed on.

Perfect gifts . . .

Each day God gives us the gift of communion with Him through prayer, the opportunity to read His Word, fellowship with other believers, sharing the gift of salvation, and the list goes on.

I pray that you and I will unwrap these gifts today, because when we are filled up with Christ, others around us can receive His perfect gifts, as well.

JANUARY 6

Peter's Epiphany

"He said to them, 'But who do you say that I am?' Simon Peter answered and said, 'You are the Christ, the Son of the living God.' Jesus answered and said to him, 'Blessed are you, Simon Bar-Jonah, for flesh and blood has not revealed this to you, but My Father who is in heaven.'" —Matthew 16:15-17

I love this passage of Scripture which illustrates Simon Peter's moment of epiphany with regard to who Jesus really was. It was an "Aha!" moment for Peter. The lightbulb came on.

Jesus had been talking with the Pharisees and Sadducees who demanded that He repeatedly show some miraculous sign as proof of His identity.

Then, Jesus asked the disciples, "But who do you say that I am?" Notice that Jesus asked all of the disciples in His presence, yet only one of them responded. It was Simon Peter. Matthew 16:16 says, *"Simon Peter answered, 'You are the Messiah, the Son of the living God.'"*

Jesus' response is beautiful. He blessed Peter, and acknowledged that no human form had revealed this to him. Peter knew who Jesus was because God had revealed this truth to him. Peter had come to know God.

Peter got it! Do you get it? The God who shone His truth into Peter's heart that day is the same God who shines His truth into your heart today.

May you seek His light to guide you in each decision you make today.

JANUARY 7

It's Not About You

"Then Jesus said to His disciples, 'If anyone desires to come after Me, let him deny himself, and take up his cross, and follow Me. For whoever desires to save his life will lose it, but whoever loses his life for My sake will find it. For what profit is it to a man if he gains the whole world, and loses his own soul? Or what will a man give in exchange for his soul?'" —Matthew 16:24-26

What Jesus tells us to do here isn't popular. It isn't always easy, either.

In fact, our feel good, have-it-all-now society constantly screams just the opposite. It says, "Why deny yourself anything?" "Look out for number one!" Use, abuse, stomp-on . . . just as long as you get what YOU want. It says, "I shouldn't have to put up with . . ."

What society fails to mention is that the death and destruction of your soul is the grand prize at the end.

But, if we desire to follow Christ, we must deny ourselves, seek Him, His kingdom, His will, His plan, His purpose, and there is eternal life with Him as the grand prize.

It's not about you.

It's all about Him.

May you find life in losing yours for Him today.

JANUARY 8

Finding Christ

"Early on Sunday morning, while it was still dark, Mary Magdalene came to the tomb and found that the stone had been rolled away from the entrance. She ran and found Simon Peter and the other disciple, the one whom Jesus loved. She said, 'They have taken the Lord's body out of the tomb, and we don't know where they have put him!'" —John 20:1-2

Have you ever misplaced something precious? Mary Magdalene did. It was very precious. It was something with immeasurable value.

It represented trust. It represented unconditional love. It represented salvation.

That precious something was the body of Christ.

She searched everywhere to find it.

Are you searching everywhere to find Him?

Proverbs 8:17 says, *"I love all who love me. Those who search will surely find me."*

And, in Hebrews 11:6, God promises to reward those who diligently seek Him.

There is nothing in all the world worth finding more than Christ.

May you search frantically to find a close personal relationship with Him today.

JANUARY 9

He Thought Of Everything

"Mary was standing outside the tomb crying, and as she wept, she stooped and looked in. She saw two white-robed angels, one sitting at the head and the other at the foot of the place where the body of Jesus had been lying. 'Dear woman, why are you crying?' the angels asked her. 'Because they have taken away my Lord,' she replied, 'and I don't know where they have put him.'" —John 20:11-13

It's beautiful. The way that God cares for every little detail of our lives—both good and bad—is simply beautiful.

There Mary was, crying, hysterical because she had no idea where Jesus' body had been taken. But God, out of a love that we can't even get our minds around, made provision for Mary. He made provision for her distress by sending two angels to speak to her, to comfort her.

God makes provision for all of us. He provides for our every care, our every concern, our every distress. He does this not only to show His love for us, but so that we can, in turn, care for others.

May you find the provision of Christ in your times of distress, and may you share that same care with someone else today.

JANUARY 10

A Case Of Mistaken Identity

"She turned to leave and saw someone standing there. It was Jesus, but she didn't recognize him. 'Dear woman, why are you crying?' Jesus asked her. 'Who are you looking for?' She thought he was the gardener. 'Sir,' she said, 'if you have taken him away, tell me where you have put him, and I will go and get him.'" —John 20:14-15

Mary thought she knew Him. They had spent so much time together. How could she possibly not recognize Him, her Savior?

Yet, it happened. She mistook Him for someone else.

What about you?

How many times have you failed to recognize Him . . . at work in your life . . . in the life of someone else . . . or, right beside you?

Do you really know and recognize Christ?

John 10:3 says, "*The gatekeeper opens the gate for him, and the sheep recognize his voice and come to him. He calls his own sheep by name and leads them out.*"

May we get to know the person of Jesus Christ so deeply that we never fail to recognize Him.

JANUARY 11

My Great Master

"'Mary!' Jesus said. She turned to him and cried out, 'Rabboni!' 'Don't cling to me,' Jesus said, for I haven't yet ascended to the Father. But go find my brothers and tell them, I am ascending to my Father and your Father, to my God and your God.' Mary Magdalene found the disciples and told them, 'I have seen the Lord!' Then she gave them his message." —John 20:16-18

It's better than any movie scene, any love story you could ever possibly imagine. I can see the scene. Can you?

Jesus calls her name, "Mary." Then, the mix of exhilaration, joy, amazement and love upon her face as she realizes the One she mistook to be the gardener is her Lord, her Savior, her Jesus.

"Rabboni," she calls him, which means, literally, *my great master*[1] in Hebrew. Oh, how she embraces Him with this one word!

It is the greatest love story of all time.

And, it's no fairy tale.

Once upon a time, God sent His one and only son, Jesus, to die on a cross for you and for me. But, death could not hold Him, and He rose from the grave!

And, if we believe and accept Him as our personal Savior, one day we will live happily ever after with Him.

---

1 Scripture Backdrops, *Relevant Historical Insights Into Scripture*, www.bible-history.com.

JANUARY 12

Holy, Holy, Holy

"This letter is from Paul, chosen by the will of God to be an apostle of Christ Jesus, and from our brother Sosthenes. I am writing to God's church in Corinth, to you who have been called by God to be his own holy people. He made you holy by means of Christ Jesus, just as he did for all people everywhere who call on the name of our Lord Jesus Christ, their Lord and ours. May God our Father and the Lord Jesus Christ give you grace and peace." —I Corinthians 1:1-3

In the Book of I Corinthians, Paul reminds the church in Corinth that they have been called by God to be His own holy people. He goes on to remind them how they have been made holy—that it was through Jesus. The entire purpose in His coming was to make us holy.

But, what does it mean to be holy? What does it look like?

Both the Hebrew word *qodesh* and the Greek word *hagios* mean, *to be separated from evil*. When God calls us to be holy, He is calling us to be completely and totally separated from evil. There is only one way that we can do that. It is to be totally and completely dependent upon God. It is to accept His agenda for our life—not our own.

What it looks like is you and me waking up every morning saying, "This is Your day, Lord. Fill me with Your Spirit. I am completely and totally dependent upon You. Guard me and protect me from evil."

The problem faced by the church in Corinth was that they were carnal, ruled by their fleshly, sin nature. They had become self-reliant, not realizing that such self-reliance is sin.

What about you? Are you depending on Christ to separate you from evil? Or, are you allowing self-reliance to creep into your life and rob you of the peace and joy that come from being dependent upon God? Self-reliance can be so subtle, and often we swallow monstrous lies because they're wrapped in one small ounce of truth.

My prayer for you today is that you will spend time in God's Word and in prayer, completely depending upon Him to make you holy.

JANUARY 13

They'll Know We Are Christians

"As soon as Judas left the room, Jesus said, "The time has come for the Son of Man to enter into his glory, and God will be glorified because of him. And since God receives glory because of the Son, he will soon give glory to the Son. Dear children, I will be with you only a little longer. And as I told the Jewish leaders, you will search for me, but you can't come where I am going. So now I am giving you a new commandment: Love each other. Just as I have loved you, you should love each other. Your love for one another will prove to the world that you are my disciples." —John 13:31-35

The well-known hymn, "They'll Know We Are Christians By Our Love," was based on this passage of Scripture. Peter Scholtes, a parish priest, was leading a youth choir out of the Church basement at St. Brendan's on the South Side of Chicago in 1966 when he penned the words and music to this song.

Fr. Scholtes was looking for an appropriate song for a series of ecumenical, interracial events. When he found none, he wrote this song in one day. Clearly, it was a divine appointment.

You have a divine appointment, too. This appointment takes place each and every day of your life and mine. It is an appointment, as the Scripture above tells us, to share the love of Jesus with each and every person we meet. It is how we prove that we are followers of Christ.

We are one in the Spirit, We are one in the Lord
We are one in the Spirit, We are one in the Lord,
And we pray that all unity may one day be restored.
And they'll know we are Christians
by our love, by our love,
Yes they'll know we are Christians by our love.

When people look at your life, do they know that you are a follower of Christ? Do they know that you're a Christian?

May your loving actions speak so loudly that others have no doubt that you are a Christian today.

JANUARY 14

Vengeance Is Mine

"Dear friends, never take revenge. Leave that to the righteous anger of God. For the Scriptures say, "I will take revenge; I will pay them back," says the Lord." —Romans 12:19

This world is an evil, vengeful place. There has even been a television program entitled, *Revenge*. In fact, society places a premium on teaching revenge and paybacks from a very early age.

The world would teach our children that if they do not take revenge and "get back" at others, they are considered weak and pathetic.

But, God's Word says something different. It says that we should never take revenge. It reminds us that God will handle things on our behalf.

I Peter 2:23 reminds us of the example that Christ set on earth when it says, *"He did not retaliate when he was insulted, nor threaten revenge when he suffered. He left his case in the hands of God, who always judges fairly."*

How awesome to know that the creator of the universe, the maker of your very soul is your defense! But, we must wait and pray.

Psalm 37:7 says, *"Be still in the presence of the LORD, and wait patiently for him to act. Don't worry about evil people who prosper or fret about their wicked schemes."*

Have you been wronged? Tempted to take revenge? Don't take matters into your own hands. Leave them in the hands of God.

JANUARY 15

The Proof Is In The Pudding

"Philip said, 'Lord, show us the Father, and we will be satisfied.' Jesus replied, 'Have I been with you all this time, Philip, and yet you still don't know who I am? Anyone who has seen me has seen the Father! So why are you asking me to show him to you? Don't you believe that I am in the Father and the Father is in me? The words I speak are not my own, but my Father who lives in me does his work through me. Just believe that I am in the Father and the Father is in me. Or at least believe because of the work you have seen me do.'" —John 14:8-11

There's an old saying from the 1400s, "the proof of the pudding is in the eating." This saying has been shortened in our day to "the proof is in the pudding," meaning the quality of something can only be proven when it is tested.

In this passage of Scripture, Jesus had already proven Himself. He had performed many miracles. Philip saw him teach publicly and privately. He watched Jesus heal the sick, the lame, the blind—even the dead. The disciples had walked with him and talked with him. They traveled with Him and lived with him. Yet, Philip still wanted more! He had tasted and seen that the Lord was good (Psalm 34:8), but it just wasn't enough.

Are you like Philip? Have you seen the good works of the Lord, and are you still selling Him short? Are you looking for more proof before you give Him complete control in every area of your life?

May you believe in the power and the person of Jesus Christ, and may He become real to you today.

JANUARY 16

Yours For The Asking

"I tell you the truth, anyone who believes in me will do the same works I have done, and even greater works, because I am going to be with the Father. You can ask for anything in my name, and I will do it, so that the Son can bring glory to the Father. Yes, ask me for anything in my name, and I will do it!" —John 14:12-14

What does it mean to ask for something in Jesus name? Does it mean that if I pray and ask God for a new car, that a Maserati will appear in my driveway, neatly wrapped with a bow? Probably not. Does it mean that if I end my prayer with, "In Jesus name" that it will seal my request, and then I'll get what I ask for? No.

Then, what does it mean?

If we examine this passage of Scripture more closely, we see in the second half of verse 13 that our requests will be granted *"so that the Son can bring glory to the Father."*

We also see in verse 12 that we must believe. In addition, I John 5:14 tells us Christ's qualifications for our requests, *"And we are confident that He hears us whenever we ask for anything that pleases Him."*

If we know Him . . . if we are His children, then we know what pleases Him. And, we can ask confidently for anything in His name, and He will do it. Now, that's powerful!

May the power of knowing Christ—REALLY knowing Him—be evident in your life today. And, may it be the best day you've ever had in your life.

JANUARY 17

God's Church

"Now I say to you that you are Peter (which means 'rock'), and upon this rock I will build my church, and all the powers of hell will not conquer it." —Matthew 16:18

Have you ever been frustrated by the conduct and behavior of your local church?

Or, have you ever been in a position to search for a local church to join?

Often the search for Christian fellowship can leave us feeling disoriented and discouraged. Though God's Word tells us not to neglect meeting together (Hebrews 10:25), it can sometimes be difficult to find the true fellowship and encouragement that God intended.

Yet, this passage of Scripture promises us that God's church will continue—the powers of hell will not prevail against it.

This is a wonderful encouragement for the believer. There is a place for you—a body of believers with whom you can and will have fellowship.

May you encourage the believers you know. May you continue meeting together in your local congregation; and, as Hebrews 13:1 tells us, may we, *"Keep on loving each other as brothers and sisters."*

JANUARY 18

The Brevity Of Life

"The brother in humble circumstances ought to take pride in his high position. But the one who is rich should take pride in his low position, because he will pass away like a wild flower. For the sun rises with scorching heat and withers the plant; its blossom falls and its beauty is destroyed. In the same way, the rich man will fade away even while he goes about his business. Blessed is the man who perseveres under trial, because when he has stood the test, he will receive the crown of life that God has promised to those who love him." —James 1:9-12

What are you clinging to today? Does having a large bank account make you feel secure? This passage in James reminds us that we can't take our money with us when we die. But are you still holding on to earthly treasures?

Recently, I had the privilege of learning about raccoons with one of my children. One particularly interesting fact about raccoons is their affinity for shiny objects.

A story we read told of a raccoon that spied a gold watch. When the owner discovered that the raccoon had taken the watch, he pursued the little robber and the spoil. Upon capturing the rascal, the owner found that the raccoon still held the gold watch tightly in its clutches. The raccoon was tranquilized, yet still held the watch in its grasp! Even upon injury, the raccoon held tightly to its prize.

Holding onto things is not necessarily wrong. It is what we hold onto that is often wrong. Are you holding onto something other than God? Like the raccoon, have you refused to release your grip?

The *Holy Bible* says in Hebrews 4:14, *"So then, since we have a great High Priest who has entered heaven, Jesus the Son of God, let us hold firmly to what we believe."*

There is nothing wrong with holding on tightly, as long as whom or what we are holding onto is our faith in the Savior. Do you have a raccoon hold on God?

My prayer is that you will hold tightly to Him—through every trial and temptation that comes your way—so that you may receive the crown of life He has promised to those who love Him.

JANUARY 19

The Goodness Of God

"When tempted, no one should say, 'God is tempting me.' For God cannot be tempted by evil, nor does he tempt anyone; but each one is tempted when, by his own evil desire, he is dragged away and enticed. Then, after desire has conceived, it gives birth to sin; and sin, when it is full-grown, gives birth to death. Don't be deceived, my dear brothers. Every good and perfect gift is from above, coming down from the Father of the heavenly lights, who does not change like shifting shadows. He chose to give us birth through the word of truth, that we might be a kind of firstfruits of all he created." —James 1:13-18

Once upon a time, in the Kitchen of Eden, Mother was preparing a feast. The kitchen counters were filled with plates, and each plate contained the most mouth-watering, delectable dishes imaginable. There was only one dish in the middle of the island that was forbidden—the plate of giant chocolate chip cookies. "From this dish," Mother said to the two children, "you shall not eat or you will receive a spanking." The children nodded in understanding, and Mother went off to do laundry.

Meanwhile, in slithered the neighbor child from next door. "Wow! Check out the spread. And, get a load of those cookies," said the neighbor child as she gazed at the kitchen dishes. "Mom said we'll get a spanking if we eat the cookies, but we can have anything else we want," said the son.

"Your mom won't spank you," said the neighbor child. "She's a big softy. She doesn't mean it."

The son ate a giant chocolate chip cookie, and handed one to his sister. The neighbor child heard her mother calling and ran home.

Just then, Mother finished folding laundry and called for the children, but they were hiding. "I see cookie crumbs," she said, following the crumbs upstairs to the children. "And, why is there chocolate all over your lips?" she said to her daughter.

"My brother gave me a cookie and I ate it," she said. "The neighbor child told me I wouldn't get a spanking, so I ate a cookie," said the son.

Mother was very disappointed. She gave both of the children a spanking, and they went to bed with a very bad tummy ache as a result of their disobedience.

The moral of the story? God never tempts us. Our own evil, selfish, prideful desires lead us into sin. God gives only good things. We need only open our eyes to see the feast of blessings He surrounds us with. His loving laws serve only to protect us.

And, He will never change. He is the same yesterday, today, and forever.

Oh, how He loves you and me.

JANUARY 20

Doers Of The Word

"Do not merely listen to the word, and so deceive yourselves. Do what it says. Anyone who listens to the word but does not do what it says is like a man who looks at his face in a mirror and, after looking at himself, goes away and immediately forgets what he looks like. But the man who looks intently into the perfect law that gives freedom, and continues to do this, not forgetting what he has heard, but doing it—he will be blessed in what he does."
—James 1:22-25

When any athlete prepares to run a race, there is a great deal of effort required in order to win. There is intense training—often accompanied by pain. A commitment is required. The runner must prepare his mind. And, he must also have endurance.

The Christian walk is no different. The *Holy Bible* says, *"Therefore, since we are surrounded by such a huge crowd of witnesses to the life of faith, let us strip off every weight that slows us down, especially the sin that so easily trips us up. And let us run with endurance the race God has set before us"* (Hebrews 12:1).

The Nike Corporation is famous for its marketing slogan, "Just do it." This slogan not only encompasses the philosophy of sports legends, like Michael Johnson, but it is the ideal of the Christian walk, as well. The *Holy Bible* tells us, *"Don't you realize that in a race everyone runs, but only one person gets the prize? So run to win"* (I Corinthians 9:24)!

God doesn't want us to make excuses for not doing what is right. He wants us to *just do it*.

What has God called you to do? Whatever it is, I'm praying that you will have focus, drive, determination, and the endurance to get it done. I'm praying that you will *just do it*—joyfully!

JANUARY 21

Purity Of The Tongue

"If anyone considers himself religious and yet does not keep a tight rein on his tongue, he deceives himself and his religion is worthless. Religion that God our Father accepts as pure and faultless is this: to look after orphans and widows in their distress and to keep oneself from being polluted by the world." —James 1:26-27

Do you ever feel as though you have foot-in-mouth disease? Me, too. Sometimes the words hang like a cartoon bubble in the air—a cartoon bubble that I wish could be taken back. But, the damage has already been done. Other times, the words shoot out of my mouth like a bazooka firing at close range—taking out the unwitting victim before they even know what's happened to them.

But, God's Word provides both the cause and the cure for Foot-in-Mouth disease. The cause is an impure heart, for out of the abundance of the heart the mouth speaks (Matthew 12:34). And, the cure is purification of our heart. How do we get a pure heart? We gain a pure heart by living in accordance with God's Word (Psalm 19:8).

My prayer for you is that you would remove the pollution from your heart, mind and soul today, and that this would be the best day you've ever had in your life.

JANUARY 22

Are You A Doubter

"As he traveled through Galilee, he came to Cana, where he had turned the water into wine. There was a government official in nearby Capernaum whose son was very sick. When he heard that Jesus had come from Judea to Galilee, he went and begged Jesus to come to Capernaum to heal his son, who was about to die. Jesus asked, 'Will you never believe in me unless you see miraculous signs and wonders?'" —John 4:46-48

I have to admit it, I have often struggled with being a *doubting Thomas*. If I were a man, I would have been Thomas, that one of the twelve who said in John 20:25, *"I won't believe it unless I see the nail wounds in his hands, put my fingers into them, and place my hand into the wound in his side."*

I would have been Peter in Matthew 14:30 when he walked on the water, but was scared by the wind and waves and shouted, *"Save me, Lord!"* I have done this so many times in life. Yet, the *Holy Bible* tells us in Hebrews 11:6 that, *"it is impossible to please God without faith."* Over and over again in Scripture we find the admonition that Christ gave to Thomas in John 20:27, *"Don't be faithless any longer. Believe!"*

Many times in life when facing challenges, I have prayed this simple prayer, "Help my unbelief." (Mark 9:24) Each time I have prayed that prayer, God has answered by strengthening my faith in ways I could never imagine. This begs the question Jesus asks above, *"Will you never believe unless you see miraculous signs and wonders?"* How many times will we require Him to demonstrate His love for us before we finally believe the substance of who Christ really is?

May you have the faith to believe that Jesus Christ is beyond able to care for your every need today and every day that follows.

JANUARY 23

In His Time

"The Lord isn't really being slow about his promise, as some people think. No, he is being patient for your sake. He does not want anyone to be destroyed, but wants everyone to repent."
—2 Peter 3:9

I don't know about you, but I tend to be a clock-watcher. In my own self-centered mind, it's just so that I can make the most of the time God has granted me. However, in an effort to make the most of the time, I often become impatient and allow my own personal schedule to override things that are more important, but aren't scheduled. Are you ever like that?

The desire to have God cater to our schedule and agenda indicates we know only a small portion of His character. But, if we knew Him fully, we would not be in such a rush for God to meet our schedule, knowing that He is beyond capable of resolving any situation and meeting any need—better than we could possibly imagine.

When we trust Him fully, we are able to rest in Him completely.

Do you try to rush God into action with your prayers? Just remember that His timing is perfect—never too fast or too slow.

May you adjust to God's timetable today, and may resting in His timing fill you with complete peace.

JANUARY 24

No Excuses

"When the king heard what was written in the Law, he tore his clothes in despair. Then he gave these orders to Hilkiah, Ahikam son of Shaphan, Acbor son of Micaiah, Shaphan the court secretary, and Asaiah the king's personal adviser: 'Go to the Temple and speak to the Lord for me and for all the remnant of Israel and Judah. Inquire about the words written in the scroll that has been found. For the Lord's great anger has been poured out on us because our ancestors have not obeyed the word of the Lord. We have not been doing everything this scroll says we must do.'" —2 Chronicles 34:19-21

I still remember my father's words. "Ignorance of the law is no excuse," he said. I was learning to drive at the age of fifteen and rolled through a right-turn-on-red without coming to a complete stop.

"I'm sorry. I didn't know," I said. His words echoed back again to remind me, "Ignorance of the law is no excuse."

"Yes, sir," I said, wanting desperately to please. But wanting to please wasn't enough.

The king in our passage of Scripture wanted desperately to please, too. He had just found out what was written in God's law and discovered that the people had not been obedient to all of God's commands. His ignorance of the law was no excuse, and he tore his clothes in despair. He had a heart that longed to be obedient to God.

What about you? Do you have a heart that longs to please God? Have you read His Word to discover what He requires of you?

May you not only learn what is pleasing to Him, but may you do everything that He requires.

JANUARY 25

A Good Reputation

"So Hilkiah and the other men went to the New Quarter of Jerusalem to consult with the prophet Huldah. She was the wife of Shallum son of Tikvah, son of Harhas the keeper of the Temple wardrobe." —2 Chronicles 34:22

Have you ever given any thought to your reputation? To how others view you? Your life?

Huldah was a prophetess who lived in the New Quarter of Jerusalem. She had a great reputation. She was known as someone who had a close personal relationship with God. Her reputation was so good that Hilkiah and the other men sent by the king knew they could count on her. They knew the king could count on her, too.

What about you?

How do others view you? Do you have a good reputation? Are you known as someone who has a close personal relationship with God? Can others count on you to deliver? What's more, can the King of Kings count on you?

The *Holy Bible* tells us in Proverbs 22:1, *"A good name is more desirable than great riches; to be esteemed is better than silver or gold."*

May you examine your heart and life before Christ, line it up with His Word, and make the necessary adjustments to improve your reputation today.

JANUARY 26

Pay Day Someday

"She said to them, 'The Lord, the God of Israel, has spoken! Go back and tell the man who sent you, 'This is what the Lord says: I am going to bring disaster on this city and its people. All the curses written in the scroll that was read to the king of Judah will come true. For my people have abandoned me and offered sacrifices to pagan gods, and I am very angry with them for everything they have done. My anger will be poured out on this place, and it will not be quenched.'" —2 Chronicles 34:23-25

The late Pastor R. G. Lee of Memphis, Tennessee is well-known for a sermon he preached over 1,200 times entitled, *Pay Day Someday*. To sum it up, the sermon reminds us that there will come a day of reckoning for all of us. We will be judged by God Almighty for our actions and inactions on this Earth—whether righteous or unrighteous.

In today's passage of Scripture, the prophetess, Huldah, tells of Israel's day of reckoning for the evil they have done—for their continued disobedience. Disaster and curses were promised to those who abandoned God and turned away from Him.

God is true to His Word. But, He is also rich in mercy, not wanting anyone to perish, but all to come to repentance (2 Peter 3:9). He longs for our return to Him, with repentant hearts.

May we live a life that looks forward to our Pay Day Someday, following Christ every day for the rest of our days—and finishing strong.

JANUARY 27

Renewed Vows

*"Then the king summoned all the elders of Judah and Jerusalem. And the king went up to the Temple of the L*ORD *with all the people of Judah and Jerusalem, along with the priests and the Levites—all the people from the greatest to the least. There the king read to them the entire Book of the Covenant that had been found in the L*ORD*'s Temple. The king took his place of authority beside the pillar and renewed the covenant in the L*ORD*'s presence. He pledged to obey the L*ORD *by keeping all his commands, laws, and decrees with all his heart and soul. He promised to obey all the terms of the covenant that were written in the scroll."*
—2 Chronicles 34:29-31

After twenty-three years, some cobwebs had grown and closets needed cleaning out in my parents' marriage. Our family was attending the Southern Baptist Convention, and pastors and their wives were being given the opportunity to renew their marriage vows.

My father didn't want anything to do with the idea, stating, "I meant it the first time," and, "I'm still here! What more do you want?"

My mother really wanted to do it. "Time can play tricks on the memory, Lindsey," she said. "It might be good to revisit what we agreed to do 23 years ago. Do you even remember our vows?"

Finally, reluctantly, my father agreed to renewing his wedding vows with my mother. I watched my father's face as he said the words to my mother. It was different than when he had been a young man, a starry-eyed dreamer, untainted by the trials and tribulations of life. He understood better the meaning behind the words he vowed before God and these witnesses. It was the same for my mother.

Now, after over fifty years of marriage, they are each glad they had the refresher.

The king in this passage of Scripture wanted to sweep out the cobwebs in the hearts of the people in Judah and Jerusalem. He read the entire Book of the Covenant aloud to them. It was, no doubt, an awakening for the people . . . a chance for all of them to recommit their lives to the Lord . . . an opportunity to solidify their union . . . a reminder of what God requires and desires.

What about you? Have you recommitted your life to Christ today? The *Holy Bible* tells us we are to take up our cross daily and follow Him (Luke 9:23).

May you renew your commitment to Christ today.

JANUARY 28

Hold The Sugar

"Our father died in the wilderness," they said. "He was not among Korah's followers, who rebelled against the Lord; he died because of his own sin. But he had no sons. Why should the name of our father disappear from his clan just because he had no sons? Give us property along with the rest of our relatives." —Numbers 27:3-4

Are you a *sugarcoater*? You know the type. Southerners are famous for it. We can sugarcoat anything. It's considered a special gift sometimes—being able to take the most awful of circumstances or sins, and smother them with sugar until they seem sweet, lovely, even heart-warming. As a child, my momma could sugarcoat Thursday night meatloaf to the point that it sounded like filet mignon. But, it still tasted like Thursday night meatloaf.

I have to tell you—I don't have the gift at all. Sugarcoating is not my specialty. I believe in calling a spade a spade, the direct approach, telling it like it is. That's what I love about this passage of Scripture. Zelophehad's daughters don't sugarcoat a thing. They acknowledge who their father was, and that he died because of his own sin. Then, they plainly, openly, and honestly lay out their request before Moses and the other leaders. The *Holy Bible* tells us in Psalm 51:6, *"But you desire honesty from the womb, teaching me wisdom even there."*

God wants us to hold the sugar.

Like Zelophehad's daughters, He wants us to communicate honestly and directly with Him. After all, He knows when it's Thursday night meatloaf, and not filet mignon.

May God hear and answer your requests, as you communicate openly and honestly with Him today.

JANUARY 29

Perfect Justice

"So Moses brought their case before the Lord. And the Lord replied to Moses, 'The claim of the daughters of Zelophehad is legitimate. You must give them a grant of land along with their father's relatives. Assign them the property that would have been given to their father.'"
—Numbers 27:5-7

The pounding gavel echoed through the courtroom as the judge took his seat. "This court is now in session. Ladies and gentlemen of the jury, have you reached a verdict?"

"We have, your Honor. We, the jury, find the defendant not guilty."

A gasp lingers throughout the courtroom. "How can this be?" one person whispers. "What?" another says in a low voice. A family sobs on one side of the courtroom, quietly clinging to each other, dismayed by the miscarriage of justice.

Sadly, it has become an all-too-familiar scene.

But, with God, things are different. His justice is perfect. In the passage of Scripture today, Moses brings the request of Zelophehad's daughters before the Lord. The Lord declares the claim legitimate and issues His pronouncement of justice. Victory for the daughters of Zelophehad!

How wonderful to know that one day there will be no more miscarriages of justice—God's perfect justice will reign supreme!

May you rest in the hope and the promise of God's perfect justice in your life today.

JANUARY 30

A Clean Slate

"Create in me a clean heart, O God, and renew a steadfast spirit within me." —Psalm 51:10

As a child in school, I loved to clean the chalkboard at the end of the school day. My fifth-grade teacher would choose two students each day to erase the blackboards and then dust the erasers outside. We took great pleasure in rubbing off every speck from the boards, and then banging the erasers together outside with all of our might, until there wasn't an ounce of chalk dust remaining.

There was something about a clean slate, ready for a new day, starting over.

There is something about a clean slate in life, too.

As this year unfolds, I reflect on the past year. There are things I'd like to do differently, mistakes made, opportunities missed, a heart that needs cleaning out.

This year, instead of all the New Year's Resolutions, I will pray as David did. I will ask God to create a clean heart in me, and to renew a steadfast spirit within me.

Do you need a clean slate? Pray with me, as David did.

I know that God will answer.

JANUARY 31

Out Of Balance

"A false balance is an abomination to the LORD, but a just weight is His delight."
—Proverbs 11:1

Have you ever driven a car with one low tire? This week as I was driving the kids to school, I noticed the "your tires are in trouble" light on my dashboard. As usual, I was in a hurry with no spare time for tire checking, so I kept going. I couldn't tell a difference in the ride as I drove.

But, the warning light was there.

A day later, and the out-of-balance light was still on. I had done nothing about it. I looked at the tires, and couldn't see a difference in them. Still in a hurry, I decided to wait until I had more time on the weekend, and continued on to work.

Leaving work the next day, I came out to find one nearly flat tire on my car. Why was I surprised?

The warning light had been on, yet I chose to ignore it.

Often when our lives become unbalanced, we choose to ignore the blaring warning light flashing in front of us, saying, "Fix this now! Before it's too late!"

Yet, all too often we continue on, full speed ahead, into disaster.

And then . . . we wonder why. It happens because our hearts are hard and we're out of fellowship with Christ. Our God-given consciences have been ignored so long that they're of little use to us anymore.

But, God can make all things new . . . even cold, hardened hearts and seared consciences.

Won't you ask Him to do just that for you today?

FEBRUARY 1

Choosing The Best

"This is what the LORD says—your Redeemer, the Holy One of Israel: 'I am the LORD your God, who teaches you what is best for you, who directs you in the way you should go.'"
—Isaiah 48:17

Do you ever have trouble making choices? Sometimes I don't see the long term results of choices I make.

Do you ever have difficulty choosing what is best?

This verse promises us that we have a God who teaches us what is best for us, and He directs us in the way we should go. If we are having difficulty making good choices, it is because we are out of fellowship with our loving Heavenly Father.

Psalm 32:8 tells us, *"The Lord says, "I will guide you along the best pathway for your life. I will advise you and watch over you."*

God wants us to make the best choices, and He will show us exactly what those are, if we will only spend time with Him through Bible study and prayer.

May you grow in fellowship with your Heavenly Father today, and may He guide you along the best pathway for your life—now and forever.

FEBRUARY 2

Bye-Bye Bottle

"Dear brothers and sisters, when I was with you I couldn't talk to you as I would to spiritual people. I had to talk as though you belonged to this world or as though you were infants in the Christian life. I had to feed you with milk, not with solid food, because you weren't ready for anything stronger. And you still aren't ready, for you are still controlled by your sinful nature. You are jealous of one another and quarrel with each other. Doesn't that prove you are controlled by your sinful nature? Aren't you living like people of the world? When one of you says, 'I am a follower of Paul,' and another says, 'I follow Apollos,' aren't you acting just like people of the world?" —I Corinthians 3:1-4

Have you ever noticed that most babies don't give up their bottles without a fight?

The bottle is so familiar to the baby. The baby often associates the bottle with security. They do not want to lose that feeling of security. Change is hard for them. They cry, scream, wail, carry on, and will even try to sneak the bottle back if they can find a way.

But, staying on the bottle is not in the baby's best interest. It will rob the baby of precious nutrients necessary for growth and development. That's why parents must go through the painful task of transitioning their precious children from milk to solid food.

Christians are often the same way. We don't like change, either. When God calls us off the bottle and into something new for our spiritual growth and development, we cry, scream, wail, and carry on, too. We like the familiar. It is comfortable for us.

The change, the growth, can be scary if we're not trusting and depending on God.

God, out of love for us, must go through the painful task of transitioning us, too. As Christians, we are to put our faith and trust in God, knowing that whatever He puts us through is in our best interest, and it will bring glory and honor to Him.

Thanks be to God who carries us no matter how scary life becomes.

FEBRUARY 3

Believe

"Then Jesus told him, 'Go back home. Your son will live!' And the man believed what Jesus said and started home." —John 4:50

Oswald Chambers wrote, "What we need more of is not more doing, it is more believing."

The *Holy Bible* tells us, *"Abram believed the Lord, and he credited it to him as righteousness"* (Genesis 15:6).

And, John 16:9 tells us, *"The world's sin is that it refuses to believe in me."*

What about you? When God speaks to your heart quietly while you read His Word each day, do you believe Him?

Simply believe.

May you listen and believe Him today. And, may you act upon that belief, just like the man in this passage of Scripture did—he started home.

Only believe.

FEBRUARY 4

A God Thing

"While the man was on his way, some of his servants met him with the news that his son was alive and well. He asked them when the boy had begun to get better, and they replied, 'Yesterday afternoon at one o'clock his fever suddenly disappeared!'" —John 4:51-52

It was a *God thing*. *God things* are those things that only God can do. You can almost hear the man whisper the time under his breath as his servants tell him what time his son began to get better.

When I was sixteen, my father accepted a pastoral position in Canada. It was heart-breaking to me because it didn't fit the plan I had. But God had a different plan for me, and He was using this circumstance to catapult me to Baylor University a year early. In two days' time, I went from being a junior in high school to a college freshman at age sixteen. It was truly a *God thing*.

God is still doing things in us and around us every moment of every day that only He can do. May you believe this truth and look expectantly for *God things* to happen in your own life every day.

FEBRUARY 5

It's All About Him

"Then the father realized that that was the very time Jesus had told him, 'Your son will live.' And he and his entire household believed in Jesus. This was the second miraculous sign Jesus did in Galilee after coming from Judea." —John 4:53-54

Jesus did it. He came through for the man in this passage of Scripture and answered his request with a miracle. This miracle caused the official and his entire household to believe in Jesus. We still experience the miracles of God in and around us every day. These miracles are used to bring glory and honor to God, and to draw others to a saving relationship with Him.

Several years ago, I was diagnosed with a brain tumor and given two years to live. God has performed a miracle in my life by allowing me to live and share His good news with others. I get so excited about it that I just want to shout sometimes.

How about you? If you have a personal relationship with Jesus Christ, that is a miracle in and of itself! Won't you share it with someone today?

I pray that the light of Christ will burn brightly in your life, and that you would share Him with everyone you meet today.

FEBRUARY 6

Free Radicals

"So if the Son sets you free, you will be free indeed." —John 8:36

Jesus came to earth preaching a radical new doctrine. That doctrine was to *love one another*—really love them. There is a freedom in this gospel, this good news of God's love. It breaks down barriers and redefines the letter of the law. It puts God and others before anything we desire, any personal agenda, any selfish pursuit.

I John 4:17-18 tells us, *"And as we live in God, our love grows more perfect. So we will not be afraid on the day of judgment, but we can face him with confidence because we live like Jesus here in this world. Such love has no fear, because perfect love expels all fear. If we are afraid, it is for fear of punishment, and this shows that we have not fully experienced his perfect love."*

Are you a free radical? If not, I pray you will discover what it means to have the freedom to really love others—with reckless abandon, and without fear.

May God drive away all doubt and fear from your life through the fulfillment of His perfect love in you.

FEBRUARY 7

Practice Makes Perfect

"Keep putting into practice all you learned and received from me—everything you heard from me and saw me doing. Then the God of peace will be with you." —Philippians 4:9

"Mom, do we have to practice the piano today?" That is a question I hear almost daily from my two children, to which I usually respond, "How do you expect to get any better if you don't practice?"

Anything we want to improve in, we practice, don't we? If you want to be a faster runner, you practice. If you want to be a better musician, you practice. Becoming a better swimmer requires practice, too.

Our walk with Christ is no different. If we want our faith to be strengthened, we must practice using it! If we want to be obedient to Christ, we must practice saying, "no" to sin. Want to be holy? Practice holiness. As each area grows and becomes stronger, the practice will become more challenging—just like anything else in life.

But, don't give up, and don't quit. For in due season we will reap, if we do not lose heart (Galatians 6:9).

May we practice all that God has taught us in His Word today.

FEBRUARY 8

The Power Of Compassion

"When the Lord saw her, his heart overflowed with compassion. 'Don't cry!' he said."
—*Luke 7:13*

Compassion is a very powerful force. If you have experienced it, you know this to be true. Perhaps you were in need of a job and someone gave you a chance when you weren't qualified for the position. Or, maybe someone gave you a strong hug at a time when you felt all hope was gone. Whatever the circumstance, to be on the receiving end of compassion is a pretty amazing thing.

The story of Jesus showing compassion to a woman who lost her only son in Luke 7:11-15 is pretty amazing, too. In this passage of Scripture, we find Jesus watching the funeral procession for this young man. When He saw the mother, Jesus was so moved with compassion for her that the Scripture tells us, *"Then he walked over to the coffin and touched it, and the bearers stopped. 'Young man,' he said, 'I tell you, get up.' Then the dead boy sat up and began to talk! And Jesus gave him back to his mother."*

You may not bring someone back from the grave, but the compassion you share through a hug, a kind word, or some other compassionate act may very well save someone's life—and you may never even realize it.

My prayer for you is that you would look past your own circumstances to show compassion to someone in need today.

Luke 6:36 says, *"You must be compassionate, just as your Father is compassionate."*

May showing compassion make this the best day you've ever had in your life.

FEBRUARY 9

Jack Be Nimble

"Unfailing love and faithfulness make atonement for sin. By fearing the LORD, people avoid evil." —Proverbs 16:6

Do you remember this nursery rhyme?

JACK BE NIMBLE[2]

Jack, be nimble,
Jack, be quick,
Jack, jump over
the candlestick.

Jack jumped high
Jack jumped low
Jack jumped over
and burned his toe.

Jack tried everything to avoid being burned in this nursery rhyme, yet he still ended up burning his toe. That's the problem with fire. If we play with it, we're going to end up getting burned. In our lives, sin is like fire. If we play with it, we're going to get burned—no matter how nimble or quick we think we are. If I were re-writing *Jack Be Nimble* to show what God can do for Jack, it would go something like this:

Jack be faithful,
cut the wick.
Jack, stay away
from the candlestick.

Jack kept praying.
Jack said "no."
Jack was unscathed
from his head to his toe.

God can protect you from the fire of sin, too. All you have to do is trust Him and say, "no" to sin.

---

[2] Author unknown.

FEBRUARY 10

A Pure Heart

"To the pure, all things are pure, but to those who are corrupted and do not believe, nothing is pure. In fact, both their minds and consciences are corrupted." —Titus 1:15

I love this verse. It reminds me of children . . . of the beautiful innocence in their eyes, the way that they trust without questioning. They believe. They haven't been hurt, calloused, and corrupted by the cold, cruel, sinful world.

This verse also reminds me of the change that happens when Christ comes and lives inside us. It really is as though we are *born again*. We become like that fresh, pure, innocent child—uncorrupted by the world and believing!

If you haven't asked God to come and live inside your heart and life, pray and ask Him to come in today. He will purify your heart and make you brand new.

If you need Him to purify your heart and life because you've allowed sin to have a stronghold there, God can give you back a pure and undefiled heart. But, you must relinquish the sin you are holding to. You must give it up and choose God's way.

This is my prayer for you, and that you would have a clean, pure conscience before God.

FEBRUARY 11

Heaven-Minded

"So remember this and keep it firmly in mind: The Lord is God both in heaven and on earth, and there is no other." —Deuteronomy 4:39

Have you ever heard the saying, "Don't be so heaven-minded that you're no earthly good"? I've heard it many times over the years, but if we examine God's Word, we find there is no truth to this saying.

In truth, the only way to be any good on this earth at all, is to be heaven-minded.

2 Corinthians 4:18 tells us, *"So we don't look at the troubles we can see now; rather, we fix our gaze on things that cannot be seen. For the things we see now will soon be gone, but the things we cannot see will last forever."*

Colossians 3:2 says it so plainly, *"Think about the things of heaven, not the things of earth."*

It is only by fixing our eyes and thoughts on heaven that we can be of any earthly good at all. Heaven-thinking causes us to shift our focus past our temporary, earthly struggles. These things no longer consume us. We consider the needs of others more, and we find it easier to trust and obey Christ.

May you fix your heart and mind on heaven today, that your life may be used for much earthly good.

FEBRUARY 12

Fine China

"But who are you, O man, to talk back to God? Shall what is formed say to him who formed it, 'Why did you make me like this?' Does not the potter have the right to make out of the same lump of clay some pottery for noble purposes and some for common use?" —Romans 9:20-21

While taking a piece of fine china from my kitchen cabinet recently, I was struck by the beauty of the plate. It was a special occasion, and the dish was just exactly what I needed, though I had not used it in quite a long time.

As the plate lingered in my hands, I was reminded of how God often waits for just the right occasion to use us, too. He doesn't leave us on the shelf forever. He doesn't really leave us on the shelf at all.

Do you ever feel as though you have gifts that no one ever sees? Do you feel you have gifts that may never be used by God?

Take heart, friend. God sees your beauty. He sees each gift He has bestowed upon you. And, He will use your life at just the right time, and for just the right purpose, if only you will surrender it all to Him.

FEBRUARY 13

Are You Ready?

"Instead, you must worship Christ as Lord of your life. And if someone asks about your Christian hope, always be ready to explain it." —I Peter 3:15

Sometime back, the media made a great deal about a pastor in Florida who planned to burn the Quran in opposition to its beliefs—which are in stark contrast to the Christian faith. I doubt this pastor ever thought his decision would receive the type of international publicity it garnered.

But, what about you? And, what about me? Are we ready to stand and face a jeering, fault-finding world for our faith? Or, are we content to sit back on the sofa and mock with the rest of the world?

In I Kings 19, Elijah had torn down the Asherah poles and killed all of the prophets of Baal. Jezebel, the evil queen, was after him. He was scared, and ran into the wilderness asking God to take his life. He ended up traveling forty days and forty nights to Mount Sinai where he hid in a cave. There was a cost involved in Elijah's obedience. There is a cost associated with our obedience, too.

This brings us back to the original question: Will you be standing in the crowd yelling "crucify Him" with the rest of the world? Or, are you be willing to face rejection, hatred, and even death to be the only one in the crowd following Christ?

In Luke 14:28, Jesus says of the Christian walk, *"But don't begin until you count the cost. For who would begin construction of a building without first calculating the cost to see if there is enough money to finish it?"*

Have you counted the cost of a life committed to following Christ? The cost may be high, but the investment has eternal rewards, with interest rates no bank could ever match.

May you always be ready to explain your Christian hope to others, and may you be the one to do what is right when no one else will.

FEBRUARY 14

Guard Your Heart

"Guard your heart above all else, for it determines the course of your life." —*Proverbs 4:23*

What does it mean for us to guard our heart?

It means that we are to protect our heart from things that would harm or corrupt it. We must keep our hearts pure in order to discover God's best for our lives.

Guarding our heart also means that we are to be faithful in all our relationships.

Are you guarding your heart, and keeping it pure?

Are you faithful to your spouse and to God?

Consider the lengths we go to in guarding important papers, stocks, bonds, jewelry, cars, precious metals, and the like. Yet, your heart is infinitely more valuable than these things.

Proverbs 4:13 says, *"Take hold of my instructions; don't let them go. Guard them, for they are the key to life."*

And, Proverbs 13:6 tells us, *"Godliness guards the path of the blameless, but the evil are misled by sin."*

Today, I pray that together we will guard our hearts above all else in order that God's purposes may be established in them.

FEBRUARY 15

Love's Perfect Timing

"Promise me, O women of Jerusalem, by the gazelles and wild deer, not to awaken love until the time is right." —Song of Solomon 2:7

There has been much conflicting commentary written about this passage of Scripture.

Some believe it is a picture of the place of peace and love Christ has in fellowship with His bride, the Church, and that the meaning is that we are not to disturb this fellowship with our own impatience. But, in fact, we are to rest in God's timing for all things.

Still others believe this verse depicts the charge given to the young, immature believer impetuously clamoring for the action and attention of the Heavenly Father, not allowing patience to have its perfect work in the believer's life.

Regardless of whether these two thoughts or still another is your belief, this verse warns us about the delicate nature of relationships. The care and patience required in maintaining true communion with another is not to be taken lightly, and it is not to be rushed.

We must wait for God's timing in all things.

Are you waiting for God's perfect timing?

Have you stirred up or awakened love before its proper time?

May we seek God when it comes to love's perfect timing in every area of our lives—today and every day.

FEBRUARY 16

The Partner

"I always thank my God for you and for the gracious gifts he has given you, now that you belong to Christ Jesus. Through him, God has enriched your church in every way—with all of your eloquent words and all of your knowledge. This confirms that what I told you about Christ is true. Now you have every spiritual gift you need as you eagerly wait for the return of our Lord Jesus Christ. He will keep you strong to the end so that you will be free from all blame on the day when our Lord Jesus Christ returns. God will do this, for he is faithful to do what he says, and he has invited you into partnership with his Son, Jesus Christ our Lord."
—*I Corinthians 1:4-9*

Imagine an invitation. The invitation is to join a partnership. The partner has unlimited resources. He will provide everything you need. The partner promises never to leave you or forsake you.

He promises to give you enough strength to get the job done.

The partner promises not to overwork you, and to give you the rest you need. He has a proven track record, too. He never lies.

This partner will even lay down His life for you.

And, He has.

Will you accept the invitation to this partnership? If so, will you do the job half-heartedly, or whole-heartedly?

I pray that you will not hold anything back from this best Partner, but will choose to commit everything to Him today.

FEBRUARY 17

Joyfully Content

"Now godliness with contentment is great gain." —I Timothy 6:6

Many times a lack of contentment can lead us into activities and pursuits which cause emotional distress in our lives. There is a story in 2 Kings 14 about a king with just such a problem.

King Amaziah of Judah suffered from a lack of contentment. He was a young man who had been successful in battle, having proudly conquered and defeated two neighboring kingdoms. He was on a roll.

Armed and freshly victorious, King Amaziah sent a message challenging his much larger neighbor, King Jehoash of Israel. Listen to King Jehoash reply to King Amaziah of Judah in 2 Kings 14:10, *"You have indeed defeated Edom, and you are very proud of it. But be content with your victory and stay at home! Why stir up trouble that will only bring disaster on you and the people of Judah?"*

Much like you and I, King Amaziah refused to listen to the warning of his wise neighbor, King Jehoash, bringing great destruction on Judah and the capture of King Amaziah.

King Amaziah forgot who gave him the victory. He didn't listen when God sent a messenger to warn him of impending disaster if he continued in his own strength. King Amaziah suffered from a lack of contentment.

Do you suffer from a lack of contentment? Sometimes God calls us to rest, trust, and become content that He is working everything to bring about good in our lives—some way, somehow.

May you trust, completely content in Him today.

FEBRUARY 18

Knowing My Purpose

"So I run with purpose in every step. I am not just shadowboxing." —I Corinthians 9:26

God created each and every one of us for a very special purpose. Proverbs 16:4 tells us, *"The Lord has made everything for his own purposes, even the wicked for a day of disaster."* He has a plan for your life.

But, that doesn't mean that we can or should go about living our lives without any thought because God is our great puppet master in the heavens. No, the Holy Bible clearly tells us in John 10:10, *"The thief's purpose is to steal and kill and destroy. My purpose is to give them a rich and satisfying life."*

We are in the midst of a spiritual battle. God longs to give us victory over sin and death, but there is a thief among us—a wolf. Many times he dresses in sheep's clothing and we fail to recognize him.

God's purpose is that none of us should perish, but that all should come to know Him. We are all a part of His divine plan, and God longs for us to be unified in this purpose for His glory. Romans 8:28 says, *"And we know that God causes everything to work together for the good of those who love God and are called according to his purpose for them."*

If we are unified in our purpose of bringing glory and honor to God, then we must set about using the abilities and talents He has given us for His glory—not our own.

C. S. Lewis once said, "Aim at heaven and you will get earth thrown in. Aim at earth and you get neither." Ask God to fulfill His purpose in your life today.

FEBRUARY 19

My Deliverer

"For I know that as you pray for me and the Spirit of Jesus Christ helps me, this will lead to my deliverance." —Philippians 1:19

There are many accounts in the *Holy Bible* of despair and deliverance. The key to unlocking the door of deliverance is faith. We must believe that God stands ready, willing, and able to deliver us and meet us at our point of need.

In my life, I can attest that God has always met me at my point of need. He has always delivered me—in every possible way imaginable. And, in each instance, God has used whatever trouble I encountered to draw me closer to Him.

The *Holy Bible* says in Psalm 40:2, *"He lifted me out of the pit of despair, out of the mud and the mire. He set my feet on solid ground and steadied me as I walked along."*

God is ready to deliver you from the pit of despair. He is ready to set your feet on solid ground—to steady you as you walk.

No matter how big the mountain, God can help you climb it. As God delivered the Israelites from the land of Egypt, He stands ready to deliver you today.

2 Corinthians 1:9-11 tells us, *"Indeed, in our hearts we felt the sentence of death. But this happened that we might not rely on ourselves but on God, who raises the dead. He has delivered us from such a deadly peril, and he will deliver us. On him we have set our hope that he will continue to deliver us, as you help us by your prayers. Then many will give thanks on our behalf for the gracious favor granted us in answer to the prayers of many."*

Are you facing a mountain today? Are you in need of someone to deliver you?

May you pray and ask God to deliver you today, and may it be the best day you've ever had in your life.

FEBRUARY 20

Sweat The Small Stuff

"If you are faithful in little things, you will be faithful in large ones. But if you are dishonest in little things, you won't be faithful with greater responsibilities." —Luke 16:10

There is a popular idea in today's culture that we shouldn't sweat the "small stuff". My friend, this premise is completely contrary to what God's Word teaches. Just as the devil takes a strand of truth and weaves a convincing web of lies around it, so he has done with this idea.

Certainly, the *Holy Bible* does teach us that we should not worry (Ecclesiastes 11:10, Matthew 6:25), and that we should have faith (Hebrews 11:6). But, one only needs to take a brief glance in any direction to see how the idea of not sweating the "small stuff" has permeated our culture in the form of a *laissez faire* mentality of anything and everything goes.

If Rip Van Winkle had fallen asleep thirty years ago and woken up today, he would wonder what planet he had gone to—and, that's not because of the iPhones and netbooks, it's because of the arrogance, immorality, narcissism, and open acceptance of every kind of sin.

Here's an analogy you've probably heard before: If you were to take a live frog and place it in a pot of boiling water, the frog would quickly and frantically hop out of the pot with every ounce of its power. But, if you were to take that same frog and place it in a pot of cold water, then slowly turn up the heat, the frog would be boiled alive.

You and I are that frog. May we wake up and jump out of the pot today.

FEBRUARY 21

No Pain, No Gain

"No discipline is enjoyable while it is happening—it's painful! But afterward there will be a peaceful harvest of right living for those who are trained in this way." —Hebrews 12:11

As a child, I can recall occasions when my father disciplined me with harsh words and actions in situations where I wanted to take the easy way out. At times, my wicked heart challenged his words with the thought that no one else was doing it this way.

Anticipating my wicked heart, my father would always remind me that this was God's way, regardless of what anyone else was doing.

He was right.

It doesn't matter what anyone else thinks. The only thing that matters is what God thinks.

God sees all, and His Word tells us that He is a rewarded of those who diligently seek Him.

Are you running away from God's painful discipline today?

May you seek Him diligently today and every day, and may you stop running from the loving hand of God's discipline in your life, now and always.

FEBRUARY 22

Dance With The Joyful

"I will rebuild you, my virgin Israel. You will again be happy and dance merrily with your tambourines." —Jeremiah 31:4

Have you ever felt as though you really messed things up in your life, and that there was no hope of joy ever returning to your life again?

This wonderful verse reminds us that we serve a God of second chances—a God who is not only a master builder, but a master *rebuilder*. He makes all things new. He brings hope to the hopeless, life to the lifeless, and fills us with abundant joy.

Isaiah 54:7-8 tells us, *"For a brief moment I abandoned you, but with great compassion I will take you back. In a burst of anger I turned my face away for a little while. But with everlasting love I will have compassion on you,' says the Lord, your Redeemer."*

May you take up your tambourine for God today, and find time to dance with the joyful.

FEBRUARY 23

God Listens

"If only someone would listen to me! Look, I will sign my name to my defense. Let the Almighty answer me. Let my accuser write out the charges against me." —Job 31:35

Do you ever feel alone, and though no one will listen to you?

In Job's story, there were three close friends of his whom, upon hearing of his tragedy, came to comfort and console him. They sat with him for seven days and nights without saying a word since they saw that his suffering was too great for words.

Yet, when Job finally spoke after the seven days, his friends did not listen. Each one, in turn, had Job's plight entirely figured out. They began rambling on and on, pouring salt in each and every one of Job's many wounds.

Not only did Job's friends not listen to what he had to say, they accused him of being arrogant, faithless, disobedient, and guilty of all manner of hidden sins! Certainly, with friends like that, Job had no need of enemies.

In desperation for someone to listen, Job cried out to God, criticizing Him and assuming He would not listen, either. But, God did listen. God did respond. He lovingly and firmly reminded Job of his place in the world, in God's divine plan.

Then, God blessed Job beyond anything he could ever hope or imagine.

He can do that for you, too.

"Because he bends down to listen, I will pray as long as I have breath" (Psalm 116:2)!

FEBRUARY 24

Joy In The Name Of Jesus

"You haven't done this before. Ask, using my name, and you will receive, and you will have abundant joy." —John 16:24

As a youngster, I took great pleasure in reading my *Holy Bible* and praying by myself before bedtime. It was just something I craved and looked forward to each day—a special time alone—just Jesus and me. One thing I would ask God for day after day, and night after night, was to use my life in some way that would bring glory and honor to Him.

Being a little kid and not really grasping that "His ways were not my ways," I often tried to figure out (for God) just how He was going to answer that prayer.

First, I figured he would make me valedictorian of my class, and I would give a grand speech giving all the praise and glory to God. But, it was not to be.

Next, I decided God needed me to be a doctor or nurse and discover a cure for some awful disease, and of course, I would give praise and glory to God in all of the medical journals. But, I couldn't even make it through one day of work in the medical profession.

After a few more two-by-fours upside the head, I began to realize how completely self-absorbed my desires were. They were *my* desires—not His. I finally prayed from a humble heart, "Lord, use me. Whatever it takes, use me."

When I finally got out of the way, God began to open doors that showed me His plan, step by step, and day by day.

God does answer our prayers. When we ask in Jesus name, and in accordance with His will, He answers and fills us with abundant joy.

FEBRUARY 25

Remove The Snakes

"Then the people came to Moses and cried out, 'We have sinned by speaking against the Lord and against you. Pray that the Lord will take away the snakes. So Moses prayed for the people."
—Numbers 21:7

The stories of the Israelites wandering in the wilderness have so many parallels to our own lives. In this part of the story, God has just given the Israelites great victory over the land of Canaan. They are traveling from Mount Hor to the Red Sea, to go around the land of Edom. Yet, like so many times before, the Israelites became impatient with the long journey and manna they were eating, and they began to complain about Moses and God.

This time, God became so angry with the Israelites for their lack of gratitude and complaining that He sent poisonous snakes among them. Many of the Israelites were bitten by the snakes and died.

Finally, the Israelites repented and asked Moses to pray to God to take away the snakes.

Are there poisonous snakes in your life because of your lack of gratitude? Do you need to repent and then ask God to take away the snakes?

May your heart be overwhelmed with gratitude for all that God has given to you, and may there be no poisonous snakes in your life.

FEBRUARY 26

Sing For Joy

"Let the whole world sing for joy, because you govern the nations with justice and guide the people of the whole world." —Psalm 67:4

What a wonderful and comforting verse.

Do you ever feel like the world is falling apart around you? Perhaps you or someone close to you has just received some very unsettling news. Or, perhaps everything you hear is doom and gloom around you. Ever want to stop the world and get off for just a little while?

There is certainly more than enough shocking and unnerving news in the world around us to cause concern.

Yet, this verse reminds us that God is still in charge.

He is governing the nations with justice and guiding the people of the whole world.

That's more than enough to sing about.

May you surprise someone today by breaking into joyful song because you know that God is still in control.

FEBRUARY 27

Joyful Psalms

"Oh, the joys of those who do not follow the advice of the wicked, or stand around with sinners, or join in with mockers." —Psalm 1:1

The Book of Psalms has more references to joy than we find in any other book in the *Holy Bible*. In fact, the New Living Translation of the *Holy Bible* contains the word *joy* or the form of the word *joy* exactly one hundred times.

The Book of Psalms is also a very practical, honest, and real book. In it, David pours out his heart to God openly, and freely shares his emotions—as well as his dirty laundry.

Regardless the trial we face, there is always a psalm that addresses the genuine longing of our heart, and the depth of emotion that we feel.

The fact that we can all relate just proves that life isn't perfect—but God is.

Open your *Holy Bible* and read in the book of Psalms today. There you will find and know the source of real joy—a relationship with Jesus Christ—the giver of all good things.

He can transform your life into a perpetual feast of joy—regardless of your circumstances.

FEBRUARY 28

Joy In Listening To God

"And so, my children, listen to me, for all who follow my ways are joyful." —*Proverbs 8:32*

There was a wonderful woman I had the privilege of knowing for many years who had a very close personal relationship with Christ. This woman exuded joy in every area of her life. She had the effervescent curiosity, exhilarating excitement, whimsy and love of all things good that only a child knows, yet she was in her nineties.

This woman was my Grandma Tis, my mother's mother. Grandma Tis taught me that there is true and complete joy in knowing, listening to, and obeying God's voice. She lived it before my eyes, and I saw that it was very real.

Do you know that listening to God can provide very real joy in every area of your life? It can and it does! That doesn't mean that our circumstances will be perfect. It just means that we know who holds our circumstances—perfectly.

May you know the joy of listening to God and following Him in a real and personal way today and every day.

And, may you do more than that.

May Jesus in you be the light in this dark world for someone else to see.

FEBRUARY 29

Knowing The Shepherd's Voice

"My sheep listen to my voice; I know them, and they follow me." —John 10:27

Do you ever wonder if thoughts inside your head are God speaking to you or simply your own ideas?

Gideon struggled with that, too. He was met by the angel of the Lord who told him that his small tribe would defeat the Midianites; yet, he had to have a sign from God to prove that he wasn't imagining things. Read Judges 6. You can probably relate to Gideon's way of thinking and feeling.

So, how do we know when God is speaking to us? How can we be certain we are hearing God's voice and not our own? Or, how can we be assured it's not the voice of evil?

The *Holy Bible* tells us very plainly in John 10:27. We must have a personal relationship with Christ in order to know Him and distinguish His voice from all the others. Read John 10. It is a beautiful picture of the loving relationship we have with Christ as our shepherd, if we will only receive it.

May you know and hear the fullness of the shepherd's voice.

And, may we follow close after Him today and every day.

MARCH 1

Loving Obedience

"But those who obey God's word, truly show how completely they love him. That is how we know we are living in him." —I John 2:5

Recently, I was a participant in a work discussion regarding a Biblical topic, and was saddened as I listened to people express opinions using philosophers, friends, popular books and personal experiences to make their various points. Yet, no one referred to the *Holy Bible* as their source. No one spoke of the answer that was clearly written upon its pages in the simplicity needed for a child to understand.

The *Holy Bible* is our guidebook. It is God's Holy Word. It is written in a manner that children can understand and know its lessons. Yet, we will never fully understand all of its lessons while on the Earth. Its lessons are designed to lead us to a close, personal relationship with God, our father.

Oh, may we never allow Satan to lead us away from these simple and complete truths, and a walk that is in obedience to Christ.

My prayer for you today is that you will read God's Word and walk in obedience to His commands to show how completely you love Him.

MARCH 2

A Higher Standard Of Living

"For just as the heavens are higher than the earth, so my ways are higher than your ways."
—Isaiah 55:9

Have you noticed the standards of today? Or, maybe you've noticed the lack of standards that exist today with regard to speech, respect, obedience, education, television, politics, tolerance, etc. We could go on and on, right?

I love the 55th Chapter of Isaiah. It is purely and simply an invitation to Christ's salvation. It is a call to raising the standard. Verse 3 says, *"Come to me with your ears wide open. Listen, and you will find life. I will make an everlasting covenant with you. I will give you all the unfailing love I promised to David."*

I don't know about you, but I find few people who actually listen anymore—to anyone except themselves. Yet, God tells us here that if we will but listen to Him, we will find life!

Verse 8 says, *"My thoughts are nothing like your thoughts,"* says the Lord. *"And, my ways are far beyond anything you could imagine."*

I challenge you to read all of Isaiah 55 and raise your standard of living—to live in obedience to Christ. You will find abundant life that is beyond anything you could possibly imagine.

I challenge you to significant change. I challenge you to turn off the questionable television program, to correct the inappropriate speech or behavior in yourself, your child. I challenge you to walk in complete obedience to God's Word.

MARCH 3

Our Just Reward

"He repays people according to their deeds. He treats people as they deserve." —Job 34:11

My family comes from a long line of ministers. My great grandfather's uncle was a humble and grateful man named George W. Truett. He was pastor of the First Baptist Church of Dallas from 1897 to 1944. My father is a preacher, my brother is a preacher, and my Uncle Billy is also a preacher. May God bless them all. Needless to say, I've heard a few sermons in my lifetime.

Growing up under my father's tutelage, he frequently drove home the point that God would repay us according to our actions, because He was always watching.

I don't know about you, but there are many times in life when I mutter to myself, *"That wasn't fair!"* or *"I wish someone else had seen that!"*

Not only does God see it all, but He pays us according to all that He sees, as the referenced passage tells us.

There is no issue of overpayment or underpayment with Christ. He pays us perfectly. Revelation 22:12 tells us, *"Look, I am coming soon, bringing my reward with me to repay all people according to their deeds."*

Yes, one day we will all receive our just reward.

May you live in such a way that you look forward to yours with joyful anticipation.

MARCH 4

What Would Jesus Do

"Don't act thoughtlessly, but understand what the Lord wants you to do." —*Ephesians 5:17*

Do you ever ask yourself in a given situation, "What would Jesus do?" What do you think would happen if you committed to asking yourself that question, before acting, for one year, no matter what the outcome?

That is the subject of a wonderful book titled, In His Steps by Charles Sheldon. The book talks about a congregation in a small town whose pastor issued just such a challenge to his congregation, and it changed their lives—all of them—in ways they never imagined.

The hard part of the challenge is searching your heart and your *Holy Bible* enough to know just what you believe Jesus would do in a given situation.

The *Holy Bible* tells us in Romans 12:2, *"Don't copy the behavior and customs of this world, but let God transform you into a new person by changing the way you think. Then you will learn to know God's will for you, which is good and pleasing and perfect."*

May we accept the challenge to ask ourselves what Jesus would do with each and every decision we face, and may we know Him well enough to be assured of the answer.

MARCH 5

Joyful Living

"Joyful are people of integrity, who follow the instructions of the Lord. Joyful are those who obey his laws and search for him with all their hearts." —Psalm 119:1-2

Psalm 119 is one of my favorite passages in the *Holy Bible*, with one hundred seventy-six verses and twenty-two stanzas. It is written as an acrostic, with each of the twenty-two stanzas beginning with the next successive letter of the Hebrew alphabet, and each verse beginning with the stanza's beginning Hebrew letter of the alphabet. The passage exudes the Spirit of God both in content and exquisite style.

If you've read it a thousand times before, stop and read Psalm 119 again. Pay close attention to King David's heart, spilled out in words across the page.

Do you have the same longing, joy, gratitude, and hunger for God? It is easy to see why God called David, *"a man after my own heart"* (Acts 13:22).

My prayer for you is that God will purify your heart and fill it with an intense longing for Him—a longing that cannot be quenched any other way.

MARCH 6

Joy In Life's Pressure Cooker

"As pressure and stress bear down on me, I find joy in your commands." —Psalm 119:143

As a little girl, my mother often made chicken and dumplings for dinner—a family favorite. To begin preparation of the meal, she would first take a whole chicken and place it in a pressure cooker with some water and vegetables, and place it on the stove.

I remember vividly the sound of what we liked to call the *screamer* on top of the pressure cooker. When the heat and pressure of the steam became strong enough, the *screamer* would shake and rattle uncontrollably, and, then make a screaming sound, indicating it was time to remove the chicken. My mother would don a potholder, and carefully remove the hot, angry *screamer* from the top of the pressure cooker. She would then remove the lid to inspect the contents inside—soft, warm, tender and beautiful. The chicken was cooked just right. Mother would say, "You just can't get the same beautiful result without the pressure cooker."

Our lives are like that chicken in the pressure cooker. When we become cold and hardened, often the only way to make the contents of our heart soft, warm, tender and beautiful again is through the pressure cooker of life. We tend to shake, rattle, and make all kinds of screaming sounds when faced with the pressures of life. Yet, if we will look to God in the midst of it all, we can see the glorious work He is accomplishing in and through us. The beauty is revealed after the *screamer* is removed.

Do you feel as though you are a chicken in the pressure cooker of life? Is your *screamer* a bit out of control? You can find joy even when sitting in the midst of the pressure cooker if you will spend time in God's Word.

May the contents of your heart become soft, warm, tender, and beautiful again through Christ.

MARCH 7

Radiant With Joy

"Those who look to him for help will be radiant with joy; no shadow of shame will darken their faces." —Psalm 34:5

My father is a wonderful example to me of real Christian love and service to others. Recently, he completed a long series of radiation treatments for prostate cancer.

Throughout the treatment process, I had the opportunity to talk with him about how things were going. Each time we talked, my father was filled with so much joy—even though the radiation process and its side effects were extremely uncomfortable and unpleasant. Daddy couldn't wait to get back to serving and doing things for others with one hundred percent of his strength.

Though my father is aging, his face is still radiant with the kind of joy that only Christ can bring.

As the Scripture above says, *"Those who look to him for help will be radiant with joy; no shadow of shame will darken their faces."*

May you be radiant with the joy of the Lord, and may that radiance be evident to everyone you meet.

MARCH 8

The Never-Ending Story

"O LORD, the God of our ancestors Abraham, Isaac, and Israel, make your people always want to obey you. See to it that their love for you never changes." —I Chronicles 29:18

Christoph Von Schmid was a parish priest and author born August 15, 1768 in Dinkelsbeuhl, Bavaria. He has written such wonderful and inspiring works for children and adults as *Easter Eggs, The Bird's Nest, Little Henri, The Forget Me Not, The Rose Bush, Christmas Eve,* and my personal favorite, *The Basket of Flowers.*

These stories have lasted through centuries as beloved favorites because they teach the simple, beautiful truths of the *Holy Bible.*

The world's belief system and trends change from day to day, but Christ's simple truths of love and obedience last forever, instilling joy and peace in all who hear and practice them.

Isaiah 51:6 says, *"Look up to the skies above, and gaze down on the earth below. For the skies will disappear like smoke, and the earth will wear out like a piece of clothing. The people of the earth will die like flies, but my salvation lasts forever. My righteous rule will never end!"*

May you find joy and peace in the never-ending righteous rule of Christ in your life, and in simple continuous obedience to Him.

MARCH 9

Joy In The Tumbler Of Life

"To all who mourn in Israel, he will give a crown of beauty for ashes, a joyous blessing instead of mourning, festive praise instead of despair. In their righteousness, they will be like great oaks that the Lord has planted for his own glory." —Isaiah 61:3

My daughter, Meredith, was an avid rock collector as a child. She could find beauty in what most would consider the oddest of places. On one occasion, she found what I would call a very plain, ugly rock which she carefully wrapped up and brought home, pronouncing it, "beautiful."

When I questioned Meredith about why she found this particular rock to be so beautiful, she responded with, "It only needs a few passes through the rock tumbler for *you* to see how beautiful it really is, Mommy."

Meredith was sure of its beauty.

God is sure of your beauty, too. Do you feel as though you are in the rock tumbler today? Remember that the rock tumbler is only going to help others see the true beauty of Christ in you.

The *Holy Bible* is full of stories in which people did not see the true beauty of Christ living within. Most people didn't even recognize God's glory in Jesus Christ, Himself!

Isaiah 53:2 tells us, *"He grew up before him like a tender shoot, and like a root out of dry ground. He had no beauty or majesty to attract us to him, nothing in his appearance that we should desire him."*

Like the first diamond ever discovered in a coal mine, like David, whom others saw as a shepherd boy and God saw as King, may you be made beautiful in God's tumbler.

MARCH 10

Joy Through The Journey

"Take nothing for your journey," he instructed them. "Don't take a walking stick, a traveler's bag, food, money, or even a change of clothes." —Luke 9:3

As a child growing up in Houston, we never had much "stuff" by the world's standard, and my parents struggled a great deal. Yet, they had God, and taught me that He was all we needed. Their struggles and endurance have shown me that it is the storm that proves the seaworthiness of the vessel.

The disciples had everything they needed. They had Christ. The *Holy Bible* tells us in 2 Corinthians 9:8, *"And God will generously provide all you need. Then you will always have everything you need and plenty left over to share with others."*

"... and plenty left over to share with others."

As we continue on the journey of our lives in Christ, may we remember that Christ is all we need for the journey. Romans 14:17 says, *"For the Kingdom of God is not a matter of what we eat or drink, but of living a life of goodness and peace and joy in the Holy Spirit."*

Chasing after wants is meaningless because this Earth is not all there is. Ecclesiastes 6:9 says, "Enjoy what you have rather than desiring what you don't have. Just dreaming about nice things is meaningless—like chasing the wind."

As hard as life can be, God provides joy throughout the journey. *"You have given me greater joy than those who have abundant harvests of grain and new wine"* (Psalm 4:7).

MARCH 11

Joy Comes With The Morning

"For his anger lasts only a moment, but his favor lasts a lifetime! Weeping may last through the night, but joy comes with the morning." —Psalm 30:5

Have you ever cried yourself to sleep? Perhaps you've done it so many times you've lost count. Maybe you're like King David who said in Psalm 42:3, *"My tears have been my food day and night, while they say to me all day long, 'Where is your God?'"*

You may feel more like this, *"I am worn out from sobbing. All night I flood my bed with weeping, drenching it with my tears"* (Psalm 6:6).

The *Holy Bible* never promises us that we won't cry while we're here on Earth, but it does promise us this, *"Those who plant in tears will harvest with shouts of joy"* (Psalm 126:5).

There's an old gospel song called, "Joy Comes in the Morning." My favorite refrain in the song says, "Hold on, my child. Joy comes in the morning!"

If you need to find a place of joy for your soul today, find it in communion with the Father through prayer and reading His Word. His glorious promises never come to an end.

MARCH 12

Dream Weaver

"He speaks in dreams, in visions of the night, when deep sleep falls on people as they lie in their beds." —Job 33:15

In the Book of Daniel, Chapter 2, King Nebuchadnezzar had such disturbing dreams that he was unable to sleep. He was so troubled by these dreams that he summoned magicians, sorcerers, astrologers, and enchanters, demanding that they tell him what he dreamed and its meaning.

The king was so adamant about his demand that he threatened to tear them limb from limb and burn their houses to the ground if they did not tell him what he had dreamed and its meaning. Yet, if they did tell him, they would receive many wonderful gifts and honors. Since none of them could meet the king's demand, he ordered them all executed.

When Daniel learned of the order, he asked for more time, and had his friends join him in prayer that God would provide an answer so that their lives may be spared.

That night, God revealed the king's dream and its meaning to Daniel in a vision.

Daniel 2:22 says, *"He reveals deep and mysterious things and knows what lies hidden in darkness, though he is surrounded by light."*

Acts 2:17 says, *"'In the last days,' God says, 'I will pour out my Spirit upon all people. Your sons and daughters will prophesy. Your young men will see visions, and your old men will dream dreams.'"*

May you hear the God of Heaven, regardless of where or when He speaks to your heart.

MARCH 13

A Heart Condition

"And I will give you a new heart, and I will put a new spirit in you. I will take out your stony, stubborn heart and give you a tender, responsive heart." —Ezekiel 36:26

I was born with a heart condition.
   You were, too.
So was everyone who was ever born after Adam and Eve—except Jesus.
This condition is a hardening of the heart, or sin. It is a fatal condition (Romans 6:23).
In spite of our heart condition, Jesus has given us the opportunity for a heart transplant.
The donor is perfect (Hebrews 4:15).
The surgery is free.
Curious about the surgeon?
His reputation is impeccable.
He is *the* physician (Mark 2:17).
Our wonderful Savior makes all things new—even cold, stony, callous, corrupt, and sinful hearts. He miraculously changes them and makes them soft, tender, loving, and sensitive—just like the heart of a child.
May you live today and every day using the new heart He has given you to its fullest potential.

MARCH 14

The Sum Of All Choices

"Wise choices will watch over you. Understanding will keep you safe." —Proverbs 2:11

How well do you consider the choices that you make each day? Do you consider the consequences of each and every decision? Or, do you stop to contemplate only certain decisions you feel are big or important?

Most of us have a choice regarding the food we eat each day, the choice of whether or not to marry and whom, and the most important choice of all—where we will spend eternity. Our lives are the sum of all the choices that we make, together with the choices that others have made on our behalf. Each and every one of them is important.

The *Holy Bible* tells us how important it is to consider even the small things in life. Luke 16:10 tells us, *"If you are faithful in little things, you will be faithful in large ones. But if you are dishonest in little things, you won't be honest with greater responsibilities."*

God cares about every little detail of our lives, and He longs for us to trust Him with them all, *"Give all your worries and cares to God, for he cares about you"* (I Peter 5:7).

If wisdom is to guide our choices, then faith must be front and center in every decision that we make, for without faith it is impossible to please Him (Hebrews 11:6).

May you have the faith to trust God, and the wisdom to consult Him with regard to every detail of your life today and every day.

MARCH 15

God's Family Style

"Children, obey your parents in the Lord, for this is right. 'Honor your father and mother'—which is the first commandment with a promise— 'that it may go well with you and that you may enjoy long life on the earth.' Fathers, do not exasperate your children; instead, bring them up in the training and instruction of the Lord." —Ephesians 6:1-4

This verse reminds us that we have a responsibility as children—to honor our parents, and we also have a responsibility as parents—to bring them up in the training and instruction of the Lord, the nurture and admonition of the Lord. Not only that, but as parents we must not provoke our children to wrath or exasperate them.

How are your parenting skills? Are you bringing up your children in the training and instruction of the Lord? Are you seeking His guidance in all you say and do with and to your children? What about your parents? Are you honoring them in word and deed?

If not, you can start today.

Recommit yourself to being the kind of child and parent God desires today.

May you honor your father and mother—that your days may be long upon the land—and may your children be blessed by your strong, loving personal relationship with the Father, today and every day.

MARCH 16

Jesus Loves The Little Children

"Then little children were brought to Jesus for him to place his hands on them and pray for them. But the disciples rebuked those who brought them. Jesus said, 'Let the little children come to me, and do not hinder them, for the kingdom of heaven belongs to such as these.' When he had placed his hands on them, he went on from there." —Matthew 19:13-15

Don't you love to watch children playing? I do, too. Recently, I was watching a group of children playing together and observed several wonderful characteristics about them: (1) they love completely, (2) they forgive and forget easily, (3) they are joyful, (4) they trust totally and without fear, (5) they say what they mean, (6) they are dependent, (7) they rest when they're tired, and (8) they hug and kiss a lot.

It's easy to see why the kingdom of heaven belongs to such as these.

Do you exhibit any of these wonderful characteristics in your life?

Matthew 18:3 says it like this, *"Then he said, 'I tell you the truth, unless you turn from your sins and become like little children, you will never get into the Kingdom of Heaven.'"*

May you take these words to heart and become like a little child that your faith in Jesus might be complete.

MARCH 17

The Blessing Of Long Life

"May the LORD bless you from Zion all the days of your life; may you see the prosperity of Jerusalem, and may you live to see your children's children. Peace be upon Israel." —Psalm 128:5-6

My mother grew up during the Great Depression. Many years have passed since that time, yet she vividly recalls picking out the feed sacks that were used to make her dresses, and how blessed her family was that her father was able to keep his job as a fireman in Van Nuys, California.

She speaks highly of the loving manner in which her parents raised her, treated her, and always honors them with her words.

Yet, when speaking with my mother's siblings, a different story emerges with regard to my grandparents—a story with unnecessary, unconstructive details, revealing the sin nature in which we were all born. Do you honor your parents—regardless of the manner and circumstance in which you were raised?

Ephesians 6:3 tells us, *"If you honor your father and mother, things will go well for you, and you will have a long life on the earth."* The *Holy Bible* tells us the same thing in Exodus 20:12 and Deuteronomy 5:16, too.

Sometimes the choices made by our parents and the legacy they leave behind may be difficult to honor. Yet, God's grace has seen fit to take even the most negative circumstance and use it for good in our lives.

May you enjoy the blessing of long life, and may peace be upon you as you honor your Heavenly Father by honoring your parents today.

MARCH 18

The Fruit Of Godly Men

"Your wife will be like a fruitful vine within your house; your sons will be like olive shoots around your table. Thus is the man blessed who fears the Lord." —Psalm 128:3-4

Have you ever known a family that epitomizes this verse?

As a youngster visiting family in Mississippi, I was always amazed at my Aunt's ability to constantly produce good things. She loved cooking, making quilts, sewing stuffed animals, teaching, telling stories, and making unique crafts. Truly, this was a fruitful vine within my Uncle's house.

Not only that, but my cousins, were just as productive. I learned so much from them, and they never seemed to run out of good things to make, do, or give to others. Even the words from their lips were a feast for the listener. They were the olive shoots around the table.

There is little wonder that the head of that home was a God-fearing man.

Do you know a family like that? A man, wife, or child like that?

I love what Psalm 67:7 says, too. *"God will bless us, and all the ends of the earth will fear him."*

What an awesome, powerful promise! May you rest in this promise as you follow after Him today.

MARCH 19

Sweet Harvest For Christ

"How joyful are those who fear the Lord—all who follow his ways! You will enjoy the fruit of your labor. How joyful and prosperous you will be!" —Psalm 128:1-2

When I was a little girl, we often visited my great-grandparents on their farm in Singleton, Texas. The farm's fence was covered with blackberries, and each summer we were recruited to pick until our pricked and bleeding hands could pick no more.

I never much enjoyed the picking. It was hot, sweaty, painful, tiring work. Not to mention the fact that I wasn't even sure I liked blackberries when we started. There were so many bug bites, prickles, chiggers, and hurts that I often wondered why we were bothering to do it at all. But, out of a healthy fear of my elders, I didn't grumble.

At the end of the day, as the sun was starting to descend on the horizon, Great-grandma, "Bees", as we called her, would smile so big every wrinkle in her lovely 80-year-old face would disappear. After hauling in and washing all of the blackberries, Bees would ask us to pick out the biggest, juiciest blackberries in the bunch, place them in a bucket of ice water, and then eat them. At that moment, there was nothing better in all the world.

The rewards of laboring for Christ are just like picking those blackberries—the work may be hard, but with regard to the harvest—there is nothing better in all the world.

May you walk in the fear of the Lord and enjoy the labor of your hands.

MARCH 20

True Blue Blood

"One day a petition was presented by the daughters of Zelophehad—Mahlah, Noah, Hoglah, Milcah, and Tirzah. Their father, Zelophehad, was a descendant of Hepher son of Gilead, son of Makir, son of Manasseh, son of Joseph. These women stood before Moses, Eleazar the priest, the tribal leaders, and the entire community at the entrance of the Tabernacle." — Numbers 27:1-2

Do you have a sense of confidence about your heritage?

Growing up, I heard often about famous family member, George W. Truett, on my father's side of the family. We listened to taped sermons and looked at old family photos. We also heard stories about my mother's second cousin (once removed), Van Cliburn. We watched video of his piano concerts, and heard endless stories. My parents shared this rich heritage with us early and often to drive home their expectation that we would grow up to do great things for God, too—it was in our blood.

The daughters in this passage of Scripture had a rich heritage. Their Great, Great, Great, Great Grandfather (once removed, perhaps) was Joseph. They were confident in their ancestry, and sure that their blue blood status was bound to continue great things for the Kingdom of God. They had so much faith in their heritage that they took their special request before Moses and all of the leaders in the entire community at the entrance of the Tabernacle.

If God is your Father, then you have the bluest blood there is. You are the truest of all blue bloods. You have a direct family relationship with Christ. No one stands between the two of you. And, you can take your requests straight to the throne of God with all the faith and confidence in the world that He will hear you.

May you realize the power of your heritage in Him today, and may His every expectation for your life be fulfilled.

MARCH 21

Plan B

"And give the following instructions to the people of Israel: If a man dies and has no son, then give his inheritance to his daughters. And if he has no daughter either, transfer his inheritance to his brothers. If he has no brothers, give his inheritance to his father's brothers."
—Numbers 27:8-10

Aren't you glad God's ways are not our ways?

This passage of Scripture reminds us that God considers more than one option for us. He has a Plan B, C, D, and beyond, if necessary. He doesn't leave us in the dark wondering what to do if our life does not fit into one neat little set of circumstances. He considers and knows all the possibilities.

Not only that, but He lovingly guides us in the way of righteousness. In this Scripture, He gives the appropriate instruction to Moses to pass on to the people of Israel. He doesn't want to leave them wondering and wandering in the darkness. He is the way, the truth, and the life.

However, when we fail to obey, we do miss out on God's blessing, His best plan for our lives.

God won't leave you in the dark with regard to His plan, either. May you find rest and peace in knowing that no matter how far you've wandered away, if you will but take that one moment to return to Him, He will meet you with love, compassion, and, yes—even a Plan B (Isaiah 54:7-8).

May you seek Him with all of your heart today, and find that His options are beyond anything you could ever imagine.

MARCH 22

Do I Have To

"But if his father has no brothers, give his inheritance to the nearest relative in his clan. This is a legal requirement for the people of Israel, just as the Lord commanded Moses." — Numbers 27:11

"Momma, do I have to?" Those are familiar words at my house. Truth be told, I'm sure I said the same to my mother, and every bit as often as I hear it. One of my children phrases it this way when given an instruction, "Is this an 'I have to' or an 'if I want to'?"

God answers the question before it's asked in this passage. His instruction for the people of Israel is a *have to*. He says it is a legal requirement. The fact that we question says a great deal about the condition of our heart and our willingness, or rather, our unwillingness to please Him. It reveals a lack of faith, and exposes our selfishness.

Are you asking, "Father, do I have to?"

May God strengthen our faith to the point that we fully trust and obey Him, without asking if we have to, but instead saying, "Yes, Father, I will go."

MARCH 23

The Best Intentions

"Simon Peter asked, 'Lord, where are you going?' And Jesus replied, 'You can't go with me now, but you will follow me later.' 'But why can't I come now, Lord?' he asked. 'I'm ready to die for you.' Jesus answered, 'Die for me? I tell you the truth, Peter—before the rooster crows tomorrow morning, you will deny three times that you even know me.'" —John 13:36-38

I had the best intentions. I told my son I would do anything for him. I said I would always be there for him—no matter what. I told him that he meant more to me than any ol' job ever would.

Then, it happened. The school nurse called. My son was sick with a fever. We were in the middle of a big project at work, and I had only been on the job for three weeks. I'm sure my boss would not have hesitated to let me tend to my son, but I didn't ask. Instead of being there for my son, I called my mother-in-law and asked if she could pick him up from school.

When I arrived home that evening, my son didn't say a word to me other than, "You said . . ."

I knew I had done wrong. I had not exercised my will to obey Christ, but I had chosen, rather, to disobey. I had the best intentions—just like Peter. But, Christ requires that we have more than just good intentions. He requires that we exercise our will in obedience to Him. He requires that we trust Him enough to know that He has our best interest in mind when He calls us to action. As a result, there is an ultimate blessing in store for us. And, there is glory and honor for Him.

May you have more than just good intentions this week. May you receive the blessing of Christ as you exercise your will in obedience to Him.

MARCH 24

One Mind

"I appeal to you, dear brothers and sisters, by the authority of our Lord Jesus Christ, to live in harmony with each other. Let there be no divisions in the church. Rather, be of one mind, united in thought and purpose. For some members of Chloe's household have told me about your quarrels, my dear brothers and sisters. Some of you are saying, 'I am a follower of Paul.' Others are saying, 'I follow Apollos,' or 'I follow Peter,' or 'I follow only Christ.'"
—I Corinthians 1:10-12

Arguments? In the church? Really? Not in *our* church.

Growing up as a preacher's kid, I was always amazed by the things people quarreled about, and even more dumbfounded that these same quarrels caused divisions and splits in the church.

Wouldn't it be beautiful if, as Paul suggests, we all lived in harmony with one another, having the same spirit—the Spirit of God—living in our midst?

Can you picture the fellowship?

Beautiful . . .

If we will depend upon Christ daily to make us holy, then that picture, that vision, that united front can become real in our church, as well as the Christian community around us.

May we seek after God with all that we have and are, that we may know the peace, joy, and power that come from unity in Him.

MARCH 25

The Good Shepherd

I am the good shepherd. The good shepherd sacrifices his life for the sheep." —John 10:11

I have always enjoyed nursery rhymes and fairy tales. One of my favorites was *Little Bo Peep*. In case you don't remember the words, the first verse goes like this:

Little Bo Peep has lost her sheep,
And, can't tell where to find them;
Leave them alone, and they'll come home,
Wagging their tails behind them.

Have you ever been lost?

The *Holy Bible* says in Isaiah 53:6, *"All of us, like sheep, have strayed away. We have left God's paths to follow our own. Yet the* LORD *laid on him the sins of us all."*

Life with Christ is better than any nursery rhyme or fairy tale could ever be.

Have you allowed Jesus Christ to be the Shepherd of your life? Or, are you still running things your own way? Bo Peep's way doesn't hold a candle to life with Christ.

If I were re-writing Little Bo Peep to show things God's way, it would go something like this:

Little Bo Peep has lost her sheep,
And, can't tell where to find them;
She calls each by name, bearing their shame,
Rejoicing when she has found them.

The *Holy Bible* tells us in John 15:13, *"There is no greater love than to lay down one's life for one's friends."*

Christ has shown us the ultimate love, the greatest love in all the world by laying down His life for us.

May we, in turn, share this love with our friends today.

MARCH 26

The Power Of Prayer

"Elijah was as human as we are, and yet when he prayed earnestly that no rain would fall, none fell for three and a half years!" —James 5:17

James 5:13-18 tells us about the power of prayer. The *Holy Bible* also tells us that the effectiveness of our prayer is a function of our faith, together with the condition of our heart (James 5:15).

God longs to answer our prayers with awesome deeds, as He did for David (Psalm 65:5), and as He did for Elijah.

I would challenge you to draw close to God, seek Him daily through His Word, and watch the amazing things that will be accomplished as a result of your faithful, heart-felt communion in prayer with Him.

"The LORD is far from the wicked, but he hears the prayers of the righteous" (Proverbs 15:29).

"Confess your sins to each other and pray for each other so that you may be healed. The earnest prayer of a righteous person has great power and produces wonderful results" (James 5:16).

May you realize the life-changing power of prayer to be real in your life today and every day.

MARCH 27

The Rescuer

"He grants the desires of those who fear him; he hears their cries for help and rescues them."
—Psalm 145:19

There is no shortcut to faithful obedience to Christ. It isn't always wrapped in a pretty little package with a bow, but it is the stuff dreams—real, lasting, eternal dreams—are made of.

Obedience and faithfulness are not always exciting. They are acts that may seem mundane and monotonous to those who do not have a personal relationship with Jesus Christ.

Yet, to the Christian, the life of faithfulness and obedience to Christ epitomizes the pinnacle of freedom. It is freedom from sin and eternal punishment. It is freedom to love others in a way only a follower of Christ can. What greater rescue could there be in all the world?

Colossians 1:13-14 says, *"For he has rescued us from the kingdom of darkness and transferred us into the Kingdom of his dear Son, who purchased our freedom and forgave our sins."*

A personal relationship with Christ rescues us from the bondage of our circumstances.

May you experience the rescuing power of Christ in your life today and every day.

MARCH 28

Palm Reading

"See, I have written your name on the palms of my hands. Always in my mind is a picture of Jerusalem's walls in ruins." —Isaiah 49:16

I grew up in a rough neighborhood on the north side of Houston. The area was riddled with crime, and a number of students in the local elementary school I attended came from homes in which various superstitions were embraced.

One such superstition was palm reading. It seemed there was always a student who longed to look at my palms and pretend to tell me the future.

In a recent business trip to New Orleans, I found the same superstition embraced in the eyes of grown women on nearly every corner of the French Quarter.

What these children and adults don't realize is that our future isn't written there. They are reading the wrong palms.

The palms that foretell my future are those of Christ. It is His nail-pierced hands that bear my name.

And, they bear your name, too.

Are you interested in knowing the future? Have you looked at the palms of Christ, the Savior, lately?

He is our lifeline.

He is our future.

And, His is a life that never ends.

MARCH 29

Leftovers

"Jesus called his disciples to him and said, 'I tell you the truth, this poor widow has given more than all the others who are making contributions. For they gave a tiny part of their surplus, but she, poor as she is, has given everything she had to live on.'" —Mark 12:43-44

God's idea of generosity is different than the world's. The world judges a person's giving by the size of the gift. But, God judges a person's giving by the amount they have left after the gift has been given.

True generosity is a sacrifice. It is more than merely giving our leftovers.

In Genesis Chapter 4, we read the story of Cain and Abel. Cain was a cultivator of the ground, and when it was time for the harvest, Cain brought some of his crops as a gift to the Lord. Yet God was not pleased with Cain's offering. Cain didn't bring God his best. He brought his leftovers.

Jeremiah 17:10 says, *"But I, the LORD, search all hearts and examine secret motives. I give all people their due rewards, according to what their actions deserve."*

Are you giving God your leftovers?

Ask God to give you a more generous heart today, and watch what He is able to accomplish through your faithful stewardship in all He has entrusted to you.

MARCH 30

Simple Simon

"The instructions of the LORD are perfect, reviving the soul. The decrees of the LORD are trustworthy, making wise the simple." —Psalm 19:7

Here's the beginning of a nursery rhyme you probably remember:

SIMPLE SIMON[3]

Simple Simon met a pie man
Going to the fair.
Said Simple Simon to the pie man
Let me try your ware.

Says the pie man to Simple Simon,
Show me first your penny.
Says Simple Simon to the pie man,
Indeed, I have not any.

The *Holy Bible* tells us in both Proverbs 22:3 and Proverbs 27:12, "*A prudent person foresees danger and takes precautions. The simpleton goes blindly on and suffers the consequences.*"

There is a difference between living a simple life, which God is pleased with (Ecclesiastes 5:12), and being a simpleton who lacks wisdom.

Following God's decrees can change even Simple Simon into a wise man. We need only trust and obey Him.

If I were rewriting Simple Simon to show what God can do for Simon, it would go something like this:

SIMPLE SIMON

Simple Simon met the Savior
Going to the city.
Said Simple Simon to the Savior
Sir, will you take pity?

---

3 Author unknown.

Focus

Says the Savior to Simple Simon,
Enter first my kingdom.
Says Simple Simon to the pie man,
Here I taste Your wisdom.

May your life be transformed by the wisdom, power and freedom of God's Word as you study it today.

MARCH 31

Hunger Monster

"For the world offers only a craving for physical pleasure, a craving for everything we see, and pride in our achievements and possessions. These are not from the Father, but are from this world." —I John 2:16

There is a bedtime story that has been told in our house when my children were little about a hunger monster. In the story, the hunger monster consumes everything in its path, and everything in sight. It gets bigger and bigger until it finally explodes into a pile of nothing.

Sadly, we've all known people like that. They eat and drink anything and consume everything they see without a thought or care for how it will affect them in the long run. Their lives are devoted to pleasure, they close their ears to the voice of criticism, and they have no thought of responsibility or the things of God. We call it living in the fast lane, or living only for the moment.

But, God calls this a life of death and destruction. When we continue this type of life, the *Holy Bible* tells us exactly what will happen in Proverbs 29:1, "Whoever stubbornly refuses to accept criticism will suddenly be destroyed beyond recovery."

Proverbs 14:12, the *Holy Bible* tells us, *"There is a path before each person that seems right, but it ends in death."*

Proverbs 22:4 tells us how to fight off the hunger monster. It says, *"True humility and fear of the LORD lead to riches, honor, and long life."*

May you resist the craving for the pleasures of this world, may you beat the hunger monster through true humility and a reverential fear of the Lord today.

APRIL 1

He Sees It All

"You spread out our sins before you—our secret sins—and you see them all." —Psalm 90:8

God sees everything.

I can still remember my mother's needed reminder when I complained about injustices experienced as a child. "God sees," she would gently remind me.

Nothing gets by Him.

Not only does He see all of our deeds, but He sees our thoughts and the intentions of our hearts, as well.

Jeremiah 17:10 tells us, *"But I, the LORD, search all hearts and examine secret motives. I give all people their due rewards, according to what their actions deserve."*

Are your thoughts and motives right? Is your heart right before God? If not, take the time right this very moment to confess your sins to the Father, repent of those sins, and live the rest of your days in the peace that passes understanding.

If your thoughts and motives are right, then thank your Heavenly Father for His loving and gracious protection of you as you seek to do His will.

David said in Psalm 17:3, *"You have tested my thoughts and examined my heart in the night. You have scrutinized me and found nothing wrong. I am determined not to sin in what I say."*

May we thank our Lord and Savior, for He sees it all.

APRIL 2

Controlling Sin

"You will be accepted if you do what is right. But if you refuse to do what is right, then watch out! Sin is crouching at the door, eager to control you. But you must subdue it and be its master." —Genesis 4:7

Sin. We were all born in it. We all struggle with it.

So, how do we subdue it and become its master, as God warns Cain here in Genesis? How do we keep sin from controlling us and dominating our lives?

First, we must invite the Spirit of the living God into our lives. Romans 8:9 tells us, *"But you are not controlled by your sinful nature. You are controlled by the Spirit if you have the Spirit of God living in you. (And remember that those who do not have the Spirit of Christ living in them do not belong to him at all.)"*

Second, we must resist the temptation to sin when it arises. James 4:7 tells us, *"So humble yourselves before God. Resist the devil, and he will flee from you."* I Corinthians 10:13 reminds us, *"The temptations in your life are no different from what others experience. And God is faithful. He will not allow the temptation to be more than you can stand. When you are tempted, he will show you a way out so that you can endure."*

Through Jesus' death on the cross, God declared an end to sin's control over us (Romans 8:3). If we allow our lives to be controlled by the Holy Spirit, sin is defeated.

Romans 8:5 says, *"Those who are dominated by the sinful nature think about sinful things, but those who are controlled by the Holy Spirit think about things that please the Spirit."*

May the Holy Spirit control your life today and always.

APRIL 3

Caught In A Whirlwind

"I, the LORD of Heaven's Armies, will act for you with thunder and earthquake and great noise, with whirlwind and storm and consuming fire." —Isaiah 29:6

Have you ever seen a whirlwind up close and personal? The power in those things is enormous, sweeping away everything and everyone in its path. You can't fight one and win.

Sometimes life's circumstances make us feel as though we are caught in a whirlwind. We feel as though we have been swept away. We keep fighting, but we feel there is no way we can win.

Let me remind you that there is a power greater than this whirlwind of circumstance you are fighting. That power is God, and He promises to fight your whirlwind with a whirlwind of His own.

He promises to act for you with thunder and earthquake and great noise, with whirlwind and storm and consuming fire.

Some circumstances in life are of our own making. But, when Satan tries to get the victory over God's redeemed, remember whose side you're on.

You have all the power of the Lord of Heaven's Armies at your disposal.

APRIL 4

Remarkable Secrets

"Ask me and I will tell you remarkable secrets you do not know about things to come." — Jeremiah 33:3

I don't know about you, but I love a good secret.

Sadly, the kinds of secrets I have often been a part of have been destructive rather than constructive. This type of secret has no redeeming value.

Yet, there are secrets and mysteries that are constructive, marvelous, and too wonderful to express in words.

These are the secrets that God has for us, and He is waiting to reveal them to us. He invites us to ask for this revelation.

How awesome to know that the Maker of the Universe has invited you and me to ask Him about the future!

And, these aren't just any secrets.

These are remarkable secrets.

They are secrets about things to come.

Rather than partaking in gossip, or any other type of destructive secrets, how about asking God to tell you remarkable secrets about things you do not know.

And, may this become the only type of secret you long to hear.

APRIL 5

The Father's Blessing

"All praise to God, the Father of our Lord Jesus Christ, who has blessed us with every spiritual blessing in the heavenly realms because we are united with Christ." —Ephesians 1:3

In the story of Jacob and Esau in Genesis 25-27, Jacob steals the blessing from his father that rightly belongs to his brother, Esau.

Scripture tells us that when Esau learned what his brother, Jacob, had done, he let out a loud and bitter cry. He then asked, *"Oh, haven't you saved even one blessing for me"* (Genesis 27:36)?

Have you felt like Esau? Do you feel as though your blessing has been taken from you? Perhaps you've made a poor choice or two, or have misplaced trust in someone who has disappointed or betrayed you.

May I remind you that your trust is never misplaced when it is rooted and grounded in your Heavenly Father?

Regardless of our circumstances—betrayal or disappointment—when our trust is in Christ, we are blessed with every spiritual blessing in the heavenly realms because we are united with Christ.

When you are at the point of letting out that loud and bitter cry, like Esau, may you rest in the truth that your Heavenly Father never runs out of blessings for you.

APRIL 6

When He Comes

"And he will send out his angels with the mighty blast of a trumpet, and they will gather his chosen ones from all over the world—from the farthest ends of the earth and heaven."
—Matthew 24:31

Christ has so much love for us that He has told us what to expect when He comes again. In Matthew 24, Jesus outlines the signs that indicate His return is soon. God doesn't want us to be deceived or misled. He outlines specific details for us regarding the events preceding His return.

Matthew 24 reminds us that wars, rumors of war, famine, and earthquakes are only the beginning of birth pains with more to come. It tells us that the followers of Christ will be arrested, persecuted, killed and hated all over the world.

We learn that many will turn away from Christ, betray and hate each other. There will be many false prophets that will appear and deceive many people. The sun and moon will be dark, and the stars will fall from the sky.

Matthew 24:12 tells us, *"Sin will be rampant everywhere and the love of many will grow cold."*

But, in all of that bad news, there is good news, too. The gospel will be preached everywhere, and everyone will have an opportunity to know and accept Christ as personal Savior.

None of us knows the day or the hour of Christ's return, but we do know that if we endure to the end, we will be saved.

May you continue in faithful, obedient service to Christ—no matter how difficult the road may be.

APRIL 7

Listen To God

"Listen to his instructions, and store them in your heart." —Job 22:22

Who are you listening to?

Our lives are surrounded by different influences—some positive, some negative, some from the forces of darkness, and some from the forces of light.

We must learn to be aware of the influences around us. Negative influences can be so subtle that they can drastically impact our life's course without our even realizing it.

Are you paying attention?

Are you listening to the instructions of Christ, and storing them in your heart?

The voice of Christ speaking to your heart is never contrary to His Word.

May you remain rooted and grounded in the Word of God. May you hide His Word in your heart.

And, may you finish strong the race He has given you to run.

APRIL 8

Forgiven Much, Loves Much

"I tell you, her sins—and they are many—have been forgiven, so she has shown me much love. But a person who is forgiven little shows only little love." —Luke 7:47

James was a man in East Texas who had lived a hard and sinful life. When I met him at the age of fifteen, I knew he was the kind of young man whom my parents would want me to avoid at all cost.

One day, James came to church with his grandmother. When the invitation was given at the end of the service, James gave his heart and life to Jesus Christ.

I never saw a man—young or old—more changed than James. He went from hardened and hateful, to humble and loving. His heart was more generous than anyone I had known up until that point.

It was the power of God that transformed James that September Sunday. He had been forgiven much, and understood the sacrifice God made in sending His one and only son to die for each and every sin—each and every sin James committed.

That same sacrifice was made for your sins and mine.

May we recognize that we all have been forgiven much, and may we be filled with the boundless, selfless love of Christ toward everyone we encounter.

APRIL 9

He Thrills Me

"You thrill me, LORD, with all you have done for me! I sing for joy because of what you have done." —Psalm 92:4

Have you ever looked out across a snow-capped mountain peak and felt the brisk air across your face? Have you watched an eagle take flight in the clear blue sky, smelled a rose, felt the skin of a newborn baby, or taken a bite from a sun-ripened strawberry?

Have you known what it is like to be rescued in times of trouble, experienced the kindness of a stranger, or, been surprised by good news on an otherwise normal day?

If you have experienced any of these things, then you know what it is to be thrilled by our Lord and Savior, Jesus Christ.

Exodus 15:11 says, *"Who is like you among the gods, O LORD—glorious in holiness, awesome in splendor, performing great wonders?"*

May you take joy in the thrilling, awesome nature of our God.

"Come and see what our God has done, what awesome miracles he performs for people" (Psalm 66:5)!

APRIL 10

No Favorites

"God knows people's hearts, and he confirmed that he accepts Gentiles by giving them the Holy Spirit, just as he did to us. He made no distinction between us and them, for he cleansed their hearts through faith. So why are you now challenging God by burdening the Gentile believers with a yoke that neither we nor our ancestors were able to bear? We believe that we are all saved the same way, by the undeserved grace of the Lord Jesus." —Acts 15:8-11

God doesn't play favorites. He cleanses us all the same way—through faith in his Son, Jesus Christ. He accepts us all the same way, too, giving us all His Holy Spirit. And, He saves us the same way—through the undeserved grace of our Lord and Savior, Jesus Christ.

Are you playing favorites, when God is not?

I am reminded of a young dairy farm boy who, as a youth, was denied membership in the local church youth group because the youth director found him to be "too worldly." This same dairy farm boy was nearly expelled from Bob Jones College before transferring to Florida Bible Institute, and finally graduating from Wheaton College with a degree in anthropology in 1943.

This young man didn't ever really fit the earthly mold that people tried to create for him. He was a square peg. Many well-meaning individuals attempted to burden this young man with a yoke of legalism that they, themselves, were unable to bear. Yet, Billy Graham believed the *Holy Bible* to be the infallible Word of God. He accepted God's grace, and honored His call to preach the gospel.

Jew or Gentile, slave or free, rich or poor, black or white, good home or no home, God's undeserved grace is available to us all.

And, where others see a shepherd boy, God may see a king.

APRIL 11

No Cliques In God's Kingdom

Everyone listened quietly as Barnabas and Paul told about the miraculous signs and wonders God had done through them among the Gentiles. When they had finished, James stood and said, "Brothers, listen to me. Peter has told you about the time God first visited the Gentiles to take from them a people for himself. And this conversion of Gentiles is exactly what the prophets predicted. As it is written: 'Afterward I will return and restore the fallen house of David. I will rebuild its ruins and restore it, so that the rest of humanity might seek the Lord, including the Gentiles—all those I have called to be mine. The Lord has spoken—he who made these things known so long ago.'" —Acts 15:12-18

It was a fulfillment of prophecy—challenging the establishment. The establishment had always been Jewish.

This was a drastic change. The Jews needed the reminder that this change was from God, it was designed by God. The Lord had spoken. There were to be no cliques in His Kingdom. It was time for all of humanity to seek the Lord. The traditional way of doing things was coming to an end.

I still remember it like it was yesterday. Having grown up with little in the way of material things, the amount of money and lavish lifestyles I encountered as a student at Baylor University were completely foreign to me, but I wanted to belong, to be a part of the establishment. Joining a sorority seemed, to me, the best course of action.

As I donned one of the three Sunday dresses from my closet and slipped out into the dorm hallway for the first Rush gathering, I was overwhelmed by the pearls, furs, fancy purses, nail polish, shiny shoes, and dresses much fancier than my Sunday best. I quickly returned to my room, replacing my Sunday dress with a favorite sweatshirt and jeans, and determining never to come back out.

Those three Greek letters I saw across multi-colored jerseys each Friday taunted me throughout the year, and again the next year as I struggled for the nerve to try again. When I finally did try again, I was rejected.

Three Greek letters, so elusive. How I wanted sorority sisters. I wanted to be a part, to belong.

As the years progressed, I observed that many of the sororities were merely cliques, and that God blessed me with something so much sweeter than sorority sisters—Kingdom sisters. My Kingdom sisters didn't care if I was rich or poor. They stood by me through thick and thin, and they're still around—just the way God planned it.

God's Kingdom has no room for cliques. May we search our hearts, and always remember to love and accept everyone whom God has called to be His own.

APRIL 12

Study To Show Yourself Approved

"Work hard so you can present yourself to God and receive his approval. Be a good worker, one who does not need to be ashamed and who correctly explains the word of truth."
—2 Timothy 2:15

Do you put forth your best effort in all that you say and all that you do? Or, are you content to do just enough to "get by".

The *Holy Bible* reminds us in Ecclesiastes 9:10, *"Whatever you do, do well. For when you go to the grave, there will be no work or planning or knowledge or wisdom."*

Our brief life on this Earth is a proving ground for our eternity, though we do not fully see or understand it. Ecclesiastes 3:11 tells us, *"Yet God has made everything beautiful for its own time. He has planted eternity in the human heart, but even so, people cannot see the whole scope of God's work from beginning to end."*

May we commit everything we have and are in hard work and devotion to Christ. May we not miss out on any aspect of God's Kingdom.

"Work hard to enter the narrow door to God's Kingdom, for many will try to enter but will fail" (Luke 13:24).

APRIL 13

Ugly Ol' Pride

"Pride goes before destruction, and haughtiness before a fall." —Proverbs 16:18

A young lady in a store dressing room came out into the open wearing a beautiful purple dress and asked her friend, "How do I look?"

Her friend quickly responded with, "The dress looks lovely, but I suggest you leave the pride on the hanger in the dressing room. It just doesn't go with the dress."

Ouch.

Those words were apples of gold in settings of silver, and though painful for the receiver, they communicated both truth and love.

So often we have no idea that we have slipped pride on in the morning along with our other garments. Sometimes it sits on our shoulders, and other times it covers everything we have on.

We usually never see it—like that white fuzzy on the back of our slacks.

Sadly, everyone else sees it.

And, it's ugly.

May we confess our pride to our Heavenly Father, repent of it, and leave it at the foot of the cross.

After all, it doesn't look good on anyone.

APRIL 14

Mirror, Mirror

"But don't just listen to God's word. You must do what it says. Otherwise, you are only fooling yourselves. For if you listen to the word and don't obey, it is like glancing at your face in a mirror. You see yourself, walk away, and forget what you look like." —James 1:22-24

One of the bittersweet aspects of being a parent is observing a reflection of yourself in your children. Very often, children reflect both the good things and the bad things they see exhibited in the lives of their parents.

Why is that?

It is because of the amount of time we spend together. We tend to imitate and emulate those with whom we spend the most time.

Our lives are also a reflection of the amount of time we spend with our Heavenly Father. If we are spending time with Him, our lives will reflect that, and the fruit of the Spirit— love, joy, peace, patience, kindness, goodness, faithfulness, gentleness, self-control—will be evident in our lives.

May we look deeply into God's mirror, and may we find in our hearts a reflection of His presence to share with each and every person we meet.

APRIL 15

No Barriers To Christ

"And so my judgment is that we should not make it difficult for the Gentiles who are turning to God. Instead, we should write and tell them to abstain from eating food offered to idols, from sexual immorality, from eating the meat of strangled animals, and from consuming blood. For these laws of Moses have been preached in Jewish synagogues in every city on every Sabbath for many generations." —Acts 15:19-21

The gospel of Christ is for everyone.

Paul knew that, and he knew that the Gentiles would face enough difficulty in their Christian walk without the Jews creating unnecessary hurdles for them. And so, he recommended a standard that would enable the Gentiles to assimilate easily with other Jewish Christians without creating resentment.

Paul's recommendation demonstrated both love and wisdom for Jewish and Gentile Christians.

But, what about us?

Do we create unnecessary barriers for others seeking a relationship with Christ?

Do we insist that they follow our manmade traditions rather than God's Word?

Do we cling to "we've always done it this way" rather than asking, "What would Jesus do?"

May we seek love and wisdom, as Paul did, removing unnecessary barriers for people of different backgrounds to incorporate with us, remembering that if we have accepted Christ as our personal Savior, we are all His children.

APRIL 16

Soothing The Savage Beast

"We understand that some men from here have troubled you and upset you with their teaching, but we did not send them! So we decided, having come to complete agreement, to send you official representatives, along with our beloved Barnabas and Paul, who have risked their lives for the name of our Lord Jesus Christ. We are sending Judas and Silas to confirm what we have decided concerning your question." —Acts 15:24-27

It happened in the workplace. Someone with inaccurate information sent an inflamed e-mail to upper management, instigating a firestorm from every direction. The beast was unleashed, and it was all based on misinformation.

By the time I became involved, the top level of the company was involved, and a squall was headed my way.

Yet, once the misinformation was corrected, the storm subsided, and the savages were soothed, for the most part. A credible source confirmed the correct information, and the last of the savages was put to rest.

It is the same today in the body of Christ. A little misinformation can set off quite a firestorm, as it did in this passage of Scripture. The misinformation was corrected, and credible sources—Paul, Barnabas, Judas, and Silas—were sent to confirm the information.

The savage beast was soothed.

May we diligently seek to learn the Scriptures so as to avoid error as we proclaim the truth of God's Word, and keep savages out of God's sanctuary.

APRIL 17

Who Do You Think You Are

"O people of Judah and Jerusalem, surrender your pride and power. Change your hearts before the LORD, or my anger will burn like an unquenchable fire because of all your sins." — Jeremiah 4:4

I am amazed by the number of people I encounter in this day and age who recount there episodes of being angry at God for the various situations and challenges they face in this life.

Friend, we ought never have the audacity, the arrogance to be angry at the Creator, the one who formed our very soul, the depth of our being.

Any anger we may feel over the many difficulties we all face in life is misdirected if directed toward God.

The *Holy Bible* tells us in James 1:20, *"Human anger does not produce the righteousness God desires."*

Hebrews 5:7 tells us that even Christ himself had reverence for God, *"While Jesus was here on earth, he offered prayers and pleadings, with a loud cry and tears, to the one who could rescue him from death. And God heard his prayers because of his deep reverence for God."*

So, just who do you think you are?

If you are God's child, your anger should never be directed at Him. He deserves your praise and honor—both now and forevermore. He is the source of all good things—every good and perfect gift (James 1:17).

"Praise the LORD, all you who fear him! Honor him, all you descendants of Jacob! Show him reverence, all you descendants of Israel" (Psalm 22:23)!

APRIL 18

No Shortcuts

"Good planning and hard work lead to prosperity, but hasty shortcuts lead to poverty." — Proverbs 21:5

There are no shortcuts to obedience where our relationship with Christ is concerned.

Many would try to rationalize or "grace away" the need for obedience to Christ.

But, it can't be done.

John 3:36 tells us, *"And anyone who believes in God's Son has eternal life. Anyone who doesn't obey the Son will never experience eternal life but remains under God's angry judgment."*

Our obedience to Christ is a demonstration of our love and commitment to Him. It is the evidence of our salvation.

The *Holy Bible* tells us in I John 2:4-5, *"If someone claims, 'I know God,' but doesn't obey God's commandments, that person is a liar and is not living in the truth. But those who obey God's word truly show how completely they love him. That is how we know we are living in him."*

Are you living in obedience to Christ today? If not, you can start today. Ask God to help you, and to give you wisdom.

He will not rebuke you for asking (James 1:5).

APRIL 19

Real Love

"There is no greater love than to lay down one's life for one's friends." —John 15:13

Do you know what real love is?

When I was a teenager, I can recall asking my mother if she thought Daddy was her *soul mate*. She didn't hesitate, but was quick to chuckle and respond with an emphatic, "no."

She went on to say, "Just how could a human being be our *soul mate*? Our *soul mate* should be God, the maker of our soul. Anyone else is just a disappointment."

As I considered that response, I realized just how accurate it was.

Who else, but Jesus, has laid down His life out of love for us (John 3:16)?

Who, but Christ, can love us even through the powers of hell (Romans 8:38)?

David, in the book of Psalms, refers repeatedly to the *unfailing* love of the Lord. In Psalm 63:3 we read, *"Your unfailing love is better than life itself; how I praise you!"*

I Corinthians 13 tells us exactly what real love looks like. Who, but Christ, possesses all of these characteristics without fail?

May you get in touch with your real soul mate, and let Him teach you what real love is all about.

APRIL 20

The Long Night

"This message came to me concerning Edom: Someone from Edom keeps calling to me, 'Watchman, how much longer until morning? When will the night be over?'" —Isaiah 21:11

Have you ever experienced a set of circumstances so difficult that they seemed to last forever? Maybe you're there now. You feel as though nothing will ever change, or that you'll never escape the dark night you're facing.

Perhaps you feel like Job felt as recorded in Job 7:4, *"Lying in bed, I think, 'When will it be morning?' But the night drags on, and I toss till dawn."*

Often the mistake we make when we encounter difficult circumstances is that we give up too soon. Because we have a lack of faith, we tend to throw in the towel too early. Our desire is to see results with our own eyes, and when we can't see, we assume nothing will ever change or get better—forgetting that all the while, God is working behind the scenes.

Romans 8:28 tells us, *"And we know that God causes everything to work together for the good of those who love God and are called according to his purpose for them."*

Remember today how much God loves you, sees you, and is busy doing things that we don't see every day.

Hold on, my friend. It is always darkest before the dawn. Ecclesiastes 11:7 says, *"Light is sweet; how pleasant to see a new day dawning."*

"For his anger lasts only a moment, but his favor lasts a lifetime! Weeping may last through the night, but joy comes with the morning" (Psalm 30:5).

APRIL 21

There's A Fork In My Road, But I Asked For A Spoon

"The whole countryside is open to you. Take your choice of any section of the land you want, and we will separate. If you want the land to the left, then I'll take the land on the right. If you prefer the land on the right, then I'll go to the left." —Genesis 13:9

I don't know about you, but I wasn't born with a silver spoon in my mouth. Although, as soon as I realized all the things a silver spoon could provide, I worked hard at scooping up all life had to offer, eager to have my fill of the finer things in life. What I failed to realize at the time was that God's definition of "the finer things" is different than the world's definition. Ecclesiastes 10:2 tells us, *"A wise person chooses the right road; a fool takes the wrong one."*

But, how do we know which fork in the road to take? How can we avoid the pitfalls of making the wrong choice?

Romans 6:16 tells us, *"Don't you realize that you become the slave of whatever you choose to obey? You can be a slave to sin, which leads to death, or you can choose to obey God, which leads to righteous living."*

Isaiah 48:17 says, *"This is what the Lord says—your Redeemer, the Holy One of Israel: "I am the Lord your God, who teaches you what is good for you and leads you along the paths you should follow."*

Psalm 25:12 tells us, *"Who are those who fear the LORD? He will show them the path they should choose."*

May we follow the fork God has chosen for us—today and every day.

APRIL 22

What's In Your Garden

"I said, 'Plant the good seeds of righteousness, and you will harvest a crop of love. Plow up the hard ground of your hearts, for now is the time to seek the LORD, that he may come and shower righteousness upon you.'" —Hosea 10:12

As a youngster growing up in Trinity, Texas, it was a family chore to assist Daddy in the planting, care, and weeding of the family garden.

Great care was taken first in the preparation of the soil. Daddy made sure it was tilled and soft, ready for the seed. Next, just the right seed was selected—a good seed that the expert gardener at the feed store recommended.

Once the seed was planted, Daddy watered it daily, making sure the roots had every opportunity to grow deep into the ground.

Then, the most difficult and painful task of gardening was the ongoing task of weeding the garden as the plants began to grow. It was a constant effort to remove the weeds, allowing the seeds to flourish. Occasionally, the weeds overtook a seed that otherwise seemed healthy before we even realized what was happening to it.

What about you and me? Has the soil of our hearts been tilled? Is it soft and ready for God's Word to be planted deep enough to take root? Are we watering it daily through prayer and more Bible study? And, are we weeding out the evil worldly influences, keeping our lives pure (Psalm 119:9)? Are we living in the world without being of the world (2 Corinthians 6:17)? May we be diligent and ever mindful of what is in our personal garden each and every day.

APRIL 23

American Idols

"You must worship no other gods, for the LORD, whose very name is Jealous, is a God who is jealous about his relationship with you." —Exodus 34:14

Chocolate is one of the things in this world that I have repeatedly thanked God for creating.

I have loved it. I have thought about it. I have spent much money on it. I even bought a cacao tree in support of my affection for it.

Some time back, I was stricken with a bacterial illness that required me to give up all chocolate and sugar for six months. Sadly, it seemed a fate worse than death to me, which would be my fate should I fail to follow the doctor's orders.

Yet, I realized through the process that it was the loving hand of God showing me that I had allowed something so silly to gain an unhealthy and sinful place in my life. I was, in a sense, a slave to chocolate.

What's your chocolate?

Is there anything in your life that is consuming your thoughts, your time, your money, your affection more than God?

Deuteronomy 4:24 tells us, *"The LORD your God is a devouring fire; he is a jealous God."*

May you examine your life before Him, and ask the Holy Spirit to guide you in purging any and all idols from your life today.

APRIL 24

Wasted Days And Wasted Nights

"A few days later this younger son packed all his belongings and moved to a distant land, and there he wasted all his money in wild living." —Luke 15:13

It is the story of the prodigal son. The younger of two brothers asks his father for his portion of the family inheritance, and leaves home. The son wastes everything he has been given in wild living, only to realize he had it good at home and has made a tragic mistake.

The prodigal son had no doubt been taught right from wrong, and knew the right path to take, yet he was one who had to learn things the hard way.

Are you like that? Do you rebel against instruction only to discover through some tragedy that you should have listened?

My friend, our days are numbered on this earth. Psalm 39:4 reminds us, *"LORD, remind me how brief my time on earth will be. Remind me that my days are numbered—how fleeting my life is."*

Proverbs 10:17 tells us, *"People who accept discipline are on the pathway to life, but those who ignore correction will go astray."* We have all known individuals who have come to the end of their lives wishing they had not wasted so much time in failing to do right.

Will that be you?

May we accept correction, choose what is right, and use wisely the brief moments God has blessed us with upon this earth.

APRIL 25

Shine It Forward

"No one lights a lamp and then hides it or puts it under a basket. Instead, a lamp is placed on a stand, where its light can be seen by all who enter the house." —Luke 11:33

In the Book of Exodus, when the Lord provides instruction to Moses regarding the building of the Tabernacle, He is very specific, providing exact measurements and materials for every detail of its construction. The instructions even indicate that the cherubim will face each other and look down upon the atonement table. There is significance in every detail of the instruction.

Of particular interest are the plans for the lampstand as recorded in Exodus 25:31-39. Verse 37 says, *"Then make the seven lamps for the lampstand, and set them so they reflect their light forward."*

Reflect their light forward . . .

Your lamp is to reflect its light forward, too.

Christ is the light of the world, and if you have a personal relationship with Him, that same light lives in you. You must share it, so that all the world can see.

John 1:5 tells us, *"The light shines in the darkness, and the darkness can never extinguish it."*

This little light of mine, I'm gonna let it shine, I'm going to let it shine forward, and how wonderful to know that the darkness can never put it out.

APRIL 26

Guilty By Association

"Walk with the wise and become wise; associate with fools and get in trouble." — Proverbs 13:20

The old saying, "birds of a feather flock together" is often true. We tend to desire the company of those most like us—people we can relate to.

But, what do we do when we find ourselves in a situation that requires us to spend time with those having convictions opposite ours, or having no conviction at all?

The *Holy Bible* tells us in 2 Corinthians 6:14, *"Don't team up with those who are unbelievers. How can righteousness be a partner with wickedness? How can light live with darkness?"*

We know, also, that evil company corrupts good habits (I Corinthians 15:33), and Proverbs 1:10 tells us, *"My son, if sinful men entice you, do not give in to them."*

If we associate with evil doers, we will often find ourselves judged and assumed to be of like mind. And, although we are called to be Christ's witnesses and to share salvation with a lost and dying world, the *Holy Bible* is clear regarding our association with those who claim to be Christians, yet do not walk the walk. I Corinthians 5:11 tells us, *"I meant that you are not to associate with anyone who claims to be a believer yet indulges in sexual sin, or is greedy, or worships idols, or is abusive, or is a drunkard, or cheats people. Don't even eat with such people."*

May you guard your heart and your associations, as Proverbs 4:23 tells us, *"Guard your heart above all else, for it determines the course of your life."*

APRIL 27

Wait And Pray

"They all met together and were constantly united in prayer, along with Mary the mother of Jesus, several other women, and the brothers of Jesus." —Acts 1:14

The Day of Pentecost was a miraculous outpouring of the Holy Spirit's power for the blessing of all who were in Jerusalem. It brought glory and honor to God, and continues to carry a blessing to us even today. The blessing lies in what we can learn from Pentecost.

One of the lessons Pentecost teaches is that when God tells us to wait, we must wait. In Acts 1:4, before Jesus ascended into heaven, the *Holy Bible* tells us, *"Once when he was eating with them, he commanded them, 'Do not leave Jerusalem until the Father sends you the gift he promised, as I told you before.'"*

Jesus' followers obeyed this command to wait. Unlike those at Pentecost, we tend to give up too quickly and miss out on God's blessing in our life and the lives of others.

A second lesson we can learn from Pentecost is to pray. Acts 1:14 tells us, *"They all met together and were constantly united in prayer, along with Mary the mother of Jesus, several other women, and the brothers of Jesus."* The *Holy Bible* repeatedly reminds us of the importance of prayer. We must pray constantly, without stopping (I Thessalonians 5:17) in order to fully realize the power of God's Holy Spirit in our lives and the lives of those around us.

Is there an area of your life in which God has asked you to wait and pray?

May you wait and pray, believing that the Holy Spirit's power is every bit as real and available to you as it was at Pentecost.

APRIL 28

The Company You Keep

"Don't envy evil people or desire their company." —Proverbs 24:1

Have you ever noticed two completely different people becoming similar in behavioral characteristics over time? We tend to develop the qualities and actions of those we spend the most time with.

So, what about you?

Who are you spending time with?

I Corinthians 15:33 reminds us, *"Don't be fooled by those who say such things, for "bad company corrupts good character."*

If we want to be like Christ, we must spend time with Him. We must not continue to keep company with those having habits contrary to the will of God.

We must also spend time with other believers in Christ for support and encouragement, as Hebrews 10:25 says, *"And let us not neglect our meeting together, as some people do, but encourage one another, especially now that the day of his return is drawing near."*

Are you spending time each day alone with God? Are you spending time reading His Word? Do you spend time with other believers who exhibit the fruit of the Spirit in a powerful way?

May you choose wisely the company you keep today and every day.

APRIL 29

War Ready

"Praise the LORD, who is my rock. He trains my hands for war and gives my fingers skill for battle." —Psalm 144:1

Ready or not, you are involved in a war every day of your life. It is a spiritual war against our adversary, the devil.

The *Holy Bible* tells us in Ephesians 6:12, *"For we are not fighting against flesh-and-blood enemies, but against evil rulers and authorities of the unseen world, against mighty powers in this dark world, and against evil spirits in the heavenly places."*

To win any war, you must be prepared. I Peter 2:11 advises, *"Dear friends, I warn you as 'temporary residents and foreigners' to keep away from worldly desires that wage war against your very souls."*

There is spiritual armor for this war that we are fighting, as Ephesians 6:13-17 entreats us, *"Therefore, put on every piece of God's armor so you will be able to resist the enemy in the time of evil. Then after the battle you will still be standing firm. Stand your ground, putting on the belt of truth and the body armor of God's righteousness. For shoes, put on the peace that comes from the Good News so that you will be fully prepared. In addition to all of these, hold up the shield of faith to stop the fiery arrows of the devil. Put on salvation as your helmet, and take the sword of the Spirit, which is the word of God."*

James 4:7 promises, *"So humble yourselves before God. Resist the devil, and he will flee from you."*

If we will but stay close to God, girded in His armor, and resist the devil, our Lord, who trains us for war, will give us the victory.

APRIL 30

The Proof Of His Love

"And have you forgotten the encouraging words God spoke to you as his children? He said, 'My child, don't make light of the Lord's discipline, and don't give up when he corrects you. For the Lord disciplines those he loves, and he punishes each one he accepts as his child.'"
—Hebrews 12:5-6

Show me a successful child or adult, and I'll show you someone who has been lovingly corrected, and who has chosen to accept this correction.

Correction is one of the many ways in which God exhibits His love for us.

No, correction is not pleasant at the time we receive it. As the *Holy Bible* says in Hebrews 12:11, *"No discipline is enjoyable while it is happening—it's painful! But afterward there will be a peaceful harvest of right living for those who are trained in this way."*

Correction is necessary in teaching us good judgment and the way to life (Proverbs 4:1, 6:23, 10:17). If we are wise, we will learn to love the discipline and correction of our Heavenly Father (Proverbs 12:1).

Correction is the evidence of God's love for us, steering us back to the straight and narrow path, guiding us in the pathway of life. If we will heed His correction, our souls will be saved from hell.

Revelation 3:19 tells us, *"I correct and discipline everyone I love. So be diligent and turn from your indifference."*

May you choose to accept the loving correction of your Heavenly Father today and every day of your life.

MAY 1

The Mysteries Of Eternity

"For who can prove that the human spirit goes up and the spirit of animals goes down into the earth?" —Ecclesiastes 3:21

There are many things about our eternity that we do not know or understand—many mysteries. Ecclesiastes 11:5 says, *"Just as you cannot understand the path of the wind or the mystery of a tiny baby growing in its mother's womb, so you cannot understand the activity of God, who does all things."*

We may not know or understand the secrets to these and other mysteries until we are in Heaven. Jesus often spoke in parables during His earthly ministry. These parables were often a mystery to those who were not His followers (Luke 8:9-10).

Yet, in Jeremiah 33:2-3 we read, *"This is what the Lord says—the Lord who made the earth, who formed and established it, whose name is the Lord: Ask me and I will tell you remarkable secrets you do not know about things to come."*

With regard to our eternity, I Corinthians 15:51 tells us, *"But let me reveal to you a wonderful secret. We will not all die, but we will all be transformed!"*

While we do not know or understand exactly what will happen to us when we die, as followers of Christ, we *do* know who holds our eternity, and that He has gone to prepare a place for us. As John 14:2 tells us, *"There is more than enough room in my Father's home. If this were not so, would I have told you that I am going to prepare a place for you?"*

May we rest in knowing who holds our eternity—it is He who reveals all mysteries. He makes all to be.

MAY 2

Let There Be Peace

"I search for peace; but when I speak of peace, they want war!" —Psalm 120:7

Have you ever had one of those days in your home that felt like World War III and the Battle of Armageddon all rolled into one?

I have.

It is at these times when we echo the cry of King David in this Scripture reference. These are the times that we long for peace the most.

So, how and where do we find it?

The *Holy Bible* answers that question for us very simply in Proverbs 16:7. It says, *"When people's lives please the LORD, even their enemies are at peace with them."*

Are you living a life that is pleasing to the Lord?

When we focus on Him, then we will find peace. It is the gift of God.

"I am leaving you with a gift—peace of mind and heart. And the peace I give is a gift the world cannot give. So don't be troubled or afraid" (John 14:27).

Are you facing a time of personal war in your life? Remember the words of Romans 5:1, *"Therefore, since we have been made right in God's sight by faith, we have peace with God because of what Jesus Christ our Lord has done for us."*

MAY 3

There Is Power

"I pray that God, the source of hope, will fill you completely with joy and peace because you trust in him. Then you will overflow with confident hope through the power of the Holy Spirit." —Romans 15:13

Do you recognize the Holy Spirit's power at work in your life?

By the Holy Spirit's power, a virgin gave birth to the Son of God. By the Holy Spirit's power, this same Son of God was raised from the dead after three days. Through the Holy Spirit's power, Jesus of Nazareth healed all those who were oppressed by the devil, for God was with Him. By the Holy Spirit's power, the apostle Paul's very plain preaching drew many thousands of people to a saving knowledge of Christ. By the Holy Spirit's power, three thousand were added to the Church at Pentecost.

The *Holy Bible* tells us in Galatians 5:16, *"So I say, let the Holy Spirit guide your lives. Then you won't be doing what your sinful nature craves."* That is a powerful promise.

2 Timothy 1:14 says, *"Through the power of the Holy Spirit who lives within us, carefully guard the precious truth that has been entrusted to you."*

God's truth is a precious gift—a powerful gift, and we must encourage each other to live within the guidance of the Holy Spirit. There is no limit to His power in and through our lives each and every day.

As we learn to be His vessel, may we encourage one another as Jude 1:20-21 entreats us, *"But you, dear friends, must build each other up in your most holy faith, pray in the power of the Holy Spirit, and await the mercy of our Lord Jesus Christ, who will bring you eternal life. In this way, you will keep yourselves safe in God's love."*

And, may you recognize the power of the Holy Spirit at work in and around you today.

MAY 4

Renew Your Mind

"Don't copy the behavior and customs of this world, but let God transform you into a new person by changing the way you think. Then you will learn to know God's will for you, which is good and pleasing and perfect." —Romans 12:2

This world has customs and habits that are completely contrary to the will of God in our lives. Revenge, using one another, hatred, holding grudges, greed, selfishness, impatience, lust, harshness, bullying, lying, cheating, stealing, these are just a few of the accepted practices in our culture, as long as we can justify them. And, according to the world's system, just about anything counts as justification.

But, God doesn't want us to think and act the way the world does. He wants us to be different. He wants our minds and our lives to be transformed. So, how do we become this transformed person? And, what does this transformation look like?

Ephesians 4:21-24 tells us, *"Since you have heard about Jesus and have learned the truth that comes from him, throw off your old sinful nature and your former way of life, which is corrupted by lust and deception. Instead, let the Spirit renew your thoughts and attitudes. Put on your new nature, created to be like God—truly righteous and holy."*

And, may we never give up, knowing that our spirits are being renewed every day (2 Corinthians 4:16).

MAY 5

Devoted Daniel

"Then the other administrators and high officers began searching for some fault in the way Daniel was handling government affairs, but they couldn't find anything to criticize or condemn. He was faithful, always responsible, and completely trustworthy." —Daniel 6:4

Daniel was completely devoted to God.

This devotion was evident in every aspect of Daniel's life. From the time he spent in prayer, down to every morsel of food he allowed to enter his body, Daniel led a disciplined life.

This was true of Daniel because he had one and only one master. That master was God. Daniel knew that in every decision he faced throughout life, he was accountable ultimately and only to God.

The *Holy Bible* tells us in Titus 2:12-13, *"And we are instructed to turn from godless living and sinful pleasures. We should live in this evil world with wisdom, righteousness, and devotion to God, while we look forward with hope to that wonderful day when the glory of our great God and Savior, Jesus Christ, will be revealed."*

Are you devoted to God?

Or, is there some area of your life that you continue to withhold from Him?

The yielded life, the devoted life is the life that is equipped to experience the Holy Spirit's power in all its fullness.

May you devote yourself completely to Him today.

MAY 6

The Power Of Kindness

"Never let loyalty and kindness leave you! Tie them around your neck as a reminder. Write them deep within your heart." —Proverbs 3:3

Kindness is powerful. Proverbs 25:21-22 says, *"If your enemies are hungry, give them food to eat. If they are thirsty, give them water to drink. You will heap burning coals of shame on their heads, and the Lord will reward you."*

This verse doesn't tell us that our actions will change our enemies and cause them to do what is right. No, in fact, Isaiah 26:10 tells us, *"Your kindness to the wicked does not make them do good. Although others do right, the wicked keep doing wrong and take no notice of the LORD's majesty."*

But, this verse does tell us that our actions will be rewarded by God.

Are you a kind person? Kindness can be defined as being considerate and having a benevolent nature. Consider the power of kindness in God's relationship with us. Romans 2:4 says, *"Don't you see how wonderfully kind, tolerant, and patient God is with you? Does this mean nothing to you? Can't you see that his kindness is intended to turn you from your sin?"*

It is God's kindness, His goodness that leads us to repentance.

May you know and understand the power of this kindness today, and may we follow God's example in extending kindness to others, regardless of their response.

"In his kindness God called you to share in his eternal glory by means of Christ Jesus. So after you have suffered a little while, he will restore, support, and strengthen you, and he will place you on a firm foundation" (I Peter 5:10).

MAY 7

A Bold Witness

"The members of the council were amazed when they saw the boldness of Peter and John, for they could see that they were ordinary men with no special training in the Scriptures. They also recognized them as men who had been with Jesus." —Acts 4:13

Are you a bold witness for Christ? Some of the boldest witnesses for Him are probably not even aware of the effectiveness of their witness and the difference that is made by the testimony of their lives.

Peter and John never really saw the complete, full and lasting impact of their bold act of obedience in speaking to the members of the Sanhedrin. They were just two men against a ruling body that was seventy-one members strong.

And, God gave them boldness.

Later, the believers prayed together for boldness in Acts 4:29, and the *Holy Bible* tells us God answered their prayer, as Acts 4:31 tells us, *"After this prayer, the meeting place shook, and they were all filled with the Holy Spirit. Then they preached the word of God with boldness."*

Paul, one of the boldest witnesses recorded in the *Holy Bible*, asked the church at Ephesus to pray that he would have boldness in Ephesians 6:19, *"And pray for me, too. Ask God to give me the right words so I can boldly explain God's mysterious plan that the Good News is for Jews and Gentiles alike."*

We can ask God to enable us to speak boldly for His sake, too.

And, may you believe that He will answer your prayer for boldness today.

MAY 8

I Am Determined

"I have chosen to be faithful; I have determined to live by your regulations." —Psalm 119:30

I am determined to live for Christ.

That statement is an open invitation for Satan to attack my life and yours from every direction and in every way known to man, and then some.

So, does that mean we should give up? If we slip along the path, should we quit?

No.

The *Holy Bible* tells us in Romans 8:35-37, *"Can anything ever separate us from Christ's love? Does it mean he no longer loves us if we have trouble or calamity, or are persecuted, or hungry, or destitute, or in danger, or threatened with death? (As the Scriptures say, 'For your sake we are killed every day; we are being slaughtered like sheep.') No, despite all these things, overwhelming victory is ours through Christ, who loved us."*

Read that again.

Have you determined to be faithful to God?

May we say with David, *"I am determined to keep your decrees to the very end"* (Psalm 119:112).

MAY 9

Stand Up For Truth

"'My people bend their tongues like bows to shoot out lies. They refuse to stand up for the truth. They only go from bad to worse. They do not know me,' says the LORD." —Jeremiah 9:3

The American twenty-first century embraces a culture of tolerance and acceptance of any and every belief, it seems, except Christianity.

We have laws and rules to defend homosexual and transgender rights, yet we can no longer post the Ten Commandments, the very foundation of our Judicial System, in our courthouses.

Yet, these struggles are no different than the struggles of our sinful society since the days of Adam and Eve. There have been struggles against the forces of evil, pagan religions, and idol worship for all time.

The joy that can be found in the midst of these struggles is knowing that God's truth stands forever (2 Timothy 2;19; Psalm 119:160).

Ephesians 6:14 encourages us by saying, *"Stand your ground, putting on the belt of truth and the body armor of God's righteousness."*

2 Corinthians 13:8 says, *"For we cannot oppose the truth, but must always stand for the truth."*

It is not always easy to stand for truth. May God grant us courage as we stand for His truth today.

"Be on guard. Stand firm in the faith. Be courageous. Be strong" (I Corinthians 16:13).

MAY 10

Signs

He replied, "You know the saying, 'Red sky at night means fair weather tomorrow; red sky in the morning means foul weather all day.' You know how to interpret the weather signs in the sky, but you don't know how to interpret the signs of the times!" —Matthew 16:2-3

Signs.

They are everywhere.

When we are driving, signs tell us when to stop, go, speed up, slow down, yield, and use caution.

But, what about in life?

The same signs are there in life, too.

Do you see them?

Can you hear them?

Isaiah 30:21 tells us, *"Your own ears will hear him. Right behind you a voice will say, 'This is the way you should go,' whether to the right or to the left."*

Jesus said in John 10:27, *"My sheep listen to my voice; I know them, and they follow me."*

There is an undeniable mystical aspect to our faith. It is not merely an exercise of brain power, but encompasses soul and spirit.

The exercise of our soul and spirit comes through daily communion with God through prayer and the reading of His Word.

May you recognize and follow the life signs surrounding you today and every day.

MAY 11

Secret Sin

"You spread out our sins before you— our secret sins—and you see them all." —Psalm 90:8

God sees everything—the good and the bad. I remember having many conversations with my son when he was very young about this subject.

My son was disturbed by the many injustices he saw in school, even in kindergarten. "Mom," he would say, "They do wrong things and they never get caught or punished!" It was upsetting to him.

But, the *Holy Bible* reminds us that we are all *caught*. God sees it all—even those sins we think no one knows anything about. God sees those, too.

And, rest assured, they will not go unpunished. Ecclesiastes 12:14 says, *"God will judge us for everything we do, including every secret thing, whether good or bad."*

Jeremiah 17:10 tells us, *"But I, the LORD, search all hearts and examine secret motives. I give all people their due rewards, according to what their actions deserve."*

In Luke 12:2 we read, *"The time is coming when everything that is covered up will be revealed, and all that is secret will be made known to all."*

And, in Romans 2:16, the *Holy Bible* warns, *"And this is the message I proclaim—that the day is coming when God, through Christ Jesus, will judge everyone's secret life."*

The converse is true, too. The day is coming when all good deeds done in secret will come to light, as well (I Timothy 5:25).

The choice is up to you.

MAY 12

Planet Me

"Don't be selfish; don't try to impress others. Be humble, thinking of others as better than yourselves." —Philippians 2:3

Do you live on your own planet?

This planet that I am referring to is one in which you are the center, and all others revolve around you. It is a planet that seeks to satisfy your own wants and desires without thought for the needs of others. It is a planet in which you reign supreme. You are all-knowledgeable, and no one else has insight or opinion that matters one iota to you.

This planet also justifies sin—any and every kind of sin it pleases. There is no consideration for consequences or impact on others' lives.

God's Word talks about this planet. It tells us that if we want to be a follower of Christ, we must turn from our selfish ways, pick up Jesus' cross daily and follow Him (Luke 9:23). And, it's not an option. It's a requirement. We can't have it both ways—there is but one way.

That one way is God's way.

The *Holy Bible* tells us in John 14:6, *"Jesus told him, "I am the way, the truth, and the life. No one can come to the Father except through me."*

If we claim to be His disciple, then we can't live on Planet Me.

We can't even vacation there.

May we humble ourselves and consider others better than us today and every day.

MAY 13

The Buzzard And The Eagle

"But those who trust in the LORD will find new strength. They will soar high on wings like eagles. They will run and not grow weary. They will walk and not faint." —Isaiah 40:31

Are you an eagle or a buzzard? Upon first sighting in the air, they appear quite similar. It is only upon closer examination that we begin to recognize the striking differences.

If you were to put an eagle in a cage and remove the lid, it would soar to the highest heights, the majestic leader of the sky. Its prior captivity seen as no deterrent to the present.

Yet, if you place a buzzard in a cage and remove the lid, it would stay in the cage, looking for a runway in which to take off and escape. It has the same ability to flap its wings and soar as the eagle. Yet, it does not.

In addition to flight differences, eagles and buzzards differ in the way they subsist. Buzzards are bottom feeders, waiting for someone else to kill their prey. Afterward, they lie in wait to steal, taking credit for what they did not earn.

Eagles, on the other hand, do not eat dead flesh killed by another. They kill and eat their own prey, that which they have earned. They soar above the buzzard and all of the other birds.

These distinctive differences are just as apparent in those who are lead by the Spirit, and those who are not. So, what about you? Do you live your life as an eagle or a buzzard? And, what about those you spend your time with? Are you spending your time with the eagles or the buzzards of the world?

May the Holy Spirit guide you to soar with the eagles.

MAY 14

Three Blind Mice

Jesus replied, "Every plant not planted by my heavenly Father will be uprooted, so ignore them. They are blind guides leading the blind, and if one blind person guides another, they will both fall into a ditch." —Matthew 15:13-14

In the nursery rhyme, *Three Blind Mice,* the mice have no idea where they are going and find themselves in danger of losing their tails to the knife-wielding farmer's wife.

In our Scripture passage, Jesus tells us to ignore those who have not been planted by the Heavenly Father, for they will be uprooted. They are the blind leading the blind, and worse than losing their tails to the farmer's wife, if we follow them, we will end up in the pit or the ditch with them, or worse—losing our very soul.

So, how do we recognize Christ and avoid these blind guides? How do we stay out of the ditch? The *Holy Bible* tells us how. John 10:3 tells us, *"The gatekeeper opens the gate for him, and the sheep recognize his voice and come to him. He calls his own sheep by name and leads them out."*

John 14:17 says, *"He is the Holy Spirit, who leads into all truth. The world cannot receive him, because it isn't looking for him and doesn't recognize him. But you know him, because he lives with you now and later will be in you."*

Christ brings us out of darkness and into his glorious light. *"For you are the fountain of life, the light by which we see"* (Psalm 36:9).

John Newton's beloved hymn, *Amazing Grace,* reminds us "I once was lost, but now am found, was blind, but now I see."

May our eyes be ever open to see God's truth.

MAY 15

Ignorance Is Bliss

"For the leaders of my people— the LORD's watchmen, his shepherds— are blind and ignorant. They are like silent watchdogs that give no warning when danger comes. They love to lie around, sleeping and dreaming." —Isaiah 56:10

There are many in today's pulpits who do not belong. They are the silent watchdogs, the blind, the ignorant, and the lazy that are described in this passage of Scripture. Yet, many of them have large, loyal congregations.

Why?

Matthew 7:13-14 tells us why. It says, *"You can enter God's Kingdom only through the narrow gate. The highway to hell is broad, and its gate is wide for the many who choose that way. But the gateway to life is very narrow and the road is difficult, and only a few ever find it."*

The blind watchmen described in Isaiah are only interested in their own personal gain. They are false prophets who, upon closer examination, have no integrity, no character, and no fruit. They tickle men's ears and use flattery to enlarge themselves and their congregations for their own advantage.

Matthew 7:15-16 reminds us to, *"Beware of false prophets who come disguised as harmless sheep but are really vicious wolves. You can identify them by their fruit, that is, by the way they act. Can you pick grapes from thornbushes, or figs from thistles?"*

May we not be blissfully ignorant, but ever sober and vigilant, for our adversary, Satan, prowls around like a roaring lion, seeking to devour us (I Peter 5:8).

MAY 16

Dissonant Chords

"Even lifeless instruments like the flute or the harp must play the notes clearly, or no one will recognize the melody." —I Corinthians 14:7

Have you ever felt as though the melody of your life was out of tune? Perhaps you feel as though every chord you play comes out sounding dissonant, despite your best efforts.

Dissonance is what happens when we try to accomplish things in our own strength, in our own power, and without the love of God in our hearts.

Just as a skilled pianist must first learn the notes of the staff, key signatures, musical signs and symbols to play the sonata, so the Christian must learn what it means to follow Christ and have a close personal relationship with Him

The skilled pianist must practice to be effective, just as the Christian must practice Christianity.

The practice of Christianity consists of spending time with Christ through prayer and reading the *Holy Bible*. There is no substitute for these things, and no short-cut to gaining a closer relationship with Christ—just as there is no substitute or short-cut for practicing the piano to become a professional pianist.

The result of this practice is a life without dissonant chords, that plays a crystal clear, beautiful melody for all who hear it.

MAY 17

The Pied Piper

"And now, just as you accepted Christ Jesus as your Lord, you must continue to follow him."
—Colossians 2:6

In "The Pied Piper of Hamelin" by Robert Browning, the town of Hamelin is overrun with rats. A stranger comes to town, promising to rid the town of its rat problem. The leaders of the town promise the man a large sum of money if he can accomplish the task. The Pied Piper takes out his pipe, charms all of the rats into following him, and all but one are drowned in the river. The leaders of Hamelin are overjoyed, yet refuse to honor their agreement, failing to pay the Pied Piper the promised amount. The Pied Piper repays the townspeople by charming away their children.

While this is certainly not a Biblical story, there is a Kingdom principle at work here with regard to following through and keeping the commitments we make.

As the Scripture reference above reminds us, we cannot take our commitment to Christ lightly. Once we have accepted Him as Savior, we must continue to follow Him.

A part of following through in our commitment to Him is keeping our word as it relates to others. Hosea 10:4, talking about the Israelites, says, *"They spout empty words and make covenants they don't intend to keep. So injustice springs up among them like poisonous weeds in a farmer's field."*

The same could be said of the people in Hamelin, who lost their children as a result of not having any intention of keeping their word.

May we follow-through, and may our word be our bond in our relationship with Christ and with others.

MAY 18

While You Were Sleeping

"Suddenly, a fierce storm struck the lake, with waves breaking into the boat. But Jesus was sleeping." —Matthew 8:24

The disciples were very frightened by the storm, and went to wake Jesus up. They shouted at Him, *"Lord, save us! We're going to drown"* (Matthew 8:25)!

But, Jesus knew they weren't going to drown. He had performed many miracles for them already. He chided them for their lack of faith. Then, he rebuked the wind and the waves and suddenly all was calm (Matthew 8:26).

What about you? Are there storms in your life? Do you feel as though you will drown from the weight of your personal storm? Do you shout at your Savior to save you?

If you've lived for any length of time at all, you have experienced some sort of difficulty. And, if you are a follower of Christ, He has proven Himself to you through the course of that difficulty and others.

So, where is our faith?

Our Savior is not sleeping.

No. He is simply waiting for us to trust that He is who He claims to be, who He has proven Himself to be in our lives.

He *is* our Savior.

Isaiah 59:1 tells us, *"Listen! The Lord's arm is not too weak to save you, nor is his ear too deaf to hear you call."*

MAY 19

We're Off To See The Wizard

"'What do you want me to do for you?' Jesus asked. 'My rabbi,' the blind man said, 'I want to see!'" —Mark 10:51

Jesus is not a wizard as some suppose Him to be, like the "Great and Mighty" Oz. He is nothing of the kind. To compare Him in this manner is complete sacrilege.

Yet, why do so many approach Him with their Christmas wish list as though He were Santa Claus or a genie in a lamp?

God *does* long to meet our deepest needs. Matthew 7:11 tells us, *"So if you sinful people know how to give good gifts to your children, how much more will your heavenly Father give good gifts to those who ask him."*

So, why shouldn't we ask Him for a heart, a brain, courage, or a home?

It isn't that we shouldn't ask, but the condition of our heart, the level of our faith, and the reasons for asking are important. Why? It is simply because our Heavenly Father is so much more, and He wants so much more for us than *just* those things on our wish list.

We must have the right motivation for requesting from God, as James 4:3 tells us, *"And even when you ask, you don't get it because your motives are all wrong—you want only what will give you pleasure."*

"Seek the Kingdom of God above all else, and live righteously, and he will give you everything you need" (Matthew 6:33).

MAY 20

The Vow

"It is better to say nothing than to make a promise and not keep it." —Ecclesiastes 5:5

The spoken word is a powerful thing.

It can break the human spirit better than a whip, or it can elevate and inspire beyond the flight of eagles.

For a wise and prudent man, his spoken word is his bond, but to the fool, vows are meaningless and meant to be broken. Or, they are made in haste, without fully realizing or understanding their cost.

In Judges Chapter 11, we read the story of Jephthah, a great warrior who made a vow to the Lord, that if He would give Jephthah victory over the Ammonites, Jephthah would sacrifice whatever came out of his house first as a burnt offering to the Lord.

Sadly, the first thing to come out of Jephthah's house was his one and only child—his precious daughter. Jephthah allowed his daughter to roam the hills in mourning for two months, as she requested.

After that time, Jephthah fulfilled his vow.

It is important to realize that God had already given Jephthah victory in battle. The Holy Spirit was on his side. There was no vow necessary.

Are you busy making promises, vows and deals with God in an effort to get Him to join your side?

The *Holy Bible* tells us in I Samuel 15:22 that, *"To obey is better than sacrifice . . ."*

And, may we remember to say a simple "yes" or "no" as anything else comes from the evil one (Matthew 5:37).

MAY 21

Progress Vs. The Progressive

"But we must hold on to the progress we have already made." —Philippians 3:16

The Christian life is a marathon journey marked by tragedy and triumph. There are hills and valleys along the way, and in order to be successful in this, our journey, we must be well-prepared.

The Pilgrim's Progress by John Bunyan outlines this journey, its pitfalls and perils, as well as its hopes and joys. This story reminds us, also, of the importance of taking great care regarding who we listen to and spend time with. There is a stark contrast between those who would enable our progress and those who would impede it. Yet, outwardly, the difference is often hard to recognize.

Take, for instance, the individual claiming to be Progressive. The Progressive individual seeks to replace Biblical morals and values with the accepted social norms of the time. At first glance, this appears as forward-motion and making progress in the journey. But, upon closer examination, it is Socialism, Communism, and all manner of evil that is contrary to the Word of God. The Progressive sugarcoats sin, accepting it as "the changing times we live in."

May we be always vigilant and mindful of what is going on around us, for our adversary the devil walks around like a roaring lion, seeking whom he may devour (I Peter 5:8).

MAY 22

Oh, Be Careful

"So be very careful to love the LORD your God." —Joshua 23:11

When I was a little girl, my mother would sing a song called, *Oh, Be Careful*, that begins like this:

Oh, Be Careful

Oh, be careful little eyes,
what you see
Oh, be careful little eyes,
what you see
For the Father up above,
is looking down in love,
So be careful little eyes
what you see.

This song goes on to talk about what we hear, do, say, and where we go.

The older I get, the more I realize how important this song is no matter what age we are. Life with God is not a trivial affair to be entered into lightly. The warning to "be careful" is used ninety-two times in the New Living Translation of the *Holy Bible*.

Proverbs 4:23 tells us, *"Guard your heart above all else, for it determines the course of your life."*

In this world of temptation at every turn, may we remember to raise our standard, being careful to guard what we see, what we hear, what we say, what we do, and where we go today and every day.

One life can make a powerful difference in eternity.

MAY 23

When Nobody's Looking

"May integrity and honesty protect me, for I put my hope in you." —Psalm 25:21

Integrity is doing the right thing when no one is watching us. And, while we think no one is watching, we know that God is always watching what we do.

Proverbs 15:3 tells us, *"The LORD is watching everywhere, keeping his eye on both the evil and the good."*

When my son was in pre-kindergarten, he was quite upset over another little boy who had a propensity for doing wrong, especially when the teacher wasn't looking. My son was disturbed because the little boy never seemed to get caught.

"It isn't fair," he would say to me.

I gently reminded him that God sees. God always sees, and the *Holy Bible* reminds us that we will all reap what we sow (Galatians 6:7).

Numbers 32:23 tells us to be sure that our sin will find us out.

And, Ecclesiastes 12:14 says, *"God will judge us for everything we do, including every secret thing, whether good or bad."*

So, what about you? And, what about me? Are we lacking in integrity? Are there things that we are doing in secret that we'd rather not have exposed?

May we bring them before the throne of God today, may we repent, and seek His mercy and forgiveness.

And, may we choose to live a life of humble service and integrity that is pleasing to God today and every day.

MAY 24

The Hidden Hand

"His splendor was like the sunrise; rays flashed from his hand, where his power was hidden."
—*Habakkuk 3:4*

There is a wonderful novel written in 1859 by Mrs. E.D.E.N. Southworth entitled, The Hidden Hand. The story is a winding tale which depicts beautifully the myriad of ways that God intervenes in our lives and circumstances to accomplish His purposes, and to right the wrongs that no one else sees.

This principle was true in a fictional novel from 1859, and it is alive and well today, too.

The *Holy Bible* tells us in Mark 4:22, *"For everything that is hidden will eventually be brought into the open, and every secret will be brought to light."*

And, may we never forget Romans 8:28 which says, *"And we know that God causes everything to work together for the good of those who love God and are called according to his purpose for them."*

There have been times in my life when I was disturbed by a wrong or misunderstanding that I experienced at the hands of someone else. And, I have always been amazed to watch as God reveals His truth to me and others in such a powerful way as to bring about a just result over time. The events that are orchestrated are so supernatural and so perfect that they could only be the hidden hand of God.

Are you disturbed by some injustice, or by another's misconception of you? Do not fret or waste your time in worry. Simply leave your concern to the hidden hand of God.

MAY 25

The New Age

"Now I will tell you new things, secrets you have not yet heard." —Isaiah 48:6b

The New Age Movement that has gained popularity in the United States in recent decades espouses two very frightening lies: (1) There are many ways to God; and, (2) Truth and power are within us all.

These ideas are clearly from Satan, himself, and seek to pull us away from the truth of God. They are ideas that are crafted using Satan's favorite *modis operandi*: Take a small truth and wrap it in a great big lie.

The *Holy Bible* tells us clearly that there is but one way to God. Matthew 7:3 says, *"You can enter God's Kingdom only through the narrow gate. The highway to hell is broad, and its gate is wide for the many who choose that way."*

John 17:3 explains, *"And this is the way to have eternal life—to know you, the only true God, and Jesus Christ, the one you sent to earth."*

Truth and power are found in God alone. We can know His truth, and His Holy Spirit living inside us can embody His truth, but the truth is *His*.

John 14:6 says, *"Jesus told him, 'I am the way, the truth, and the life. No one can come to the Father except through me.'"*

May we fill our hearts and minds with God's truth today and every day, and may His Spirit flow freely from every pore in our being.

MAY 26

Grace On Display

"The wise don't make a show of their knowledge, but fools broadcast their foolishness." — *Proverbs 12:23*

When I was a little girl, there was a woman in the church I grew up in named Bettie. Bettie was a fine example of grace. She was kind, gentle, joyful, loving, peaceful, patient, she held her tongue when needed, and spoke when needed, as well. I wanted to be like Bettie when I grew up. She was an excellent example of grace on display, exhibiting the fruits of the Spirit in every aspect of her life.

Yet, the true epitome of grace on display was Jesus Christ, who was in all ways tempted as we are. And, He remained sinless.

Do you long to live a life that displays the grace of God to others?

The *Holy Bible* tells us in James 4:6, *"But he gives us even more grace to stand against such evil desires. As the Scriptures say, 'God opposes the proud but favors the humble.'"*

The secret to living a life of grace on display is being rightly-related to God. We must live a life of faith and devotion to Him in order to experience His grace fully in our lives. And, when we do this, we share His grace with others, as well.

May your life display His grace today and every day that follows.

MAY 27

Silence Of The Lamb

"When the Lamb broke the seventh seal on the scroll, there was silence throughout heaven for about half an hour." —Revelation 8:1

It is sad when honest, truth-telling, God-fearing people are silenced. Those who are paying attention to the world around them see this happening more and more each day. Clearly, there is a time to keep silent and a time to speak.

But, the silence of the God-fearing is nothing new. The shouting of fools is not new, either.

Consider the example of Christ, the Lamb of God, regarding silence. Jesus chose to remain silent when questioned by the high priest. And when elders and priests of the church brought accusations against Him, He continued in silence (Matthew 26:63; 27:12; Mark 14:61).

Jesus knew His response would not change the outcome, nor would it change the will of His Father in ransoming your life and mine through His Son.

One day it will be the accusers who will be silenced, as God turns the tables, as Isaiah 54:17 tells us, *"But in that coming day no weapon turned against you will succeed. You will silence every voice raised up to accuse you. These benefits are enjoyed by the servants of the LORD; their vindication will come from me. I, the LORD, have spoken!"*

May the way in which we live our lives silence our accusers, as I Peter 2:15 says, *"It is God's will that your honorable lives should silence those ignorant people who make foolish accusations against you."*

MAY 28

Too Late

"When the master of the house has locked the door, it will be too late. You will stand outside knocking and pleading, 'Lord, open the door for us!' But he will reply, 'I don't know you or where you come from.'" —Luke 13:25

There are a number of popular Christian songs out today containing the line "it's never too late." And, while I know the writers have the best of intentions and mean nothing but encouragement, the words are not true.

The *Holy Bible* teaches us that one day it will be too late for us to turn to Christ. One day it will be too late for us to choose to be obedient to Christ. And, one day the door to the Master's house will be closed and locked.

So often, we want to paint our picture with a broad brush that accepts everyone into God's Kingdom because God is love (I John 4:8). But, the road that leads to Him is a narrow road, and only few ever find it (Matthew 7:14). It is the road of obedience, and there is no substitute for that obedience. We cannot choose our own way and God's way, too.

Satan would have you to believe that a loving God would not make you give up your own way and your own desires, but it is a lie. It is the love of God that requires you to give up your own way—your way of selfishness and sin.

May we realize the truth and communicate this truth to everyone we come into contact with, that this truth will set them free from the bondage of sin, death, and hell both now and forever.

MAY 29

The High Road

"And I will make my mountains into level paths for them. The highways will be raised above the valleys." —Isaiah 49:11

We've heard it said before, that when someone treats us badly we should not stoop to their level, but should take the high road. But, what exactly does it mean to "take the high road"?

The *Holy Bible* is very clear.

Matthew 5:39-40 tells us, *"But I say, do not resist an evil person! If someone slaps you on the right cheek, offer the other cheek also. If you are sued in court and your shirt is taken from you, give your coat, too."*

The road that Christ has for us is different. It is beyond anything we could ever envision for ourselves, and the requirements are different, too.

To the person who does not know Christ and has no relationship with Him, taking the high road is difficult and is often inconceivable.

But for the Christian, the high road is the only way to live, and in following it, God grants us His peace and joy that passes all understanding.

Isaiah 35:8 says, *"And a great road will go through that once deserted land. It will be named the Highway of Holiness. Evil-minded people will never travel on it. It will be only for those who walk in God's ways; fools will never walk there."*

May we follow the high road, the Highway of Holiness, and though it may not be easy, we have Christ as our companion on the journey.

MAY 30

Good Medicine

"A cheerful heart is good medicine, but a broken spirit saps a person's strength." — Proverbs 17:22

Proverbs 15:30 tells us, *"A cheerful look brings joy to the heart; good news makes for good health."*

It is a proven scientific fact that laughter releases endorphins, which are the feel-good chemical of the brain. These endorphins are also natural pain and stress fighters in the body, contributing to a person's overall health and well-being.

In contrast, sadness causes a rise in blood pressure and blood sugar which can eventually lead to heart disease, coronary artery disease and other illnesses.

When we have a relationship with Christ there is always a reason to rejoice and be cheerful. We have a Heavenly Father who adores us, longs to spend time with us, and always has our back. Regardless the difficulty of circumstance we face, He is there with us throughout the storm, and will lead us through.

What could possibly be better than that?

Are you struggling with bouts of depression and sadness? Don't let the lies of the Devil drown out God's truth.

The *Holy Bible* tells us in Psalm 94:19, *"When doubts filled my mind, your comfort gave me renewed hope and cheer."*

"The LORD is my strength and shield. I trust him with all my heart. He helps me, and my heart is filled with joy. I burst out in songs of thanksgiving" (Psalm 28:7).

MAY 31

The Eye Of The Beholder

"How beautiful you are, my darling, how beautiful! Your eyes are like doves." — Song of Solomon 1:15

They say that beauty is in the eye of the beholder. There is something within each of us that longs for affection—longs for someone to find us beautiful in their eyes.

The *Holy Bible* tells us that God takes delight in us, and even rejoices over us with singing. Zephaniah 3:17 says, *"For the Lord your God is living among you. He is a mighty savior. He will take delight in you with gladness. With his love, he will calm all your fears. He will rejoice over you with joyful songs."*

Considering that we were created by God for His good pleasure (Ephesians 1:5), and in His own image (Genesis 1:27), if we desire to be adored, then how much more does our Heavenly Father desire our adoration?

Psalm 50:2 says, *"From Mount Zion, the perfection of beauty, God shines in glorious radiance."*

When we behold our Heavenly Father, how perfect, how beautiful, and how gloriously radiant we find Him.

May we see our gracious God always in the beauty of His holiness (I Chronicles 16:29).

"Yours, O LORD, is the greatness, the power, the glory, the victory, and the majesty. Everything in the heavens and on earth is yours, O LORD, and this is your kingdom. We adore you as the one who is over all things" (I Chronicles 29:11).

JUNE 1

The Man God Made

"Then God said, 'Let us make man in our image, to be like us. They will reign over the fish in the sea, the birds in the sky, the livestock, all the wild animals on the earth, and the small animals that scurry along the ground.'" —Genesis 1:26

Before the fall of man, God had a plan. He created man in His own image, to be like Him. He gave man dominion over all living things.

Genesis 2:7 explains, *"Then the Lord God formed the man from the dust of the ground. He breathed the breath of life into the man's nostrils, and the man became a living person."*

So, what was the man God made *really* like? First, Genesis 2:15 tells us, *"The Lord God placed the man in the Garden of Eden to tend and watch over it."* We can assume that the man God made found joy in this work that God had given him, as this was the perfect environment—with no thorns and no fallow ground.

We know, also, that Adam had to be highly intelligent. Genesis 2:19-20 tells us that God brought all of the creatures He made to Adam for naming. One would have to be equipped with extreme intelligence and language capacity to name and remember the names for all living things.

Adam's DNA was perfect—with none of the mutations that exist in all of us today, having been born into sin. Imagine the musical prodigy, art prodigy, and mathematical genius all rolled into one. He had full use of the brain power scientists tell us we utilize at only a fraction of capacity. May we praise our glorious Maker for the loving plan in which we were created. And, may we praise Him for the hope that is yet to come.

JUNE 2

The Woman God Made

"Then the Lord God said, 'It is not good for the man to be alone. I will make a helper who is just right for him.'" —Genesis 2:18

The *Holy Bible* tells us that God caused a great sleep to fall upon Adam, that He took a rib from Adam's side and formed from him and for him, a companion. (Genesis 2:21-22). Adam called her woman, the Hebrew transliteration *ezer*, meaning helper, or "one who helps." What a powerful position.

When God brought the woman to Adam, he exclaimed, *"At last! This one is bone from my bone, and flesh from my flesh! She will be called 'woman,' because she was taken from 'man'"* (Genesis 2:23). It is significant that she was flesh of his flesh and bone of his bone, depicting the bond that God intended between the two.

Adam went on to give this woman the name, Eve, which means *life* or *living* because she would be the mother of all living (Genesis 3:20). Genesis 2:24 tells us, *"This explains why a man leaves his father and mother and is joined to his wife, and the two are united into one."*

The woman that God made is also described in Proverbs 31:11-12; and Proverbs 31:25-29, *"Her husband can trust her, and she will greatly enrich his life. She brings him good, not harm, all the days of her life. She is clothed with strength and dignity, and she laughs without fear of the future. When she speaks, her words are wise, and she gives instructions with kindness. She carefully watches everything in her household and suffers nothing from laziness. Her children stand and bless her. Her husband praises her: 'There are many virtuous and capable women in the world, but you surpass them all!'"*

This is the woman that God made.

JUNE 3

The Marriage God Made

"'Haven't you read the Scriptures?' Jesus replied. 'They record that from the beginning God made them male and female.' And he said, 'This explains why a man leaves his father and mother and is joined to his wife, and the two are united into one. Since they are no longer two but one, let no one split apart what God has joined together.'" —Matthew 19:4-6

The marriage God made was for life (Romans 7:2).

It was the union of one man and one woman (Genesis 2:24).

God declared marriage to be an honorable estate (Hebrews 13:4).

A husband and wife are each to submit to one another out of reverence for the Lord (Ephesians 5:21).

A husband is to love his wife as Christ loved the church and gave His life for her (Ephesians 5:25).

A wife is to respect her husband (Ephesians 5:33).

As the church submits to Christ, so the wife should submit to her husband in everything (Ephesians 5:24).

Husbands are to love their wives as they love their own bodies, because a man who loves his wife actually shows love for himself (Ephesians 5:28).

A husband is to never treat his wife harshly (Colossians 3:19).

A wife is to accept the authority of her husband (I Peter 3:5), and the husband is to give honor to his wife (I Peter 3:7).

This is the marriage that God designed.

JUNE 4

Biblical Money Management

"The wicked borrow and never repay, but the godly are generous givers." —Psalm 37:21

The *Holy Bible* talks in great detail about the way we should handle the money and belongings that God has entrusted to us.

The idea of giving God a thank offering of the first and best of all He has entrusted to us began with Cain and Abel in Genesis 4. Jacob vowed to give God one-tenth of all he received from the Lord for protecting him on his journey in Genesis 28. The idea of giving one-tenth of all one had was added to the Jewish law in Leviticus 27.

We should pay our government taxes, as required, even if we think they are unfair, as Jesus said in Matthew 22:21, *"give to Caesar what belongs to Caesar, and give to God what belongs to God."*

Our Lord also taught us the importance of giving to the poor. Proverbs 28:27 tells us, *"Whoever gives to the poor will lack nothing, but those who close their eyes to poverty will be cursed."* And, in I Corinthians 16, Paul advised the believers in Corinth to set aside an amount they purposed in their heart on the first day of each week for the poor in Jerusalem.

The attitude with which we handle the Lord's wealth is also important. 2 Corinthians 9:7 tells us, *"You must each decide in your heart how much to give. And don't give reluctantly or in response to pressure. 'For God loves a person who gives cheerfully.'"* If we realize but a fraction of the generous nature of our Heavenly Father, this will be no problem for us. These are only a few of the passages in Scripture that tell us how to handle our Master's money.

May we be ever mindful of our Lord's principles in managing financial affairs.

JUNE 5

One Guarantee

"He has paid a full ransom for his people. He has guaranteed his covenant with them forever. What a holy, awe-inspiring name he has!" —Psalm 111:9

We've heard it said that in this life the only sure things are death and taxes. But, there is one certainty, one guarantee that is eternal, and it easily eclipses these two earthly events.

That guarantee is that nothing can separate us from the love of God.

Romans 8:38-39 explains, *"And I am convinced that nothing can ever separate us from God's love. Neither death nor life, neither angels nor demons, neither our fears for today nor our worries about tomorrow—not even the powers of hell can separate us from God's love. No power in the sky above or in the earth below—indeed, nothing in all creation will ever be able to separate us from the love of God that is revealed in Christ Jesus our Lord."*

That is an amazing guarantee and promise—far beyond what our earthly minds can truly comprehend.

Just think about it for a moment.

There is nothing you can do that will make God stop loving you—ever. What does that mean? I Corinthians 13 tells us exactly what love looks like, and I John 4:8 tells us that God *is* love.

May we allow this love to permeate our souls, transform our lives, and be reflected in every interaction of our existence.

JUNE 6

Hidden Treasure

"The Kingdom of Heaven is like a treasure that a man discovered hidden in a field. In his excitement, he hid it again and sold everything he owned to get enough money to buy the field." —Matthew 13:44

In the offshore oil and gas industry, an amazing amount of money and manpower is expended in an effort to find the elusive treasures of oil and natural gas.

Staffs of geologist pour over seismic data for months determining the best areas to drill. The data is often re-processed to ensure the most accurate results.

Drilling professionals are consulted to determine the necessary equipment and operations personnel for the project.

Partners are brought in to spread the risk and provide additional insight and expertise.

Still, with all of this effort, there is no promise that the hidden treasure beneath the ground will be found.

The Kingdom of Heaven is infinitely more valuable than oil or natural gas, yet God does give us a promise that if we seek, we will find it.

Jeremiah 29:13 tells us, *"If you look for me wholeheartedly, you will find me."*

Oh, that we might recognize the hidden treasure that is our Heavenly Father's Kingdom.

There is no staff of geologists or drilling operators needed to find this greatest of all hidden treasures.

May we look for Him with all of our heart, for we know He promises to be found.

JUNE 7

Are We There Yet

"I have traveled on many long journeys. I have faced danger from rivers and from robbers. I have faced danger from my own people, the Jews, as well as from the Gentiles. I have faced danger in the cities, in the deserts, and on the seas. And I have faced danger from men who claim to be believers but are not." —2 Corinthians 11:26

As a youngster on family vacations, I vividly remember asking my father time and again, "Are we there yet?" The trip back home made me even more anxious.

My own children have been no different—especially as we travelled from Southeast Texas to Yellowstone one summer.

Often throughout my journey with Christ, I have asked my Heavenly Father the same thing. "Are we there yet, Father? How much longer? When will we be there?"

Each time, our patient, compassionate, gentle, and loving Heavenly Father responds. Always, His response is far beyond my expectations.

We aren't there yet, and often the road is long, exhausting, and we want to stop or even quit.

John 14:2 says, *"There is more than enough room in my Father's home. If this were not so, would I have told you that I am going to prepare a place for you?"*

Keep going. You'll get there. And, God will have your place ready.

JUNE 8

God's Lovingkindness

"As long as the earth remains, there will be planting and harvest, cold and heat, summer and winter, day and night." —Genesis 8:22

In Genesis 8, we read the account of Noah exiting the ark after the floodwaters subsided, and offering a sacrifice of thanksgiving to God. God promises Noah that he will never again curse the ground because of the human race, and He will never again destroy all living things.

It is a display of God's lovingkindness. The Hebrew transliteration of lovingkindness is *chesed*. It is the idea of a never-ending, unfailing, compassionate love that is active. This word also embodies the notion of rescuing one in times of extreme distress. It is God's lovingkindness, His *chesed*, that has borne witness to all humanity through His mercy, patience, and sacrifice for us, as well.

Psalm 36:7 says, *"How precious is your unfailing love, O God! All humanity finds shelter in the shadow of your wings."*

Jeremiah 31:3 tells us, *"Long ago the Lord said to Israel: 'I have loved you, my people, with an everlasting love. With unfailing love I have drawn you to myself.'"*

The great hymn, "He Lifted Me," written by Charles Gabriel, aptly reminds us:

In lovingkindness Jesus came
My soul in mercy to reclaim.
And from the depths of sin and shame
Thro' grace He lifted me.

Regardless of how low we feel we have sunk; God's lovingkindness can reach us wherever we are.

JUNE 9

The Daily Work

"Anyone who does not provide for their relatives, and especially for their own household, has denied the faith and is worse than an unbeliever." —I Timothy 5:8

The daily work of the Christian life is not glamorous. It is the stuff borne out of necessity and obedience. For the most part, it is unnoticed by man, but it is always noticed by God.

God wants us to work, and not to be idle.

John 9:4 tells us, *"We must quickly carry out the tasks assigned us by the one who sent us. The night is coming, and then no one can work."*

No, the bands don't always play for us while we carry out these tasks. There is no applause. Men won't necessarily pat us on the back, either. The kind of attention sought by Hollywood wannabes and the like is foreign to the Christian's daily walk.

Romans 2:29b reminds us, *"And a person with a changed heart seeks praise from God, not from people."*

Yet, there is a reward.

James 1:12 promises us, *"God blesses those who patiently endure testing and temptation. Afterward they will receive the crown of life that God has promised to those who love him."*

Not only that, but when our work on earth is through and we accomplish God's purposes, *"The master said, 'Well done, my good and faithful servant. You have been faithful in handling this small amount, so now I will give you many more responsibilities. Let's celebrate together'"* (Matthew 25:23)!

JUNE 10

Behind The Curtain

"This hope is a strong and trustworthy anchor for our souls. It leads us through the curtain into God's inner sanctuary." —Hebrews 6:19

Behind the Iron Curtain of communism in the post-World War II era was capitalism. The boundary line was marked by the Berlin Wall. The Iron Curtain fell on November 9, 1989, when Eastern bloc countries were liberated from communism and allowed to cross into West Germany. They were no longer separated from one another, but were now opened to a new way of life. Yet, some continue living as though the wall is still there—even today.

Behind the curtain of the Tabernacle, the Ark of the Covenant was housed. Behind this curtain was the Most Holy Place, the Holy of Holies. It was a place separating God and the High Priest from the Jews.

When Jesus, the Christ, died on the cross, Mark 15:38 tells us, *"And the curtain in the sanctuary of the Temple was torn in two, from top to bottom."*

The *Holy Bible* goes on to tell us, in Hebrews 10:20, *"By his death, Jesus opened a new and life-giving way through the curtain into the Most Holy Place."*

Jesus death and resurrection opened to all of us a new way of life. We are now free to enter into God's inner sanctuary. We are free to go behind the curtain. We are free to dwell with Him. Yet, some continue living as though the curtain was never rent. They fail to receive the gift of God's Son.

May we take full advantage of this freedom to dwell with Him today and every day.

JUNE 11

Words That Are Never Wasted

"It is the same with my word. I send it out, and it always produces fruit. It will accomplish all I want it to, and it will prosper everywhere I send it." —Isaiah 55:11

Have you ever wondered if what you say really matters or makes a difference to someone else?

There are words that you never have to wonder about. They always make a difference to the listener. They always produce fruit. And, they always accomplish God's purposes.

What words do I refer to?

I am referring to God's Word, the *Holy Bible*. The words in this book are never wasted. His Word always prospers.

Isaiah 40:8 says, *"The grass withers and the flowers fade, but the word of our God stands forever."*

That is a powerful promise.

Are you in a dilemma wondering what to say or do? Do you wonder how you will be received?

Let God's Word do the talking for you.

His Word will never fail.

JUNE 12

No Hesitation

"As Jesus walked beside the Sea of Galilee, he saw Simon and his brother Andrew casting a net into the lake, for they were fishermen. 'Come, follow me,' Jesus said, 'and I will send you out to fish for people.' At once they left their nets and followed him." —Mark 1:16-18

This passage of Scripture has always been remarkable to me because when Simon and his brother, Andrew, were called by Jesus, they didn't hesitate to go with Him.

Verse 18 tells us, "At once" they followed him. There was no delay.

When Jesus called others in Luke 9:59-61, they hesitated. One simply wanted to bury his father. Another wanted to bid farewell to those in his household. Luke 9:62 says, *"But Jesus told him, 'Anyone who puts a hand to the plow and then looks back is not fit for the Kingdom of God.'"*

Do you look longingly back at the world instead of plowing ahead in the task that God has called you to?

If so, the *Holy Bible* tells us that we are unfit for God's Kingdom. This is a stern, yet loving, warning that Jesus gives.

I am reminded of Lot's wife as the angels led her from the burning land of Sodom. Lot, his wife, and daughters were warned not to stop anywhere or to look back. But, Lot's wife looked back, and she became a pillar of salt (Genesis 19).

My mother often said to me as a child growing up, "Delayed obedience is disobedience." These same words have been echoed to my own children.

May we obey God's call on our life at once—with no hesitation—that we might be fit for the Kingdom of God.

JUNE 13

What Ever Happened To Making A Difference

"But among you it will be different. Those who are the greatest among you should take the lowest rank, and the leader should be like a servant." —Luke 22:26

One life does make a difference.

One life invented the electric light. One life worked to develop a vaccine for polio. One life discovered that the Sun, not the Earth, was at the center of the Solar System. One life discovered that genes were located on chromosomes. One life discovered a new world called, America, and dared to believe that the Earth was round.

One life obeyed God and built an ark out of gopher wood. One life believed and became the voice of one crying in the wilderness, preparing the way of the Lord. One life was a life after God's own heart. One life was the most humble man that ever lived. One life was used by God to save Egypt and Israel from famine. One life listened to God for the interpretation of dreams.

And, one life was created like you and me, was tempted in all ways like you and me, yet was without sin. One life was given so that you might find life.

One life.

Your life.

Every life makes a difference.

What difference will be made through your life today?

JUNE 14

Hardening Of The Heart

"I said, 'Plant the good seeds of righteousness, and you will harvest a crop of love. Plow up the hard ground of your hearts, for now is the time to seek the LORD, that he may come and shower righteousness upon you.'" —Hosea 10:12

The precious, tender heart of a child is like no other. It trusts. It believes. It loves. It is loyal.

Over time, this same heart is hurt. It learns it cannot trust, so it fails to be loyal. It often stops believing because it has been disappointed. It is betrayed and experiences hatred, and pride, impeding its ability to love.

Doctors often explain that a literal hardening of the heart precedes its failure as we age.

But, there is a beautiful rebirth that God can bring to this heart. Ezekiel 36:26 tells us, "And I will give you a new heart, and I will put a new spirit in you. I will take out your stony, stubborn heart and give you a tender, responsive heart."

When we turn our lives over to Christ, we enter into a covenant relationship with Him, and He puts His laws in our heart, and writes them on our minds (Hebrews 10:16).

No matter how bad your past sin, a relationship with Christ actually has the power to make our spiritual heart pure, innocent, and soft again—like that of a little child. That is the kind of heart that God desires. That is the power of a right relationship with Him.

May you allow Him to cleanse you of sin, purify your mind, and soften your heart today.

JUNE 15

In Season

"They are like trees planted along the riverbank, bearing fruit each season. Their leaves never wither, and they prosper in all they do." —Psalm 1:3

While picking lemons in our yard last fall, I was struck by the fact that God's timing for their harvest season is so very perfect. They ripen in late fall, just before the cold and flu season, and as I squeeze a bit into my water each day, I find this wondrous gift keeps me from taking ill as we are so prone to do this time of year.

The same is true for the timing of other fruits, nuts, berries and vegetables—God times their harvest season perfectly.

When we are rightly related to God, He causes our lives to bring forth a harvest that is perfectly timed, as well. It is just the right crop, produced in just the right season.

There is also a harvest that is ripe and ready for picking right now. John 4:35 tells us, *"You know the saying, 'Four months between planting and harvest.' But I say, wake up and look around. The fields are already ripe for harvest."*

May we labor for our Master, bringing in the sheaves that are white unto harvest, while we patiently wait for our Lord's return.

James 5:7 says, *"Dear brothers and sisters, be patient as you wait for the Lord's return. Consider the farmers who patiently wait for the rains in the fall and in the spring. They eagerly look for the valuable harvest to ripen."*

His return, too, will be in the perfect season.

JUNE 16

More Believing

"Abraham never wavered in believing God's promise. In fact, his faith grew stronger, and in this he brought glory to God." —Romans 4:20

There is a quote by Oswald Chambers in My Utmost for His Highest that says, "The great need is not to do things, but to believe things."

Do you need to believe things? The disciples had the need to believe.

They were quite a bit like you and I. Give me a checklist of things that need to get done, a To-Do list, and I'm your girl. But, ask me to believe something extraordinary, something I've never seen happen before, and I often have difficulty.

But, why?

The disciples experienced the extraordinary with Jesus every day. Yet truly grasping His death and resurrection was remarkable and difficult for them. Knowing this, Jesus even said to them in John 14:12, *"I tell you the truth, anyone who believes in me will do the same works I have done, and even greater works, because I am going to be with the Father."*

God wants to do something extraordinary—something never seen before—in and through your life today.

Won't you simply believe?

JUNE 17

The Spirit Is Willing, But The Flesh Is Weak

"Jesus and his disciples went on to the villages around Caesarea Philippi. On the way he asked them, 'Who do people say I am?' They replied, 'Some say John the Baptist; others say Elijah; and still others, one of the prophets.' 'But what about you?' he asked. 'Who do you say I am?' Peter answered, 'You are the Messiah.' Jesus warned them not to tell anyone about him. He then began to teach them that the Son of Man must suffer many things and be rejected by the elders, the chief priests and the teachers of the law, and that he must be killed and after three days rise again. He spoke plainly about this, and Peter took him aside and began to rebuke him. But when Jesus turned and looked at his disciples, he rebuked Peter. 'Get behind me, Satan!' he said. 'You do not have in mind the concerns of God, but merely human concerns.'"
—MARK 8:27-33

There they were, walking on the road to Philippi. Jesus asked the disciples who they thought He was. Peter answered correctly, *"You are the Messiah."* Matthew's account of the story adds, *"Jesus replied, 'You are blessed, Simon son of John, because my Father in heaven has revealed this to you. You did not learn this from any human being'"* (Matthew 16:17). Peter got it. He understood who Jesus really was.

Yet, almost immediately Peter's flesh took over, and he had the audacity to rebuke his master, his teacher, the Messiah.

It is no different with us. I can recall several occasions when I was certain I would never fall prey to a certain sin—like so-and-so had—only to be guilty of the very same thing in my next breath.

In Matthew 26:41, Jesus tells us, *"Watch and pray, lest you enter into temptation. The spirit indeed is willing, but the flesh is weak."*

May we heed the warning of our Messiah to watch and pray, lest we fall into temptation today.

JUNE 18

Correcting The Master

"'You will all fall away,' Jesus told them, 'for it is written: I will strike the shepherd, and the sheep will be scattered. But after I have risen, I will go ahead of you into Galilee.' Peter declared, 'Even if all fall away, I will not.' 'Truly I tell you,' Jesus answered, 'today—yes, tonight—before the rooster crows twice you yourself will disown me three times.' But Peter insisted emphatically, 'Even if I have to die with you, I will never disown you.' And all the others said the same." —Mark 14:27-31

Jesus had earned a position of trust with the disciples. They watched and were astounded by the many miracles He performed. Yet still, they corrected Him, insisting that He was wrong about them falling away, insisting He had misjudged their devotion to Him, insisting He did not know their true nature, commitment, and character.

Not only are they insistent, but when Jesus tells them exactly when and how it will happen, they continue to argue with Him. It was all because they simply did not like what He had to say.

Do you ever argue with God? Do you ever try to correct His understanding of things, just because you don't like what He has to say?

Sadly, I have been known to try to convince my Savior of that which He knows otherwise. The *Holy Bible* reminds us in Matthew 10:24, *"A disciple is not above his teacher, nor a servant above his master."*

What about you?

Oh, that we might humble ourselves to receive our Master's truth—without argument, edits, or correction.

JUNE 19

Not I

"While Peter was below in the courtyard, one of the servant girls of the high priest came by. When she saw Peter warming himself, she looked closely at him. 'You also were with that Nazarene, Jesus,' she said. But he denied it. 'I don't know or understand what you're talking about,' he said, and went out into the entryway. When the servant girl saw him there, she said again to those standing around, 'This fellow is one of them.' Again he denied it. After a little while, those standing near said to Peter, 'Surely you are one of them, for you are a Galilean.' He began to call down curses, and he swore to them, 'I don't know this man you're talking about.' Immediately the rooster crowed the second time. Then Peter remembered the word Jesus had spoken to him: 'Before the rooster crows twice you will disown me three times.' And he broke down and wept." —Mark 14:66-72

Do any of these sound familiar to you?

"I didn't do it!"

"I didn't eat the last cookie!"

"I didn't break the vase!"

"I don't know how that dent got in the car!"

"I have no idea how that happened!"

For Peter, it was, *"I don't know what you're talking about! I don't know him! I don't know this man you're talking about!"* He was so adamant in his denial as to curse.

Jesus had predicted that before the rooster crowed twice, Peter would deny Him three times. Yet, Peter denied he would deny the Messiah. Then, when he recalled the words of Jesus, he wept.

Have you ever done that?

What is the solution? The cure?

The solution is remaining in a right relationship with Christ, moment by moment, and day by day.

There is a wonderful gospel song by Phil McHugh, entitled, One Day Jesus Will Call My Name, in which the chorus goes like this:

Not I

One day Jesus will call my name
As days go by, I hope I don't stay the same
I wanna get so close to Him that it's no big change
On that day that Jesus calls my name.

May we never deny knowing our Savior, but continue to grow closer to Him until that day that He calls our name.

JUNE 20

Widening The Road

"But the gateway to life is very narrow and the road is difficult, and only a few ever find it."
—Matthew 7:14

There is a tendency we have as Christians to change God's requirements. We do this in an effort to bring everyone to Heaven that we can. We don't want anyone to miss out, and we reason that a loving God does not want anyone to miss out, either. Right?

It is true that God is not willing that any should perish (Matthew 18:14; 2 Peter 3:9).

But, we must remember not to distort God's truth in an effort to increase His harvest.

Luke 3:8 reminds us, *"Prove by the way you live that you have repented of your sins and turned to God. Don't just say to each other, 'We're safe, for we are descendants of Abraham.' That means nothing, for I tell you, God can create children of Abraham from these very stones."*

Christ reminds us that we can tell a true Christian by the fruit that is produced in and through their life (Matthew 7:15-20). We must guide others in the knowledge of this truth.

May we remember that, *"You can enter God's Kingdom only through the narrow gate. The highway to hell is broad, and its gate is wide for the many who choose that way"* (Matthew 7:13).

JUNE 21

The Experience Of His Love

"And as we live in God, our love grows more perfect. So we will not be afraid on the day of judgment, but we can face him with confidence because we live like Jesus here in this world. Such love has no fear, because perfect love expels all fear. If we are afraid, it is for fear of punishment, and this shows that we have not fully experienced his perfect love."
—I John 4:17-18

Have you experienced difficulty in life? If you have, and if you have depended upon God to get you through it, then you know and have experienced the love of God.

The more we experience that love, the more our faith grows because His love has been tested and proven to us. As a result, we become more loyal to Christ based on this trust we have in Him.

And, when we experience His love, we know that there is nothing in all the world to fear.

Romans 8:38-39 tells us, *"And I am convinced that nothing can ever separate us from God's love. Neither death nor life, neither angels nor demons, neither our fears for today nor our worries about tomorrow—not even the powers of hell can separate us from God's love. No power in the sky above or in the earth below—indeed, nothing in all creation will ever be able to separate us from the love of God that is revealed in Christ Jesus our Lord."*

May your love grow more perfect as you continue to live in and depend upon your Savior.

JUNE 22

To Infinity And Beyond

"The grass withers and the flowers fade, but the word of our God stands forever." —Isaiah 40:8

It is the cycle of life—new life, this life fades, and the cycle is repeated. Yet, there is one thing that never fades with the passage of time. It is never outdated. It is never irrelevant. And, it never loses its power—the power to transform the lives of those it touches. It is the Word of God.

Hebrews 4:12 tells us, *"For the word of God is alive and powerful. It is sharper than the sharpest two-edged sword, cutting between soul and spirit, between joint and marrow. It exposes our innermost thoughts and desires."*

This power is infinite, as we are reminded in Ephesians 3:20, *"Now all glory to God, who is able, through his mighty power at work within us, to accomplish infinitely more than we might ask or think."*

Are you allowing His living, powerful Word to accomplish infinitely more than you might ask or think through your life? Do you believe?

Perhaps it's time for a bit of mid-year reflection to determine what areas of your life you are still holding on to.

Recommit every area of your heart and life to Christ today, and He will use you to accomplish His purposes—to infinity and beyond.

JUNE 23

Angels Watching Over Me

"For he will order his angels to protect you wherever you go." —Psalm 91:11

In the book entitled, *The Boy Who Came Back From Heaven*, Alex Malarky describes seeing angels catch his father as he is thrown from their automobile after a near-fatal car accident. Throughout Alex's battle to survive in the hospital after the accident, he describes numerous accounts of angels ministering to him and comforting him in his hospital room, and protecting him from evil.

Billy Graham's book, Angels, describes his own personal encounters with God's messengers, as well as the encounters of many other individuals Mr. Graham met throughout his ministry.

The *Holy Bible* tells us that angels are God's servants, and messengers. They are spirits sent to care for people who will inherit salvation (Hebrews 1:14).

Matthew 13:41-42 says, *"The Son of Man will send his angels, and they will remove from his Kingdom everything that causes sin and all who do evil. And the angels will throw them into the fiery furnace, where there will be weeping and gnashing of teeth."*

If our Savior has entrusted his angels with such a task, how much more will he charge them in caring for and ministering to us as His children each and every day.

JUNE 24

Hopefully Devoted

"I will walk in freedom, for I have devoted myself to your commandments." —Psalm 119:45

How devoted are you to following Christ? Do you have one foot in the cares of this world and one foot in God's Kingdom? If so, you are lukewarm, as the church at Laodicea described in Revelation 3. Our Lord says that He will spew out its members from His mouth because they are neither hot nor cold. Their wealth has caused them to grow indifferent to their need for Him. They no longer care, and they no longer have hope.

The *Holy Bible* also tells us in the Parable of the Farmer Scattering the Seed found in Mark 4:19, *"but all too quickly the message is crowded out by the worries of this life, the lure of wealth, and the desire for other things, so no fruit is produced."*

But, there is a hope beyond earthly comprehension when we devote our lives in service to Christ. It is a hope limited only by our faith.

Romans 5:5 reminds us, *"And this hope will not lead to disappointment. For we know how dearly God loves us, because he has given us the Holy Spirit to fill our hearts with his love."*

May you not be a lukewarm Christian, but may you be totally devoted to Christ, who is our hope, as we read in Hebrews 10:23, *"Let us hold tightly without wavering to the hope we affirm, for God can be trusted to keep his promise."*

JUNE 25

Easy Does It

"For my yoke is easy to bear, and the burden I give you is light." —Matthew 11:30

Do you feel overwhelmed with the tasks and circumstances before you today? Do others around you seem to have life so much easier? Do you ever wonder how you can possibly get some peace and sanity in your daily existence?

The *Holy Bible* offers hope for daily burdens and difficulties that are too great for us to carry on our own.

Psalm 55:22 promises, *"Give your burdens to the LORD, and he will take care of you. He will not permit the godly to slip and fall."*

Matthew 11:28 promises, *"Then Jesus said, "Come to me, all of you who are weary and carry heavy burdens, and I will give you rest."*

God requires simply that we love Him and keep His commandments.

I John 5:3 tells us, *"Loving God means keeping his commandments, and his commandments are not burdensome."*

If your life is overloaded and out-of-control, stop and take the time in all of the craziness to pray. Ask God to help you prioritize the things which must be done, and ask Him to help you release the things that are too much for you to bear.

May you allow Him to have complete control over every area of your life today, and may it be the best day you've ever had in your life.

JUNE 26

Lessons Learned

"Then the Lord said, 'Learn a lesson from this unjust judge. Even he rendered a just decision in the end. So don't you think God will surely give justice to his chosen people who cry out to him day and night? Will he keep putting them off?'" —Luke 18:6-7

When we walk through trials and difficulties of life with God, we learn to trust Him. We learn that His word is true, that He never abandons us, and that He carries us when the way becomes too difficult. Our fears diminish because we know without a shadow of a doubt that no matter what circumstance comes our way, we have God, and we are all-encompassed by His love.

The *Parable of the Persistent Widow* in Luke 18 tells the story of an unjust judge who does not care about the things of God, and a widow who daily and persistently demands justice in a dispute she has with her enemy.

Luke 18:4-5 tells us, *"The judge ignored her for a while, but finally he said to himself, 'I don't fear God or care about people, but this woman is driving me crazy. I'm going to see that she gets justice, because she is wearing me out with her constant requests!'"*

The squeaky wheel got the grease.

Prayer is a powerful gift. Our Heavenly Father has allowed us each the opportunity to commune and communicate with Him through prayer.

Have you temporarily forgotten how much God loves you and longs to answer your prayers?

May you be reminded today of the loving and perfect justice of God, and may you be persistent in your request for it.

JUNE 27

Repeat Offenders

"Anyone who continues to live in him will not sin. But anyone who keeps on sinning does not know him or understand who he is." —I John 3:6

When we are walking with Christ, allowing Him to take up residence in us, we do not sin. It is only when we push Christ aside, when we insist on our own way, that we sin.

Having Christ as our shepherd, when this happens, He convicts us of our selfishness, our sin. We then have the choice to repent, and welcome Him back to take up residence once again in our lives.

The lack of repentance and continuing to sin reveals our lack of understanding with regard to the person of Jesus Christ.

Do we know and understand who He really is?

If we have experienced any level of God's goodness, then we realize that nothing on this earth, no selfish desire can ever come close to measuring up to the joy that comes from living in complete communion with Him.

Isaiah 54:8 says, *"In a burst of anger I turned my face away for a little while. But with everlasting love I will have compassion on you," says the Lord, your Redeemer."*

May we seek to cleanse our lives of sin, to understand the person of Jesus Christ, and to walk with Him all the days of our life.

JUNE 28

Real Religion

"Pure and genuine religion in the sight of God the Father means caring for orphans and widows in their distress and refusing to let the world corrupt you." —James 1:27

Every day we are bombarded with messages through television, radio, the internet, and others that are completely contrary to the Word of God. When we allow these messages to infiltrate our lives, they corrupt us.

How can we avoid this corruption and practice the pure and real religion that James 1:27 is talking about?

We must stay focused on our relationship with Christ through daily prayer and reading His Word. There is no substitute for this.

We must also seek to care for the needs of others, including those in our own family, and trust that God will provide for our daily needs.

It is an active, disciplined process. It does not mean sitting idly and doing nothing.

Real religion is an active pursuit of righteousness, day-in and day-out. It isn't glamorous or filled with fame, but it does provide a deep, abiding joy that cannot be compared to anything else on earth.

Psalm 106:3 says, *"There is joy for those who deal justly with others and always do what is right."*

May your life reflect the pure and genuine religion that pleases God the Father today and every day.

JUNE 29

Let The Whole World Know

"O Zion, messenger of good news, shout from the mountaintops! Shout it louder, O Jerusalem. Shout, and do not be afraid. Tell the towns of Judah, "Your God is coming!" —Isaiah 40:9

There is a radiance that shines from the face of one who is rightly-related to Christ. They need not even speak, because their smile and every pore in their being seems to exude the Heavenly Father's love.

Your life and my life should exude our Heavenly Father's love. The way in which we daily live our lives should shout to the world that Jesus Christ is Lord of all.

But, that is not enough.

Jesus commands us all in Matthew 28:19-20 saying, *"Therefore, go and make disciples of all the nations, baptizing them in the name of the Father and the Son and the Holy Spirit. Teach these new disciples to obey all the commands I have given you. And be sure of this: I am with you always, even to the end of the age."*

We must share our faith with others. We must tell them about Christ.

Romans 10:14 tells us, *"But how can they call on him to save them unless they believe in him? And how can they believe in him if they have never heard about him? And how can they hear about him unless someone tells them?"*

May yours be the voice that tells someone about Christ today.

JUNE 30

Lasting Riches

"Teach those who are rich in this world not to be proud and not to trust in their money, which is so unreliable. Their trust should be in God, who richly gives us all we need for our enjoyment." —I Timothy 6:17

Jesus reminds us often not to lay up our treasures here on earth (Matthew 6:19-21; Luke 12:34). His truth teaches us that where our treasure is, our heart will follow closely behind (Matthew 6:21).

Yet, to deny the desire for good things—treasures—is to deny a basic part of who we are. Jesus redefines our definition of treasure and our definition of riches.

Real riches and real treasure is found in giving away our earthly possessions to the poor who are in greater need. In doing this, we learn what real love is all about—the very essence of God—and, we gain treasure in Heaven that is lasting, eternal.

So often we are afraid to give our things away. Our lack of faith and understanding of who our Father is causes us to wonder where our next meal will come from, yet Jesus reminds us that this is how unbelievers think—not His children.

In Matthew 6:31-33 Jesus tells us, *"So don't worry about these things, saying, 'What will we eat? What will we drink? What will we wear?' These things dominate the thoughts of unbelievers, but your heavenly Father already knows all your needs. Seek the Kingdom of God above all else, and live righteously, and he will give you everything you need."*

May we remember we are stewards and trust God with everything He has entrusted to us for the good of others.

JULY 1

Sweet Dependence Upon Christ

"The LORD is good to those who depend on him, to those who search for him." — Lamentations 3:25

It is good to recognize that we are dependent upon God, and that every good and perfect gift comes from Him (James 1:17).

Yet, it is so very dangerous and easy to claim responsibility and independence as we swell with pride over personal accomplishments, failing to realize the one who ultimately makes all good things possible.

Take the time to stop and count the blessings God has given you—just today.

Search for Him in the face of everyone you encounter today, in every place that you find yourself.

May you depend upon His goodness to sustain you when times are plentiful and when they are lean.

May you acknowledge His presence making a way for you in each and every moment of the day.

JULY 2

Serve The Lord With Gladness

"Worship the Lord with gladness. Come before him, singing with joy." —Psalm 100:2

In serving the Lord, is your heart filled with gladness? Or, are you weary and burdened out of an obligation to serve? How about your prayer life? Do you approach the throne of grace with song? Or, are you always filled with sadness of heart because you are in constant need of the Savior's "fixing" power?

After recently attending an event at a world-renowned country club in Houston, I was struck by the fact that there is no luxury quite like that of human service. I was waited on by people with gladness of heart from the moment I stepped in the door. The service was not intrusive, nor did it impede anyone's movement in the business conference taking place; yet, it was constant from the checking of my jacket to the refreshing of my glass the moment it was set upon the table. Each server was intent on fulfilling the desires of each guest, nothing more and nothing less.

What about you?

Are you intent on fulfilling the desires of your Heavenly Father? Are you serving with gladness of heart?

Or, do you have an ulterior motive in your service? Is selfish ambition hindering your effectiveness? We are all much more transparent than we might think.

Philippians 2:3 encourages us, *"Don't be selfish; don't try to impress others. Be humble, thinking of others as better than yourselves."*

May we serve the Lord with gladness by serving others each and every day.

JULY 3

Summer Burn

"They will never again be hungry or thirsty; they will never be scorched by the heat of the sun."
—*Revelation 7:16*

In Texas, our summers are long and hot. No matter how much sunscreen my mother slathered on my fair skin as a child, and much to her chagrin, I never failed to come into the house burned to a crisp by the end of the day.

The aftermath was a miserable experience of ice baths, Noxzema, aloe vera, and other home remedies—all aimed at soothing my sun-scorched body.

In stark contrast, Revelation 7 is a beautiful picture of God's mercy lavished on His followers prior to the tribulation. Before the angels are unleashed to bring destruction upon the earth, God shouts for them to wait until each of His children can receive the seal of God upon their foreheads.

When the tribulation is over, John sees them as a great crowd, with their faces down, falling before the throne of God in worship, praise and song.

The Scripture goes on to say that God will be their shelter, and Revelation 7:16-17 says, *"They will never again be hungry or thirsty; they will never be scorched by the heat of the sun. For the Lamb on the throne will be their Shepherd. He will lead them to springs of life-giving water. And God will wipe every tear from their eyes."*

I don't know about you, but I am longing for the day when I will never be scorched by the sun, where there are springs of living water, and where God will wipe away every tear from our eyes.

JULY 4

Independent Thinking

"Trust in the LORD with all your heart; do not depend on your own understanding." — *Proverbs 3:5*

Rational, logical thought has little, if any, place in the life of faith that Christ requires us to live.

Those individuals who consider themselves to be intellectuals and rational thinkers in their own right often encounter great difficulty in the Christian walk because they cannot reconcile dependence upon their own understanding of things with the life lived by faith.

Time after time in the *Holy Bible*, God called people to do things that made no logical or rational sense from a human perspective. Yet, in each instance, God's plan was infinitely greater and more rewarding than anything they could have imagined.

When we follow after Christ in obedience, a blessing is sure to follow us. The ultimate blessing may not be something that we see completed in our lifetime, but we have the promise of God working all things together for the good of those who love Him and are called according to His purpose (Romans 8:28).

Are you struggling to rationalize and intellectualize God's plan for your life? That approach will never work.

Simply trust Him and obey.

JULY 5

Hell's Fire

"If your hand causes you to sin, cut it off. It's better to enter eternal life with only one hand than to go into the unquenchable fires of hell with two hands." —Mark 9:43

Do you have a pet sin? Is there something that you struggle with and refuse to truly repent from, comforting yourself with God's grace as an excuse not to totally obey Him?

This New Testament verse reminds us that being a half-committed Christian is simply not good enough. God's expectations for us are higher than that. He requires more. And, He loves us enough to discipline us when we continue unrepentant of pet sins.

He doesn't do this in an effort to be a mean dictator, but because He loves us so much that He does not want us to miss out on the blessing of a life lived in accordance with His plan and purpose.

We are all too often aware of the specific circumstances that lead us into the temptation to sin, yet we do nothing about it.

There must be a conscious decision on our part to avoid those people, places, and circumstances that continue to lead us into sin.

Do you want to avoid hell's unquenchable fire?

Then, go and sin no more.

I Corinthians 15:34 says, *"Think carefully about what is right, and stop sinning. For to your shame I say that some of you don't know God at all."*

JULY 6

Hell, Fire And Brimstone

"But cowards, unbelievers, the corrupt, murderers, the immoral, those who practice witchcraft, idol worshipers, and all liars—their fate is in the fiery lake of burning sulfur. This is the second death." —Revelation 21:8

I've observed that many pastors and members of the clergy today neglect to mention things that they perceive as unpleasant in the *Holy Bible*, namely, Hades.

But, the fact that pastors fail to mention it, doesn't make hell any less real. There is much to be said for the reverential fear in knowing that this place is a reality.

Luke 12:5 tells us, *"But I'll tell you whom to fear. Fear God, who has the power to kill you and then throw you into hell. Yes, he's the one to fear."*

Knowing this should cause us to believe and to repent of the sins named in Revelation 21:8 that lead us into the second death.

And, there is something else that should cause us to believe and repent. It is the love of God, and the reality of this love's power in our lives.

Romans 8:38 says, *"And I am convinced that nothing can ever separate us from God's love. Neither death nor life, neither angels nor demons, neither our fears for today nor our worries about tomorrow—not even the powers of hell can separate us from God's love."*

May the fear of God and the reality of His love lead us to repentance regarding anything in our life that is not pleasing to Him today.

JULY 7

The Refiner's Fire

"I have refined you, but not as silver is refined. Rather, I have refined you in the furnace of suffering." —Isaiah 48:10

It is a marvelous thing to experience the furnace of suffering and to be brought into a place of extraordinary fellowship with Christ. 2 Timothy 2:3 tells us, *"Endure suffering along with me, as a good soldier of Christ Jesus."*

But, why?

Hebrews 5:8 is one of many verses that answers this question. It says, *"Even though Jesus was God's Son, he learned obedience from the things he suffered."*

Not only do we learn obedience through the things we suffer, as Christ did, but we also receive comfort, and are able to comfort others through our suffering.

2 Corinthians 1:5 says, *"For the more we suffer for Christ, the more God will shower us with his comfort through Christ."*

We become members of the fellowship of His suffering, as we experience just a portion of what Jesus experienced on the cross.

2 Corinthians 4:10 tells us, *"Through suffering, our bodies continue to share in the death of Jesus so that the life of Jesus may also be seen in our bodies."*

"And since we are his children, we are his heirs. In fact, together with Christ we are heirs of God's glory. But if we are to share his glory, we must also share his suffering" (Romans 8:17).

One day we will experience the wonderful joy of His glory revealed.

JULY 8

The Dark Ages

"Jesus replied, "My light will shine for you just a little longer. Walk in the light while you can, so the darkness will not overtake you. Those who walk in the darkness cannot see where they are going." —John 12:35

The real *Dark Ages* are not the period of intellectual and economic regression some suppose them to be after the collapse of the Roman empire. The real *Dark Ages* existed in the past and exist today in the lives of those who do not walk in the light of Jesus Christ.

These individuals may think that they know where they are going as they follow a plan of their own design and making. Yet, they do not see where their own road is truly leading them.

Those who choose their own way, the way of darkness, may see the fine trappings along the side of the road they are travelling, and the journey may even appear to be somewhat smooth. However, the final destination has been obscured from their view. Satan does this intentionally. He does not want them to step out of the *Dark Ages* and into the *Age of Enlightenment*.

May we never allow the corruption of the world to crowd out the enlightenment of God, causing us to walk in spiritual darkness.

May we work diligently every day to allow the light of Christ to penetrate our lives, giving light to everyone who might be in the dark around us.

JULY 9

Our Forefathers' Education

"Put on your new nature, and be renewed as you learn to know your Creator and become like him." —Colossians 3:10

The New England Primer was the first reading primer designed for the American colonists, and it became the foundation for most American schooling prior to the 1790s.

The primer was first published between 1687 and 1690 by Benjamin Harris in Boston, Massachusetts. Its text consisted of 90 pages, much of which was theology.

There were original works in the primer, such as the prayer we have all come to know as *Now I Lay Me Down to Sleep*. And, there were many passages drawn directly from the King James Bible.

The primer reflected strongly the Puritans concern for the uncontrolled speech of children which they felt led to depravity. The New England Primer instructed children in the loving and protective authority found in abiding under the authority of Christ and their parents.

They were being taught to know their Creator and be like Him.

I think they had it right.

What about you?

Do you know your Creator?

Are you becoming more like Him each day?

May you dig deeply into His Word that you might be more like Him each day.

JULY 10

Defending The Gospel

"They preach because they love me, for they know I have been appointed to defend the Good News." —Philippians 1:16

An apologist is a defender of the gospel of Jesus Christ. The apostle Paul was one of the first. He was appointed to defend the Good News, as this Scripture tells us.

If you are God's child, then you have been appointed to defend the gospel, too. So, just how are you doing that?

Do you correct the blatant misrepresentation of God and His Word when you hear it in the workplace?

Do you turn off the crude television program, movie, or video game?

Are you careful with the words that you speak?

Do you live in accordance with God's Word, exhibiting the fruit of the Spirit in your life?

Matthew 3:8 tells us, *"Prove by the way you live that you have repented of your sins and turned to God."*

This is the greatest defense of the Good News of Jesus Christ—what others see in your life and mine.

JULY 11

The Emporer's New Clothes

"And all who have been united with Christ in baptism have put on Christ, like putting on new clothes." —Galatians 3:27

In Jeremiah 52:31-34, we learn the story of King Jehoiachin of Judah. He had been in exile for thirty-seven years after being captured by the Babylonians who destroyed the Temple in what has become known as the Babylonian Exile.

When a new King, Evil-merodach, took the throne in Babylon, he was anything but evil to King Jehoiachin. King Evil-merodach spoke kindly to Jehoiachin and gave him a higher position than any of the other exiled kings. He also released Jehoiachin from prison after those thirty-seven years.

King Evil-merodach did something else for Jehoiachin. He replaced Jehoiachin's prison garb with new clothes, and the Scripture tells us he was allowed to dine in the king's presence for the rest of His life (Jeremiah 52:33).

Imagine King Jehoiachin's feelings. The putting on of new clothes—clothes that are beautiful and fit just right—is such a wonderful feeling. We feel special, pure, clean, and like we can do anything. Imagine beautiful new clothes after thirty-seven years of wearing prison clothes.

Now, imagine dining in the presence of the king for the rest of your life.

When we are united with Christ, we are clothed in the beauty of His righteousness. And, we are invited to the marriage supper of the lamb (Revelation 19:9), to dine in the presence of the King forever.

JULY 12

Won't You Be My Neighbor

"The man wanted to justify his actions, so he asked Jesus, 'And who is my neighbor?'" — Luke 10:29

In Luke 10:25-37, an expert in religious law came to test Jesus by asking Him what must be done to inherit eternal life. Jesus responded by asking the man what the law of Moses said, and how he interpreted it.

Luke 10:27 tells us, *"The man answered, "'You must love the Lord your God with all your heart, all your soul, all your strength, and all your mind.' And, 'Love your neighbor as yourself.'"*

Jesus told the man he was right, and that if he did this he would live. But, in an effort to justify his own sin, the man asked Jesus, *"Who is my neighbor?"*

Jesus responded by telling the parable of the good Samaritan, in which a Jewish man was beaten, robbed, and left for dead on the roadside. A priest and a Levite each passed the man by without helping. Then, a Samaritan, whom the Jewish people despised, came and helped the man, bandaging his wounds, and paying for the man's care at a local inn.

Is there someone who despises you and is in need of your help today?

Perhaps their own circle of friends has passed them by, ignoring their need.

Won't you be their neighbor?

JULY 13

A Friend In Need

"A friend is always loyal, and a brother is born to help in time of need." —*Proverbs 17:17*

This verse doesn't say that a friend is *sometimes* loyal. It doesn't say that a friend is loyal when it is *deserved*. And, it doesn't say a friend is loyal when they *feel* like it, either.

It says, *"a friend is always loyal."*

The second half of this verse is equally important.

When a member of our family is in need, the Scripture tells us that we are not to turn our back on them. It says, *"a brother is born to help in time of need."*

Part of your purpose in the life that God has given you is to help your brother in time of need.

So, who is our brother?

A brother would be someone that we have a blood relationship with, right?

Think about that for a moment.

If Jesus Christ is my Savior, and if He is your Savior, then we have a blood relationship, too.

You are my brother, my sister, my family.

Part of my God-given purpose and yours is for us to help each other in time of need.

May we practice true friendship that is loyal *always*, and may we help our brothers and sisters in time of need—with no reservation.

JULY 14

Focus

"Until I get there, focus on reading the Scriptures to the church, encouraging the believers, and teaching them." —I Timothy 4:13

To be considered successful at most things in life, a commitment is required. We must focus on the mission, the assignment.

The Christian life is no different. If we want to be the kind of Christian that God desires, we must first learn the Scriptures and what is required of us.

We must also put into practice what we have read in the Scriptures. Just as a good runner must train and practice. He/she does not become a champion overnight—it takes time learning, practicing, training, and being encouraged by others running the race.

It is often painful and difficult, and we may want to give up. This is why the support of other Christians is so vital and necessary.

We need each other in order to keep the proper focus.

Until Christ returns, may we keep focused on the Scriptures, on encouraging one another in love and good works, and may we put into practice all that we have learned.

JULY 15

Footprints Of Jesus

"Indeed, he loves his people; all his holy ones are in his hands. They follow in his steps and accept his teaching." —Deuteronomy 33:3

There is a wonderful hymn with words penned by Mary B. C. Slade and music written by Asa Everett in 1871 entitled, *Footprints of Jesus*.

The refrain of the song goes like this:

> *Footprints of Jesus,*
> *That make the pathway glow;*
> *We will follow the steps of Jesus*
> *Where'er they go.*

The more time we spend with Christ in prayer and reading His Word, the more obvious and clear (glowing) are the steps He would have us to take in life.

We begin to see, step by step and day by day, the plans that He has for our life.

We may never have the full picture of His plan and purpose for our life while we are on this earth, but what we can clearly see is a taste of how utterly and completely He loves us and holds us in His hands, gently guiding us and caring for us all along this earthly journey.

Are you following the steps of Jesus, wherever they go?

Or, are you following your own path, fearful of the unknown?

May you find the freedom to follow Christ—with every step—knowing that there is no safer place in all the world.

JULY 16

Playing Nicely With Others

"Accept other believers who are weak in faith, and don't argue with them about what they think is right or wrong." —Romans 14:1

Have you ever been involved in a disagreement with another believer over a theological matter?

Perhaps it was a discussion on the consumption of alcohol. Or, maybe you and another believer had a strong disagreement on whether true baptism was immersion or sprinkling.

While it is important to follow the teachings of God's Holy Word and not cut corners, the *Holy Bible* does command us to seek love above all else. We are not to split hairs when the intent of the heart is a loving, faithful, and righteous intent.

I Timothy 1:5 tells us, *"The purpose of my instruction is that all believers would be filled with love that comes from a pure heart, a clear conscience, and genuine faith."*

John 13:35 says, *"Your love for one another will prove to the world that you are my disciples."*

And, I Peter 4:8 reminds us, *"Most important of all, continue to show deep love for each other, for love covers a multitude of sins."*

May we seek love above all when dealing with each other, in misunderstandings, disagreements, and in learning to understand the Scriptures.

JULY 17

For The Visual Learner

"At that time I gave Joshua this charge: 'You have seen for yourself everything the Lord your God has done to these two kings. He will do the same to all the kingdoms on the west side of the Jordan.'" —Deuteronomy 3:21

Are you a visual learner? Do you long to see things with your own eyes in order to grasp the concept? Or, do you tend to visualize yourself accomplishing certain things in life?

In this passage of Scripture, Moses encourages Joshua to visualize what he has already seen God do before.

Throughout Scripture, God speaks to the visual learner. He shows Himself real, and helps us to visualize the place He has for us in His kingdom. But, this visualizing, this seeing, requires faith.

When Jesus was resurrected from the dead, Thomas did not witness His resurrected body with the other disciples at the beginning, and failed to believe the witnesses. Yet God, out of great love, showed Himself to Thomas.

The Scripture says in John 20:26-28, *"Eight days later the disciples were together again, and this time Thomas was with them. The doors were locked; but suddenly, as before, Jesus was standing among them. 'Peace be with you,' he said. Then he said to Thomas, 'Put your finger here, and look at my hands. Put your hand into the wound in my side. Don't be faithless any longer. Believe!'"*

"My Lord and my God!" Thomas exclaimed.

May we have the faith to believe and visualize God's truth at work in our lives today and every day.

JULY 18

Wait, What?

"What are you waiting for? Get up and be baptized. Have your sins washed away by calling on the name of the Lord." —Acts 22:16

The New Testament story of Saul, aka Paul, and his conversion is miraculous. He was the chief persecutor of the Christians, but now he had become a Christian, himself, and found God calling him into immediate action of the opposite kind. Now, he was to become a minister of the gospel to the Gentiles, and a mediator between the Jews and the Gentiles.

This calling defied all rational thought.

Has God ever called you to something that defied all rational thought?

Is He calling you to something *now* that defies all rational thought?

When you hear His voice calling you to action, you must answer—without hesitation.

After Paul accepted Christ and was praying in the Temple in Jerusalem, he heard God's voice speaking to him and telling him to leave Jerusalem because his testimony would not be received there.

Paul argued with God, not understanding His call (Acts 22:19-22), and this hesitation nearly led to him being lashed with whips. God confirmed to Paul that he would be sent far away, as a messenger to the Gentiles.

What about you?

Where has God called you today?

May you respond to the loving plea of your Heavenly Father—no matter how abnormal it may seem.

JULY 19

Go West, Young Man

"After this, David asked the Lord, 'Should I move back to one of the towns of Judah?' 'Yes,' the Lord replied. Then David asked, 'Which town should I go to?' 'To Hebron,' the Lord answered." —2 Samuel 2:1

Do you ever wonder which direction God wants you to take, or where He wants you to go?

David did.

It wasn't even a matter of going east or west. David wanted to know exactly which town God wanted him in, and he asked God that very question.

And, God answered.

Are you surprised?

We shouldn't be surprised when God answers our prayers and our questions.

We shouldn't be surprised that He listens to us, or that He hears our prayers.

Psalm 116:2 says, *"Because he bends down to listen, I will pray as long as I have breath!"*

Psalm 65:5 tells us, *"You faithfully answer our prayers with awesome deeds, O God our savior. You are the hope of everyone on earth, even those who sail on distant seas."*

If you are longing to know the direction that God wants you to go, may you ask Him today, believing that He will answer you.

JULY 20

Catapult

"Hegai was very impressed with Esther and treated her kindly. He quickly ordered a special menu for her and provided her with beauty treatments. He also assigned her seven maids specially chosen from the king's palace, and he moved her and her maids into the best place in the harem." —Esther 2:9

Esther was an orphaned Jewish girl who was being raised by her cousin, Mordecai, in the fortress of Susa after the period of time known as the Babylonian Exile.

When King Xerxes, who ruled one hundred twenty-seven provinces from India to Ethiopia, banished Queen Vashti and began searching for a replacement, Esther found herself being catapulted from a regular Jewish household to the position of Queen, where she would put a stop to the annihilation of the Jewish race.

David, too, was catapulted from shepherd, the lowliest of all positions in his day, to being anointed King.

And, Moses, the son of a Jewish slave, raised by the Egyptian Pharaoh's daughter and exiled for murder, finds himself catapulted to the position of serving as the leader who would deliver God's chosen people from Egypt.

Perhaps God seeks to catapult you to a new position of service. Are you arguing with Him, as Moses did?

Do you question whether or not you are really the one God wants to use, as Esther did?

Remember 2 Corinthians 12:9, *"Each time he said, 'My grace is all you need. My power works best in weakness.' So now I am glad to boast about my weaknesses, so that the power of Christ can work through me."*

JULY 21

Softly And Tenderly

"The Lord is like a father to his children, tender and compassionate to those who fear him."
—Psalm 103:13

The world screams constantly to get our attention. Every direction we turn, there is someone or something demanding our attention. There are crises at every corner, business activities calling us to action, and constant distractions from these hoarders of our time.

All the while, Jesus is calling to us, softly and tenderly He calls to us.

Are we listening?

It is easier to hear the screaming of the immediate need, the siren, the child's cry, the television, the dryer buzzer, the microwave alarm, the bill needing payment.

We must stop and focus. We must listen for God's voice.

We must be still.

Psalm 46:10 says, *"Be still, and know that I am God! I will be honored by every nation. I will be honored throughout the world."*

Stop and focus on Him.

Focus on Christ.

Focus on the One who saved your soul.

Focus on the One who loves you more than anyone else in all the world.

Focus on Jesus.

And, may you hear Him speaking to you today.

JULY 22

Saddle Up Your Horses

"Harness the horses, and mount the stallions. Take your positions. Put on your helmets. Sharpen your spears, and prepare your armor." —Jeremiah 46:4

Ecclesiastes 3:8 tells us that there is *"a time for war and a time for peace."*

When it comes to our dealings with Satan, it is always a time for war. This monster is a serious foe with all manner and method of heinous attack just waiting to take you down.

And, don't think for a moment that you will ever make a peace treaty with this enemy.

I Peter 5:8 tells us, *"Stay alert! Watch out for your great enemy, the devil. He prowls around like a roaring lion, looking for someone to devour."*

Yet, the *Holy Bible* encourages us, and it provides the best means and method of combating this foe. When Jesus was tempted by Satan in the wilderness, he quoted Scripture (Matthew 4), and was able to correct the intentional misquotations of Satan.

James 4:7 reminds us, *"So humble yourselves before God. Resist the devil, and he will flee from you."*

When we walk with our Savior and resist Satan, he moves on to an easier target. But, rest assured, the war is not over. The beautiful thing in all of the struggle is that when we remain in Christ, He gives us victory.

Psalm 144:1 says, *"Praise the Lord, who is my rock. He trains my hands for war and gives my fingers skill for battle."*

May you live in the victory that only Christ can give.

JULY 23

The Champion

"We do this by keeping our eyes on Jesus, the champion who initiates and perfects our faith. Because of the joy awaiting him, he endured the cross, disregarding its shame. Now he is seated in the place of honor beside God's throne." —Hebrews 12:2

Don't you love a champion?

Whether it's an Olympic champion, a football champion, or a spelling bee champion, we love seeing someone triumph.

Jesus is the champion of all champions.

He is perfect, flawless.

And, He wants to be your personal trainer.

He has initiated the training, and He wants you to join Him to continue this training to perfection.

This training isn't for the faint-hearted. It requires patience, endurance.

Hebrews 12:1 tells us, *"Therefore, since we are surrounded by such a huge crowd of witnesses to the life of faith, let us strip off every weight that slows us down, especially the sin that so easily trips us up. And let us run with endurance the race God has set before us."*

Jesus Christ, our Champion, will help us to complete the necessary training to be victorious with Him.

Philippians 1:6 says, *"And I am certain that God, who began the good work within you, will continue his work until it is finally finished on the day when Christ Jesus returns."*

JULY 24

The Evangelist

"I solemnly urge you in the presence of God and Christ Jesus, who will someday judge the living and the dead when he appears to set up his Kingdom: Preach the word of God. Be prepared, whether the time is favorable or not. Patiently correct, rebuke, and encourage your people with good teaching." —2 Timothy 4:1-2

The term *evangelist* has been defined as "one who proclaims the gospel" or "one who seeks to convert others to the Christian faith."

You have been called by God to be an evangelist.

This passage of Scripture in 2 Timothy reminds us of the importance of being prepared—whether the timing is favorable or not—to preach the word of God.

When we are rightly-related to God, evangelism is natural. It is something that exudes out of every single pore in our being. We can't help but share the good news of Jesus Christ with others at work, at school, at the store, at the ball game, on the airplane, at the theater, and the list goes on and on.

The early Christians were excellent evangelists, as Acts 6:7 tells us, *"So God's message continued to spread. The number of believers greatly increased in Jerusalem, and many of the Jewish priests were converted, too."*

May you realize your role as an evangelist today, and may God guide you as you share the good news of Jesus Christ with others today.

JULY 25

Ear Tickling

"For a time is coming when people will no longer listen to sound and wholesome teaching. They will follow their own desires and will look for teachers who will tell them whatever their itching ears want to hear. They will reject the truth and chase after myths." —2 Timothy 4:3-4

Have you noticed the number of comedians that have made their way to the pulpit these days? Humor and ear tickling in the pulpit has become so commonplace that it gives one reason to question what is being taught in seminaries today.

And, what about sin and repentance?

If you heard them from the pulpit in your last church service, then thank your Father in Heaven for the pastor He has given you.

This Scripture tells us that a day is coming when people will no longer listen to sound and wholesome teaching.

Sadly, that day is here, my friend.

All around us are people who are presented with the truth, yet they reject it. They would rather listen to foolishness and myths. The things they choose to believe are so ridiculous it is shocking.

So, what are we to do? Are we to give up, to quit?

The *Holy Bible* tells us absolutely not.

2 Timothy 4:5 says, *"But you should keep a clear mind in every situation. Don't be afraid of suffering for the Lord. Work at telling others the Good News, and fully carry out the ministry God has given you."*

May we be encouraged to carry on in proclaiming God's truth to others as long as we have breath.

JULY 26

The Unity Of The Body

"Now I am departing from the world; they are staying in this world, but I am coming to you. Holy Father, you have given me your name; now protect them by the power of your name so that they will be united just as we are." —John 17:11

I love the prayer of Jesus in John 17. It is remarkable. What I love most about this prayer is simply who and what Jesus prays for.

He prays for His disciples, asking God not to remove them from the world, but to keep them safe from the evil one.

Jesus prays not only for the disciples, but *"for all who will ever believe in me through their message"* (John 17:20).

That's me! If you believe in Christ as your Savior, that's you, too!

Jesus prayed for us—all those years ago.

He prayed that we would all be one.

And, He didn't just stop there.

He prayed, *"that they will all be one, just as you and I are one—as you are in me, Father, and I am in you."*

He prayed, *"May they experience such perfect unity that the world will know that you sent me and that you love them as much as you love me"* (John 17:23).

Oh, that we might be so united as to be the fulfillment of the prayer of our Lord and Savior, Jesus Christ, today.

JULY 27

A Bumper Crop

"So, my dear brothers and sisters, this is the point: You died to the power of the law when you died with Christ. And now you are united with the one who was raised from the dead. As a result, we can produce a harvest of good deeds for God." —Romans 7:4

The year was 1981. The old gardeners in the small town our family lived in said it couldn't be done. They said my father couldn't get a good crop of vegetables out of that hard, briar-filled clay soil in East Texas.

He had tried the year before, and there were many old-timers who said, "I hate to say it, but I told you so."

But, this year was different. Daddy studied the soil, and found out what additive was needed to provide the proper nourishment for the plants to grow. He tilled the soil a little earlier, giving the plants an opportunity to take strong root before the weather turned too hot. And, this year proved to have more than ample rainfall.

It was a bumper crop!

May you fill your life with all the right nourishment: time alone with God in prayer, Scripture reading, and good Christian fellowship, so that your life will produce a bumper crop of good works for God.

JULY 28

Permanent Marker

"Do not cut your bodies for the dead, and do not mark your skin with tattoos. I am the Lord."
—*Leviticus 19:28*

I'll never forget it. I was only six, but I knew better. I took a marker and wrote my name all over the dresser in my bedroom. And, it was permanent. It wasn't coming off.

I loved it at first. It was *my* special touch. My mother was not happy with me for doing it. And over time, I wished I had not scribbled on the dresser—destroying its intended beauty.

There are millions of people in the world with tattoos of all shapes and sizes, and they get them for all manner of reasons.

But, I wonder if they don't change their minds over time, wishing they hadn't marked their skin—altering its natural beauty.

I also think of the inner tattoo God has placed upon my heart. It reminds me that I am His, and it will never come off. He placed it there with permanent marker. It is a change of heart and life.

And, I have never once changed my mind about that mark.

May others see the permanent mark that God has placed upon your heart and life today.

JULY 29

The Voice

"And I assure you that the time is coming, indeed it's here now, when the dead will hear my voice—the voice of the Son of God. And those who listen will live." —John 5:25

Writers are often instructed on the importance of finding their *voice*—that uniqueness in one's writing style.

There is a television program entitled, "The Voice," in which vocalists train and compete to find the uniqueness in their own vocal talent, that special something that sets them apart from the crowd.

But, there is a voice so special, so unique, so set apart from the crowd as to provide life to the hearer. The *Holy Bible* tells us that the dead can even hear this voice.

It is the voice of God.

Can you hear Him when we speaks to you?

Do you listen when he speaks softly to your heart?

The *Holy Bible* tells us in Isaiah 30:21, *"Your own ears will hear him. Right behind you a voice will say, 'This is the way you should go,' whether to the right or to the left."*

Do you ignore God's voice when you hear it, rebelling against Him?

Hebrews 4:7 encourages us, *"So God set another time for entering his rest, and that time is today. God announced this through David much later in the words already quoted: 'Today when you hear his voice, don't harden your hearts.'"*

May you soften your heart to hear God's voice as He speaks to you today, that you might find life in answering His call.

JULY 30

The King's Ranch

"For all the animals of the forest are mine, and I own the cattle on a thousand hills." — Psalm 50:10

The legendary King Ranch in Kingsville, Texas was founded by an impoverished, indentured jeweler's apprentice from New York City who stowed away on a ship heading south. After much hard work, diligence, and vision, the King Ranch was born, and eventually became one of the largest cattle ranches in the world at 825,000 acres, handling cattle, horses, farming, publishing, and many other endeavors. It is a wonder to behold.

Yet, the King Ranch pales in comparison to our King's ranch.

He is the King of kings and Lord of lords.

Our King owns all the animals of the forest, and the cattle on a thousand hills.

Who could boast more?

Are you in need?

2 Corinthians 9:8 tells us, *"And God will generously provide all you need. Then you will always have everything you need and plenty left over to share with others."*

God is generous with us in order that we might share this generosity with others.

Psalm 112:4 says, *"Light shines in the darkness for the godly. They are generous, compassionate, and righteous."*

May you live in the knowledge that your Father owns all the animals of the forest and the cattle on a thousand hills, and may you share this generosity with everyone you meet.

JULY 31

Rubber Baby Buggy Bumpers

"But Moses pleaded with the Lord, 'O Lord, I'm not very good with words. I never have been, and I'm not now, even though you have spoken to me. I get tongue-tied, and my words get tangled.'" —Exodus 4:10

Rubber baby buggy bumpers . . . that tongue twister always stumped me. Can you say it three times fast? I'm guessing that Moses probably couldn't say it three times fast.

The *Holy Bible* tells us that not only did Moses get tongue-tied, but he was more humble than any man on earth (Numbers 12:3). God called Moses to lead the people of Israel out of their slavery and bondage in Egypt. But, Moses resisted God's call. He didn't feel he was good enough for the job. He tried every excuse in the book, even pleading, *"Lord, please! Send anyone else"* (Exodus 4:13). Do you ever resist God's call on your life?

Do you feel as though you're not good enough for the job? Perhaps you think someone else is better suited for the position He is calling you to. Do you beg God to send anyone but you?

Moses' response caused God's anger to burn against him. His disobedience eventually led to Moses missing out on the blessing of entering the promised land. Don't miss out on God's promised land for you.

When Paul had the same issue, the *Holy Bible* tells us in 2 Corinthians 12:9 God responded, *"Each time he said, 'My grace is all you need. My power works best in weakness.' So now I am glad to boast about my weaknesses, so that the power of Christ can work through me."*

May you allow God to work through your weakness today.

AUGUST 1

Time And Wounds

"He heals the brokenhearted and bandages their wounds." —Psalm 147:3

There is an old saying that, "Time heals all wounds." But, that isn't necessarily true. There are some wounds that no amount of time can heal. These wounds run deep—to the core of our being.

These are the wounds that only Christ can heal. He can heal them because He has experienced them firsthand. God knows the deepest, most gut-wrenching wounds.

I Peter 2:24 tells us, *"He personally carried our sins in his body on the cross so that we can be dead to sin and live for what is right. By his wounds you are healed."*

Are you wounded today?

Do you find yourself in need of His healing today?

Our Father is the God who heals us.

Isaiah 57:19 says, *"I will comfort those who mourn, bringing words of praise to their lips. May they have abundant peace, both near and far,' says the* LORD, *who heals them."*

May you come near to Him today, allowing Him to carry you in His arms.

"He will feed his flock like a shepherd. He will carry the lambs in his arms, holding them close to his heart. He will gently lead the mother sheep with their young" (Isaiah 40:11).

AUGUST 2

Honor Bound

"I will bring honor to your name in every generation. Therefore, the nations will praise you forever and ever." —Psalm 45:17

Honor can be defined as: to hold in high esteem; revere, dignify; glorify.

The *Holy Bible* talks a great deal about honor. In fact, honor or a form of honor is used three hundred sixty-six times in the New Living Translation of the *Holy Bible*.

Being honor bound is to be obliged to one's personal integrity. That is, doing what is honest, right, and true whether anyone else is watching us or not. It is about the legacy we leave by the way we live the life God has blessed us with—each and every day.

God is always watching.

Are your actions bringing honor to the name of Christ?

Will your actions today bring honor to God for generations to come?

In 2 Chronicles 2:4, King Solomon said, *"I am about to build a Temple to honor the name of the LORD my God. It will be a place set apart to burn fragrant incense before him, to display the special sacrificial bread, and to sacrifice burnt offerings each morning and evening, on the Sabbaths, at new moon celebrations, and at the other appointed festivals of the Lord our God. He has commanded Israel to do these things forever."*

May your life be a fragrant offering that honors the name of the Lord your God today and for many generations to come.

AUGUST 3

I Will Remember You

"Remember him before you become fearful of falling and worry about danger in the streets; before your hair turns white like an almond tree in bloom, and you drag along without energy like a dying grasshopper, and the caperberry no longer inspires sexual desire. Remember him before you near the grave, your everlasting home, when the mourners will weep at your funeral." —Ecclesiastes 12:5

I have had the privilege of seeing several of the elderly accept Christ as their personal Savior just prior to their passing from this life. It was a blessing I can't put into words—just to witness the event.

Yet, in each case, the individuals expressed regret at having not made the decision to accept and follow Christ while still in their youth. There was sadness over the many lost opportunities to do right and to reap the benefits of a life well-lived in obedience to Christ.

Ecclesiastes 12:1 says, *"Don't let the excitement of youth cause you to forget your Creator. Honor him in your youth before you grow old and say, 'Life is not pleasant anymore.'"*

When we are young, we often think of ourselves as invincible and untouchable. We also have a tendency to procrastinate and say, "I have plenty of time to come to Christ. I'll do it tomorrow." But, 2 Corinthians 6:2b says, *"Indeed, the 'right time' is now. Today is the day of salvation."*

We are never guaranteed tomorrow or even this evening.

May we remember Christ now, today, and always.

AUGUST 4

Divided Loyalty

"Come close to God, and God will come close to you. Wash your hands, you sinners; purify your hearts, for your loyalty is divided between God and the world." —James 4:8

Where is your loyalty?

Are you loyal to your family first and foremost? Your job? Leisure? What about God?

While it is good to be loyal to our family and our work, our loyalty to God is to be first in our life. We aren't to allow our work, our family, or anything else in the world to jeopardize the call that Christ has placed upon each of our lives.

To some, this may sound like a radical concept, but it is what the *Holy Bible* teaches.

God's Word tells us in Deuteronomy 4:24 and other passages that the Lord our God is a jealous God.

The *Holy Bible* also tells us in Luke 14:26, *"If you want to be my disciple, you must hate everyone else by comparison—your father and mother, wife and children, brothers and sisters—yes, even your own life. Otherwise, you cannot be my disciple."*

Have you examined your loyalty to Christ lately? Perhaps it is time for you to re-evaluate where your loyalty truly lies, and recommit your life to Christ—every closet, nook and cranny.

He remains faithful, and He will never let you down.

AUGUST 5

The Almighty Dollar

"No one can serve two masters. For you will hate one and love the other; you will be devoted to one and despise the other. You cannot serve both God and money." —Matthew 6:24

What are you doing with the money God has entrusted to you? What are you spending it on?

There is a saying that if you want to find out where a man's loyalty lies and what type of person he is, you need only to open his checkbook and see where he's spending his money. I have found this to be true in many respects.

God does not bless us with wealth so that we can hoard it and only enrich our personal lifestyles. We are to use the money that God has entrusted to us wisely—not trusting in it, but trusting in God, and blessing others with all He has given.

Ecclesiastes 7:12 says, *"Wisdom and money can get you almost anything, but only wisdom can save your life."*

Proverbs 11:28 tells us, *"Trust in your money and down you go! But the godly flourish like leaves in spring."*

I Timothy 6:17 says, *"Teach those who are rich in this world not to be proud and not to trust in their money, which is so unreliable. Their trust should be in God, who richly gives us all we need for our enjoyment."*

Jesus spoke in parables about money, and using what our Master has entrusted to us for the growth of His Kingdom. He also reminded us that our real treasure is in Heaven.

"Jesus told him, 'If you want to be perfect, go and sell all your possessions and give the money to the poor, and you will have treasure in heaven. Then come, follow me'" (Matthew 9:21).

AUGUST 6

Opportunity Knocks

"Look! I stand at the door and knock. If you hear my voice and open the door, I will come in, and we will share a meal together as friends." —Revelation 3:20

Life is full of opportunities to serve Him each and every day. If we ignore God's voice, or if our lives are so full of sin that we do not hear His voice, we miss out on these opportunities—we miss out on deepening the joy of knowing Him and experiencing Him fully and intimately.

We miss the fellowship of God.

We miss the friendship of God.

We miss the sheer bliss of His presence.

Colossians 4:5 reminds us to, *"Live wisely among those who are not believers, and make the most of every opportunity."*

When we take advantage of the opportunities that God sets before us, we not only enrich our own lives, souls, spirits and emotions, but we also enrich the lives of others.

God uses each and every opportunity to effect eternity.

Do you hear Him knocking at your heart's door?

Won't you accept the opportunity He's giving you today?

AUGUST 7

Living In The Land Of The Lost

"I have wandered away like a lost sheep; come and find me, for I have not forgotten your commands." —Psalm 119:176

In the world, you are surrounded by sheep who have no shepherd. They are truly lost.

When we miss our daily communion time with God, it is easy to become lost, and wander away from the truth—becoming disconnected from our Good Shepherd.

But, the *Holy Bible* tells us in Matthew 18:12-14, *"If a man has a hundred sheep and one of them wanders away, what will he do? Won't he leave the ninety-nine others on the hills and go out to search for the one that is lost?"*

When we wander away from the truth, our loving Heavenly Father calls us back to Himself.

John 10:3 tells us, *"The gatekeeper opens the gate for him, and the sheep recognize his voice and come to him. He calls his own sheep by name and leads them out."*

And, once our Good Shepherd has led us safely back to His pasture, we must avoid the corrupt practices of those around us, because, *"bad company corrupts good character"* (I Corinthians 15:33b).

We must be in the world, but not of the world. We are not to ignore the needs—especially the need for Christ—in those around us, but we must stay true to the law of God (I Corinthians 9:19-27).

May we realize we are living in the land of the lost, and may we seek to bring them to Christ while remaining true to Him each day.

AUGUST 8

On The Fence

"Their loyalty is divided between God and the world, and they are unstable in everything they do." —James 1:8

When we fail to totally commit to Christ, our fence-riding is pretty obvious to everyone around us. But, what causes us to ride the fence? And, what can be done about it?

The cause, the *Holy Bible* tells us in James 4, is our own selfishness and evil desires that are at war within us.

So, what can be done to get us off the fence and fully committed to Christ? What can be done to purge the selfishness and evil desires?

The Book of James provides these answers for us, as well.

James 4:7-10 tells us, *"So humble yourselves before God. Resist the devil, and he will flee from you. Come close to God, and God will come close to you. Wash your hands, you sinners; purify your hearts, for your loyalty is divided between God and the world. Let there be tears for what you have done. Let there be sorrow and deep grief. Let there be sadness instead of laughter, and gloom instead of joy. Humble yourselves before the Lord, and he will lift you up in honor."*

May we follow the words of James in this passage of Scripture and get off the fence today. May we humble ourselves, purify every aspect of our lives, come close to God, and resist the devil today and every day.

May we take up our cross this day and follow Him (Luke 9:23).

AUGUST 9

Part Time Christian

"Not everyone who calls out to me, 'Lord! Lord!' will enter the Kingdom of Heaven. Only those who actually do the will of my Father in heaven will enter." —Matthew 7:21

Are you treating your relationship with Christ as though it were a part time job? If so, be forewarned: There is no such thing as a part time Christian.

Christ requires a full time commitment from us.

Does that mean that we must be gainfully employed by a church or other Christian organization?

No.

The world is a mission field. God calls each of us into different tasks for His honor and glory.

These different tasks also serve to encourage and benefit our fellow Christians and those who are yet to come to know Him.

Romans 6:13 reminds us that we are to give ourselves completely to God. It says, *"Do not let any part of your body become an instrument of evil to serve sin. Instead, give yourselves completely to God, for you were dead, but now you have new life. So use your whole body as an instrument to do what is right for the glory of God."*

May we not hold anything back from God, but commit everything we have and are to Him, in complete and total devotion, remembering our full time wage.

"For the wages of sin is death, but the free gift of God is eternal life through Christ Jesus our Lord" (Romans 6:23).

AUGUST 10

Busy Man

"Plant your seed in the morning and keep busy all afternoon, for you don't know if profit will come from one activity or another—or maybe both." —Ecclesiastes 11:6

We live in a very busy world. The busyness around us is sometimes needless, sometimes not.

Ecclesiastes 5:19-20 says, *"And it is a good thing to receive wealth from God and the good health to enjoy it. To enjoy your work and accept your lot in life—this is indeed a gift from God. God keeps such people so busy enjoying life that they take no time to brood over the past."*

So, how do we know the difference between the kind of busyness that is a gift from God, and our own self-created busyness?

Often, all of our busy scurrying around is simply mimicking the patterns of behavior we see exhibited in the world around us. This busyness has no rhyme or reason. It is simply *doing to do*.

Whereas, the busy life that comes from God is purposeful. It is not necessarily easy, but it is always accompanied by a deep, abiding joy.

Romans 12:2 reminds us, *"Don't copy the behavior and customs of this world, but let God transform you into a new person by changing the way you think. Then you will learn to know God's will for you, which is good and pleasing and perfect."*

When God is in control of the way we think, we will easily know when our busy life is purposeful and when it is just busy.

AUGUST 11

His Home

"Don't you realize that your body is the temple of the Holy Spirit, who lives in you and was given to you by God? You do not belong to yourself, for God bought you with a high price. So you must honor God with your body." —I Corinthians 6:19-20

The word *temple* means sacred or holy place. The Hebrew word for temple is *hekal*, which means palace. The Old Testament temple was the dwelling place of God.

Your body is to be a sacred, holy palace for the Holy Spirit to come and make His home inside.

When Christ is your personal Savior, your life is no longer yours—you belong to Him. He paid the ultimate price for your life. He gave His one and only Son.

This means we are to be mindful of the Holy Spirit's presence dwelling inside us.

Does this realization change what you eat, say, think, or do?

If not, it should.

What about the places that you go?

Are all of these things honoring to God?

If not, pray and recommit yourself to God as His sacred, holy dwelling place—His *home sweet home*.

"I pray that from his glorious, unlimited resources he will empower you with inner strength through his Spirit. Then Christ will make his home in your hearts as you trust in him. Your roots will grow down into God's love and keep you strong" (Ephesians 3:16-17).

AUGUST 12

Disoriented

"And let us not neglect our meeting together, as some people do, but encourage one another, especially now that the day of his return is drawing near." —Hebrews 10:25

Churches aren't perfect.

You don't need to hear that from me. You know that churches are filled with imperfect people.

But, it is easy to become disoriented with church when we encounter groups of people who do not seem to have a desire to grow closer to Christ and become more like Him. They simply embrace their imperfection. It becomes their personal crutch.

They love to talk about God's grace covering their sin, and they just keep right on sinning, too, reminding everyone who sees their sin about that grace.

The *Holy Bible* talks about these people in Romans 6:1-4. It says, *"Well then, should we keep on sinning so that God can show us more and more of his wonderful grace? Of course not! Since we have died to sin, how can we continue to live in it? Or have you forgotten that when we were joined with Christ Jesus in baptism, we joined him in his death? For we died and were buried with Christ by baptism. And just as Christ was raised from the dead by the glorious power of the Father, now we also may live new lives."*

But, what do we do when we become disoriented with these people in church?

James 5:19-20 tells us, *"My dear brothers and sisters, if someone among you wanders away from the truth and is brought back, you can be sure that whoever brings the sinner back will save that person from death and bring about the forgiveness of many sins."*

"Let us think of ways to motivate one another to acts of love and good works" (Hebrews 10:24).

May we grow in His grace (2 Peter 3:18), rather than remaining stagnant. Things that are stagnant have a very unpleasant fragrance.

And, may you be encouraged by Galatians 6:9, *"So let's not get tired of doing what is good. At just the right time we will reap a harvest of blessing if we don't give up."*

AUGUST 13

We're All In This Together

"We are in this struggle together. You have seen my struggle in the past, and you know that I am still in the midst of it." —Philippians 1:30

"No man is an island," so goes the famous quote taken from John Donne's 1624 prose work entitled *Meditation XVII*.

It is true. God did not intend that any of us spend our lives in isolation.

We need each other.

So often I am helped when I begin to share my personal struggles with someone else. I find that they, too, have been where I am, and we may have words of wisdom to share with each other.

Galatians 6:2 tells us, *"Share each other's burdens, and in this way obey the law of Christ."*

We can also pray for each other in times of struggle. There is such a peace that comes when we take the time to pray together through our difficulties.

Remember that James 5:16 says, *"Confess your sins to each other and pray for each other so that you may be healed. The earnest prayer of a righteous person has great power and produces wonderful results."*

And, Matthew 18:20 says, *"For where two or three gather together as my followers, I am there among them."*

May you experience the joy and blessing of knowing the fellowship of other believers today and every day.

AUGUST 14

The Momma Bear And The Fool

"It is safer to meet a bear robbed of her cubs than to confront a fool caught in foolishness."
—Proverbs 17:12

Which is worse—an angry momma bear or a fool? Clearly, the *Holy Bible* tells us here—the fool in his folly is worse. That's really saying something. Have you ever seen a momma bear robbed of her cubs?

I haven't seen a momma bear robbed of her cubs, but I have been in Yellowstone National Park when a momma bear thought a car was in the way of her cubs crossing the road. She reared up on her hind legs, opened her mouth wide, flashed a monstrous mouth of teeth, and lunged at the vehicle. I definitely wouldn't have wanted to be in that car. But, a fool in his foolishness is worse than that.

A fool is unreasonable. A fool gives no consideration to consequences. Fools think about no one but themselves.

That *is* scary.

Psalm 53:1 tells us, *"Only fools say in their hearts, 'There is no God.' They are corrupt, and their actions are evil; not one of them does good!"*

How comforting to know that when we walk the Highway of Holiness, there are no fools there. For, Isaiah 35:8 says, *"And a great road will go through that once deserted land. It will be named the Highway of Holiness. Evil-minded people will never travel on it. It will be only for those who walk in God's ways; fools will never walk there."*

May we travel the King's Highway—away from fools—today and every day hereafter.

AUGUST 15

Pretty Please With Sugar On Top

"After leaving the synagogue that day, Jesus went to Simon's home, where he found Simon's mother-in-law very sick with a high fever. 'Please heal her,' everyone begged." —Luke 4:38

When I was a youngster asking for something from my brother or sister, I wasn't above begging. "Pretty please?" I would ask. When the answer was still, "no," the final plea was, "Pretty please with sugar on top?" I reasoned that the extra sugar might change their response.

In this Scripture, when Simon's mother-in-law was very sick with a fever, the people begged Jesus to heal her. Jesus rebuked the fever and immediately she got up and cooked a meal for them. There was no sugar necessary.

Moses spent a great deal of time begging and pleading with the Lord to change His mind. In each instance, God knew Moses' heart, and He knew what would bring glory and honor to His name. God's answers were dependent upon this, rather than any amount of sugar we might pour upon our request.

It is the same with us. God is not manipulated by a smooth tongue or any outward display. He looks on the heart.

When Daniel earnestly prayed for an understanding regarding his vision, God sent an angel with this message, *"Then he said, 'Don't be afraid, Daniel. Since the first day you began to pray for understanding and to humble yourself before your God, your request has been heard in heaven. I have come in answer to your prayer'"* (Daniel 10:12).

May our sugar be replaced with humility and a loving heart atop our every plea to God.

AUGUST 16

Eat Your Veggies

"It's not what goes into your mouth that defiles you; you are defiled by the words that come out of your mouth." —Matthew 15:11

Are you a healthy eater?

Or, are you one of those folks who would prefer a plate of chocolate chip cookies for breakfast?

God wants us to honor Him with everything that we have and are, including what we put into our bodies.

But, this verse reminds us that equally important are the words that we speak and the intent with which we speak them.

When Jesus spoke these words to the disciples, they didn't understand them, and were concerned that Jesus had offended the Pharisees by what He said.

Consider Jesus words in Matthew 15:16-20 when Peter asked Jesus to explain, *"'Don't you understand yet?' Jesus asked. 'Anything you eat passes through the stomach and then goes into the sewer. But the words you speak come from the heart—that's what defiles you. For from the heart come evil thoughts, murder, adultery, all sexual immorality, theft, lying, and slander. These are what defile you. Eating with unwashed hands will never defile you.'"*

How can we keep wholesome words coming from our lips, our heart? The answer: by feasting on healthy words, God's Word, daily. For, when our heart is right with God, everything in our being longs to please Him.

"Taste and see that the Lord is good. Oh, the joys of those who take refuge in him" (Psalm 34:8)!

AUGUST 17

Expect A Miracle

"He does great things too marvelous to understand. He performs countless miracles." — Job 9:10

A man teaching a Sunday School class I attended recently stated that God doesn't perform miracles anymore—like He did in Bible days.

I was heartbroken by the comment, and could not keep silent because, my friend, God still performs countless miracles every day.

We need only open our eyes to see them . . . and we must believe.

The level of miracles that God performs in and around us occur in direct proportion to the level of our faith.

When Jesus encountered doubters in his hometown of Nazareth, the Scripture tells us in Matthew 13:58, "And so he did only a few miracles there because of their unbelief."

The same thing is recounted in Mark 6:5-6, *"And because of their unbelief, he couldn't do any miracles among them except to place his hands on a few sick people and heal them. And he was amazed at their unbelief."*

Each day, God performs countless miracles in and around us for those who believe, those who expect Him to act.

Do you need a miracle today?

Are you expecting a miracle today?

May we believe and expect a miracle today and every day.

AUGUST 18

His Perfect Strength

"Each time he said, 'My grace is all you need. My power works best in weakness.' So now I am glad to boast about my weaknesses, so that the power of Christ can work through me."
—*2 Corinthians 12:9*

There is a song written by Steven Curtis Chapman, entitled "His Strength is Perfect," in which the chorus says:

> *His strength is perfect when our strength is gone;*
> *He'll carry us when we can't carry on.*
> *Raised in His power, the weak become strong;*
> *His strength is perfect, His strength is perfect.*

I recall many years back hearing Billy Graham recount his lack of professional seminary training, and how God had empowered him and given him the necessary strength to preach the gospel message. At the time I heard these words, I did not understand their importance.

As I grew older and became more aware of all the ways in which God has used Billy Graham's life, I was awed by the power of God to use a single life that is devoted to Him. I also understood the importance of boasting in our own weaknesses, as Paul did in the referenced passage.

Our personal story, with all of its imperfections, shortcomings, and flaws, can bring honor and glory to our Heavenly Father when others realize who we are—both with Him and without Him.

May you put aside—once and for all—any personal agenda you may have, and recommit everything you have and are to Him whose strength is made perfect in our weakness.

AUGUST 19

High-Powered Hogwash

"Don't let anyone capture you with empty philosophies and high-sounding nonsense that come from human thinking and from the spiritual powers of this world, rather than from Christ."
—*Colossians 2:8*

My daddy was born in Houston, Texas and grew up on a dairy farm in Anderson, South Carolina. He is about as southern as people get.

He has often used colloquialisms from his farm days. One of my personal favorites is, "That is nothin' but high-powered hogwash!" This was used most often in reference to some intellectual idea espoused by someone who felt their mind was too advanced for the concept of faith or other truths of the *Holy Bible*.

Hogwash is the garbage fed to pigs, in the literal sense, swill.

This passage of Scripture is reminding us that any such notion that is contrary to the truths of the *Holy Bible*, is coming from the spiritual forces of this world, the devil and his demons, and it is nothing more than high-powered hogwash.

We must always test the teaching that we receive against God's Word.

I Thessalonians 5:21-22 tells us, *"but test everything that is said. Hold on to what is good. Stay away from every kind of evil."*

May you be filled with God's perfect truth today.

AUGUST 20

The King's Right-Hand Man

"Then the King will say to those on his right, 'Come, you who are blessed by my Father, inherit the Kingdom prepared for you from the creation of the world.'" —Matthew 25:34

In days of old, a man was thought to have little difficulty defending himself from an attacker approaching on his left side—assuming he was right-handed. He was much more vulnerable to an attacker approaching his right side—considering the same assumption.

With this thought in mind, the king always kept his most trustworthy servants on his right. They had proven themselves to be of impeccable character and integrity. They had proven themselves faithful.

These were the king's right-hand men.

What about you?

Are you trustworthy?

Have you proven yourself to be of impeccable character and integrity?

Are you faithful to Him?

Jesus tells us in Matthew 25:35 what this faithful servant looks like, *"For I was hungry, and you fed me. I was thirsty, and you gave me a drink. I was a stranger, and you invited me into your home. I was naked, and you gave me clothing. I was sick, and you cared for me. I was in prison, and you visited me."*

May we live a life worthy of being called to our King's right-hand.

AUGUST 21

The Hills Are Alive With The Sound Of Music

"You will live in joy and peace. The mountains and hills will burst into song, and the trees of the field will clap their hands!" —Isaiah 55:12

Isaiah 55 provides an illustrious description of what it is like to be invited to the richness of God's salvation.

"You will live in joy and peace..."

This is not conditioned upon our circumstance. It is a glorious place of complete contentment, with the Holy Spirit living and breathing inside of us. It is knowing that His Spirit can and will handle anything that comes our way.

All of God's creation rejoices that we are in Him and He is in us.

That is how it is meant to be, yet so often we suffocate the Holy Spirit's presence in our lives. We act ashamed of our Savior, like a teenager embarrassed to be seen with their parents—neither picture is God's design.

I Thessalonians 5:19 provides a loving command for us by saying, *"Do not stifle the Holy Spirit."*

May we allow the Holy Spirit's power to have complete and total access to every chamber of our hearts.

As Psalm 21:13 tells us, *"Rise up, O Lord, in all your power. With music and singing we celebrate your mighty acts."*

AUGUST 22

Contented Living

"So if we have enough food and clothing, let us be content." —I Timothy 6:8

Are you a contented person?

Or, do you allow selfishness and personal ambition to steal away the peace and contentment that God longs to give you?

King Amaziah (2 Kings 14) had been victorious in battle, yet could not find contentment and waged war against Israel's King Jehoash. Prior to the battle, King Jehoash sent a letter to King Amaziah saying, *"You have indeed defeated Edom, and you are very proud of it. But be content with your victory and stay at home! Why stir up trouble that will only bring disaster on you and the people of Judah"* (2 Kings 14:10)?

He did, indeed, bring disaster on himself and the people of Judah. Why? It was all due to a lack of contentment.

The apostle, Paul, learned to be content. In Philippians 4:11 he tells us, *"Not that I was ever in need, for I have learned how to be content with whatever I have."*

Are you always reaching for more: Bigger house, pool, nicer car, different job, bigger paycheck, keeping up with the Joneses?

May we heed the words of Solomon in Proverbs 30:8, when he says, *"First, help me never to tell a lie. Second, give me neither poverty nor riches! Give me just enough to satisfy my needs."*

AUGUST 23

The Big Bad Wolf

"The thief's purpose is to steal and kill and destroy. My purpose is to give them a rich and satisfying life." —John 10:10

Once upon a time, I was a little pink pig who had built a beautiful house of straw—not fully understanding how powerful the Big Bad Wolf (Satan) really was.

In a short time and just a few huffs and puffs, he blew through my flimsy protection. After all, what I thought was a beautiful straw house was only a few Scripture verses here and there—when it was convenient for me—and regular church attendance, plus a prayer or two, now and then.

So, I added some Christian fellowship, visiting with my brother in his house of sticks. I was sure the Big Bad Wolf was no match for us there. I was wrong.

When the Big Bad Wolf blew that house down, my brother and I ran straight to our Teacher's house—the Master—and joined him in His house made of bricks. We could hear the Big Bad Wolf huffing and puffing outside the door, yet he never made it inside.

Our Master explained that we must remain vigilant, tending always to loose bricks and mortar, keeping the roof and gutters repaired, and properly sealing the chimney to guard against the Wolf's attacks.

I Peter 5:8 tells us, *"Stay alert! Watch out for your great enemy, the devil. He prowls around like a roaring lion, looking for someone to devour."*

May we tend to the condition of our heart, allowing Christ to protect us always from the devil's schemes.

AUGUST 24

We Belong To Him

"A hired hand will run when he sees a wolf coming. He will abandon the sheep because they don't belong to him and he isn't their shepherd. And so the wolf attacks them and scatters the flock." —John 10:12

How wonderful to know that our shepherd, Jesus Christ, is not a hired hand. The hired hand runs away because he's working only for the money and doesn't really care about the sheep (John 10:13).

But, Jesus is our master, our owner.

He will never abandon us, because He has too much invested.

We belong to Him.

He has given everything for us—His one and only Son, Jesus Christ.

John 10:11 tells us, *"I am the good shepherd. The good shepherd sacrifices his life for the sheep."*

John 10:14-15 says, *"I am the good shepherd; I know my own sheep, and they know me, just as my Father knows me and I know the Father. So I sacrifice my life for the sheep."*

May we listen always to our shepherd's voice, and may we follow Him wherever He may lead us (John 10:27).

Savior, like a shepherd lead us, for we belong to You.

AUGUST 25

Back To School

"Teach me your ways, O Lord, that I may live according to your truth! Grant me purity of heart, so that I may honor you." —Psalm 86:11

As a youngster, I was one of those kids who couldn't wait to be finished with school. I went to college at age sixteen, finished in three and a half years, and celebrated that I was done with school for life.

It was quite a surprise to my perfectly-planned world when I learned soon after landing my first job that I would have to hit the books again . . . permanently. Continuing education is a part of life—not just in business—but, in our spiritual life, as well.

Joshua 1:8 tells us, *"Study this Book of Instruction continually. Meditate on it day and night so you will be sure to obey everything written in it. Only then will you prosper and succeed in all you do."*

When we study God's Word, we begin to grow deeper in our understanding of His plan and purpose for our lives. He communicates with us, teaches, and leads us through His Word.

2 Peter 1:8 tells us, *"The more you grow like this, the more productive and useful you will be in your knowledge of our Lord Jesus Christ."*

Let us not be like those addressed in Hebrews 5:12, which says, *"You have been believers so long now that you ought to be teaching others. Instead, you need someone to teach you again the basic things about God's word. You are like babies who need milk and cannot eat solid food."*

May we continue to grow in the knowledge of our Lord and Savior, Jesus Christ, every day.

AUGUST 26

Out Of The Darkness

"Then the Lord said to Moses, 'Lift your hand toward heaven, and the land of Egypt will be covered with a darkness so thick you can feel it.'" —Exodus 10:21

When we intentionally walk in sin, it is a darkness so thick, so deep, it can be felt. In this place, we are unable to grasp the reality of where we are, and where God is in relation.

The darkness of sin shrouds the truth from our eyes.

In John 8:12, Jesus showed us the way out of the darkness, *"Jesus spoke to the people once more and said, 'I am the light of the world. If you follow me, you won't have to walk in darkness, because you will have the light that leads to life.'"*

He also tells us in John 12:46, *"I have come as a light to shine in this dark world, so that all who put their trust in me will no longer remain in the dark."*

Jesus is the light that dispels all darkness.

As we allow His Holy Spirit to fill our lives, His light fills our lives, His truth fills our lives, and there is no darkness.

Won't you remain in Him?

Won't you allow Him to remain in you?

May the Lord send out His light and His truth, that they may guide us. May His light lead us to His holy mountain, the place where He lives (Psalm 43:3).

AUGUST 27

Healthy Spirit

"Dear friend, I hope all is well with you and that you are as healthy in body as you are strong in spirit." —3 John 1:2

We hear a great deal of talk regarding physical fitness—especially at each New Year.

But, what about our spiritual fitness?

If you went to the Great Physician for a spiritual well check, what do think He would say to you?

Are you strong in spirit?

And, what exactly does it mean to be strong in spirit?

The *Holy Bible* tells us that John the Baptist was strong in spirit (Luke 1:80). It tells us that Barnabas was full of the Holy Spirit and strong in faith (Acts 11:24).

I believe that in order to be strong in spirit we must first acknowledge our own personal weakness without the Holy Spirit's power living and working in our lives. We must also have faith in Him, and a reverential fear of His power.

In Ephesians 6:10, Paul says, *"A final word: Be strong in the Lord and in his mighty power."*

What about you?

Are you strong in the Lord?

May you come before Him today for your own spiritual check-up.

May you grow in faith, and may you grow strong in spirit, remembering that no matter what circumstance comes your way, our God is greater (Isaiah 63:1).

AUGUST 28

Count Your Blessings

"All praise to God, the Father of our Lord Jesus Christ, who has blessed us with every spiritual blessing in the heavenly realms because we are united with Christ." —Ephesians 1:3

When was the last time you *really* took stock of your blessings?

Perhaps you are in a difficult place in life, and find it hard to see the good. Or, perhaps you have been counting your blessings just before reading this.

Wherever you find yourself in life, there are always blessings to be counted. No matter how difficult the day or the night, God's love remains.

Isaiah 54:10 promises us, *"For the mountains may move and the hills disappear, but even then my faithful love for you will remain. My covenant of blessing will never be broken,' says the Lord, who has mercy on you."*

John 1:16 reminds us, *"From his abundance we have all received one gracious blessing after another."*

We are surrounded by blessings. We need only to stop and recognize them, acknowledging them, and praising God for them.

Have you counted your blessings today?

May you count your many blessings, naming them one by one.

I am sure it will surprise you what the Lord has done.

AUGUST 29

Plea Bargain

"You boast, "We have struck a bargain to cheat death and have made a deal to dodge the grave. The coming destruction can never touch us, for we have built a strong refuge made of lies and deception." —Isaiah 28:15

Do you ever try to bargain with God, make deals with Him? God is not one to play such games with any of us.

But, the devil will.

Sadly, many have sold their souls to the devil to get things they believe will satisfy.

But, it is a lie.

The devil, himself, is the one trying to convince them that their evil desire is actually a good thing.

We must remember the truth in order to counter these attacks from the evil one.

In Matthew 16:26, Jesus asked, *"And what do you benefit if you gain the whole world but lose your own soul? Is anything worth more than your soul?"*

The devil knows the value of your soul.

But, he doesn't want you to know its value.

Remember the words of I Peter 2:11 which says, *"Dear friends, I warn you as 'temporary residents and foreigners' to keep away from worldly desires that wage war against your very souls."*

May we thank God, our Savior, for being the Guardian of our souls (I Peter 2:25), and may we listen to His voice, as He seeks to protect us from the evil one.

AUGUST 30

Never Stop Praying

"Never stop praying." —I Thessalonians 5:17

Prayer is the most powerful form of communication we have. It is communication with the Master of the Universe, our Heavenly Father.

Never underestimate the power of prayer.

And, there is no greater example of how to pray than that provided by Jesus.

In Matthew 6:5-7, Jesus tells us, *"When you pray, don't be like the hypocrites who love to pray publicly on street corners and in the synagogues where everyone can see them. I tell you the truth, that is all the reward they will ever get. But when you pray, go away by yourself, shut the door behind you, and pray to your Father in private. Then your Father, who sees everything, will reward you. When you pray, don't babble on and on as people of other religions do. They think their prayers are answered merely by repeating their words again and again."*

Jesus then gives us the example that we refer to as "The Lord's Prayer" in Matthew 6:9-13.

He also reminds us that we should never give up praying in Matthew 7:7, when he pronounces, *"Keep on asking, and you will receive what you ask for. Keep on seeking, and you will find. Keep on knocking, and the door will be opened to you."*

May you have the faith to believe that our sovereign Lord hears your every prayer, that His answer will come, His timing will be perfect, and the end result will be better than you could ever imagine it to be.

AUGUST 31

No Secrets

"But don't be afraid of those who threaten you. For the time is coming when everything that is covered will be revealed, and all that is secret will be made known to all." —Matthew 10:26

Are you good at keeping secrets?

I'm not.

The *Holy Bible* tells us that God knows the secrets of every heart (Psalm 44:21). It tells us that He sees every secret sin, too (Psalm 90:8). He even knows about secret motives that we try to cover up (Jeremiah 17:10).

Are you trying to keep secrets from God?

It won't work.

Mark 4:22 tells us, *"For everything that is hidden will eventually be brought into the open, and every secret will be brought to light."*

Luke 8:17 says, *"For all that is secret will eventually be brought into the open, and everything that is concealed will be brought to light and made known to all."*

Are there things you think you've gotten away with? Things you think no one will ever know about?

Romans 2:16 soberly advises, *"And this is the message I proclaim—that the day is coming when God, through Christ Jesus, will judge everyone's secret life."*

May we live our lives in such a way as to have no concern for these secrets. May we humbly repent of any unconfessed sin in our lives, and may we work toward complete holiness because we fear God (I Corinthians 7:1).

SEPTEMBER 1

Never Alone

"And I will ask the Father, and he will give you another Advocate, who will never leave you."
—John 14:16

She was a young mother. Her father abandoned their family when she was twelve, and she had to go to work to help support the family shortly thereafter. They lived in Mexico City, and didn't have much.

Now that she had her own children, the old wounds from her childhood began to haunt her. Would her husband abandon the family? He wasn't exactly the most responsible man she knew, and hadn't kept a job for more than a year at a time.

Fear gripped her heart and began to take hold of her mind. She had convinced herself that she, too, would end up alone to care for her young family.

It was her worst nightmare.

But, it was a lie.

She ended up in church with her young family and heard the truth.

She heard that God would never fail her or abandon her (Hebrews 13:5).

She heard Lamentations 3:31, *"For no one is abandoned by the Lord forever."*

And, she heard that the Father would send another Advocate, who would never leave her (John 14:16).

Do you feel alone today?

Remember that the Holy Spirit is always with you, He will never leave you, and is your comfort, your peace, and your advocate.

SEPTEMBER 2

Onward Christian Soldiers

"Endure suffering along with me, as a good soldier of Christ Jesus." —2 Timothy 2:3

There are many wonderful soldiers who have defended our country, our freedom, our lives, our personal honor.

But, what defines a *good* soldier?

The *Holy Bible* tells us in 2 Timothy 2:4 that, *"Soldiers don't get tied up in the affairs of civilian life, for then they cannot please the officer who enlisted them."*

Clearly, a good soldier's focus is on pleasing the enlisting officer, regardless of the amount of sacrifice and suffering that may be required. The good soldier puts aside his own plans, his own agenda to follow the enlisting officer's every command. He gives up everything—up to and including his very life.

Are you a good soldier?

Are you focused on pleasing your enlisting officer, Jesus Christ, no matter what the sacrifice?

Have you put aside your own plans?

How about your own personal agenda?

Are you following His every command?

Perhaps you feel ill-equipped to follow His commands. Remember that Psalm 144:1 tells us, *"Praise the LORD, who is my rock. He trains my hands for war and gives my fingers skill for battle."*

SEPTEMBER 3

Faith Hope Love

"Three things will last forever—faith, hope, and love—and the greatest of these is love."
—I Corinthians 13:13

Few things are built to last these days.

In fact, most manufacturers intentionally limit the shelf life of various products to generate repeat business.

But, God gives us things that will last forever: faith, hope, and love.

"Faith is the confidence that what we hope for will actually happen; it gives us assurance about things we cannot see" (Hebrews 11:1).

Hope is defined by the Merriam-Webster Dictionary as, "to cherish a desire with anticipation."

Love is vividly described for us in I Corinthians 13, which outlines every attribute.

Scripture tells us in 2 Corinthians 4:18 that we are to fix our gaze on these things, to focus on them, rather than on the temporary earthly problems that we can now see. It says, *"So we don't look at the troubles we can see now; rather, we fix our gaze on things that cannot be seen. For the things we see now will soon be gone, but the things we cannot see will last forever."*

When we focus on the things that will last forever, we accept our circumstances with joy, knowing that there are better things waiting for us (Hebrews 10:34).

SEPTEMBER 4

Not Of This World

"We are here for only a moment, visitors and strangers in the land as our ancestors were before us. Our days on earth are like a passing shadow, gone so soon without a trace."
—I Chronicles 29:15

It was Christy's first trip in an airplane. At twenty-two, she was long past the typical age for a first flight, and it was overseas, to boot.

She buckled in, listened to the flight attendant's safety message, and drank in a deep breath in an effort to still her cat-like nerves. During the flight, she practiced the language she would soon be immersed in.

When the plane landed, she prayed her way through the chaos. Each successive day, Christy did her best to assimilate within the culture, but each passing moment only served to increase her homesickness more and more.

But, Christy's was not a homesickness for the country she left, for it was not her real home. She was a foreigner there, too. Hebrews 11:14-16 tells us, *"Obviously people who say such things are looking forward to a country they can call their own. If they had longed for the country they came from, they could have gone back. But they were looking for a better place, a heavenly homeland. That is why God is not ashamed to be called their God, for he has prepared a city for them."*

Christy longed for the city that God has prepared for her—her heavenly home.

What about you? Are you feeling as though you are not of this world? Remember that God has prepared a city for you. And one day, both you and Christy will enjoy that heavenly homeland—forever.

SEPTEMBER 5

Delightful

"Take delight in the Lord, and he will give you your heart's desires." —Psalm 37:4

The Hebrew transliteration of the word *delight* in this verse is *oneg*, which carries with it the idea of an exquisite delicacy from which one derives extreme pleasure. It is something to be celebrated and rejoiced over.

Do you celebrate and rejoice over your relationship with Christ?

Having such a relationship with Him causes us to be of the same mind. It changes the way that we think, removing selfishness and pride, and allows our desires to become one with the desires of Christ.

When this happens, our glorious Heavenly Father causes these dreams and desires to become a reality.

Christ has become delightful to us.

Matthew 7:11 tells us, *"So if you sinful people know how to give good gifts to your children, how much more will your heavenly Father give good gifts to those who ask him."*

May you delight yourself in the Lord, realizing how many of your heart's desires he has already fulfilled.

SEPTEMBER 6

He Speaks Softly To My Heart

"And after the earthquake there was a fire, but the Lord was not in the fire. And after the fire there was the sound of a gentle whisper." —I Kings 19:12

I've noticed as I begin to get older, that I do not hear as well as I used to. I must ask repeatedly for things to be restated in a louder volume. "I can't hear you, Dear. What was that again?"

It can be a bit like my relationship with the Father. As a young follower of Christ, my heart was sensitive and closely attuned to the gentle whisper of the Savior. We spent time together regularly, and I couldn't wait to hear from Him, as He communicated His thoughts and instructions to my heart and soul.

Yet, when sin takes a toehold in any area of my life, I no longer hear the still small voice of my beloved Savior speaking softly to my heart. The bitter roots of sin take hold, serving to harden my heart and deafen my soul to His gentle whisper. The thoughts of sin crowd out His gentle whisper.

Hebrews 12:25 warns us of the serious consequences of not listening to our Savior, *"Be careful that you do not refuse to listen to the One who is speaking. For if the people of Israel did not escape when they refused to listen to Moses, the earthly messenger, we will certainly not escape if we reject the One who speaks to us from heaven!"*

May we incline our heart to His still, small voice, and heed His every direction to our heart, rejecting sin—today and always.

SEPTEMBER 7

Stop The World

"Be still, and know that I am God! I will be honored by every nation. I will be honored throughout the world." —Psalm 46:10

Do you ever feel as though you'd like the world to stop so that you can get off?

Perhaps you are overwhelmed with your circumstances. Or, maybe you just feel as though you cannot go on in your present situation.

God does want us to stop and be still at times, but not so that we can get off this crazy ride called life. It is so that we can recognize His sovereign, loving control of things—all things. It is so that we can know but a taste of all that He is doing in and around us. And, it is so that we may honor our Lord and Savior for all that He is.

Psalm 104:1 says, *"Let all that I am praise the Lord. O Lord my God, how great you are! You are robed with honor and majesty."*

Often we want the world to stop out of frustration that we do not see the justice of the Lord. Yet, the *Holy Bible* tells us in Psalm 37:7, *"Be still in the presence of the Lord, and wait patiently for him to act. Don't worry about evil people who prosper or fret about their wicked schemes."*

May we honor our God by acknowledging His sovereign ability to act on our behalf at the perfect time, and in the perfect way.

SEPTEMBER 8

Jack And Jill

"Two people are better off than one, for they can help each other succeed. If one person falls, the other can reach out and help. But someone who falls alone is in real trouble." — Ecclesiastes 4:9-10

In the nursery rhyme, *Jack and Jill,*[4] Jack and Jill go up a hill to fetch a pail of water. Jack falls down and breaks his crown, and then Jill comes tumbling after.

Hopefully, after Jill finished tumbling, she was able to help Jack get back up. If he needed medical attention, she could get that, too. And then, together, they could go after that pail of water again. Imagine if poor Jack had gone after the water all by himself. No one would have known he fell and cracked his head open for quite some time, and he would've been in some serious trouble.

This passage in Ecclesiastes reminds us that we need each other.

Sometimes in life when we are hurt or betrayed by someone we trust with all of our heart, it leaves a very deep wound—a wound that never wants to trust or depend upon anyone else ever again.

But, the love of God can heal even the deepest wounds of betrayal, so that we may allow others into our life once again.

Psalm 147:3 says, *"He heals the brokenhearted and bandages their wounds."*

May you allow His love to heal you today.

---

[4] Author unknown.

SEPTEMBER 9

My BFF

"There are 'friends' who destroy each other, but a real friend sticks closer than a brother."
—Psalm 18:24

Do you have a BFF?

My favorite story of Biblical BFFs is that of David and Jonathan.

I Samuel 18:1 tells us, *"After David had finished talking with Saul, he met Jonathan, the king's son. There was an immediate bond between them, for Jonathan loved David."*

I Samuel 18:3 says, *"And Jonathan made a solemn pact with David, because he loved him as he loved himself."*

The pact between the two BFFs proved very important, as Jonathan's father, King Saul, became jealous of David and sought to kill him.

Jonathan risked his life to protect David from his father's jealous rage, renewing his pact of loyalty and friendship with him on more than one occasion.

When the Philistines finally took the life of Saul and Jonathan, David honored his pact of friendship by showing kindness to Jonathan's crippled son, Mephibosheth (2 Samuel 9:7).

John 15:13 tells us, *"There is no greater love than to lay down one's life for one's friends."*

I pray that God will bless your life with such a true friend, and I pray that God will make you this kind of friend to someone else, as well.

SEPTEMBER 10

To The Death

"Then Nebuchadnezzar said, 'Praise to the God of Shadrach, Meshach, and Abednego! He sent his angel to rescue his servants who trusted in him. They defied the king's command and were willing to die rather than serve or worship any god except their own God.'" —Daniel 3:28

If you are familiar with the story of Shadrach, Meshach, and Abednego in the fiery furnace, then you know it is the kind of story that legends are made of. Yet, it is true.

These three men and Daniel were part of a select group chosen from the tribe of Judah to be trained for three years in order to serve in the king's royal palace in Babylon.

Some time later, King Nebuchadnezzar made a ninety-foot gold statute and issued a decree that everyone should bow to the statue whenever they heard the sound of musical instruments. But, Shadrach, Meshach, and Abednego refused to bow down to the statue, as this was against God's command.

When King Nebuchadnezzar found out, he was enraged, and ordered them thrown into the fiery furnace. Not only that, but he ordered the furnace to be heated seven times hotter than normal, and had the men bound and thrown into the fire fully clothed. The fire was so hot that the soldiers were killed by the fire as they threw the men in.

Daniel 3:25 tells us what happened next, *"Look!"* Nebuchadnezzar shouted. *"I see four men, unbound, walking around in the fire unharmed! And the fourth looks like a god!"*

They honored God to the death, and He rewarded them with life. May we remember their example in every choice we make.

SEPTEMBER 11

Pinocchio

"Telling lies about others is as harmful as hitting them with an ax, wounding them with a sword, or shooting them with a sharp arrow." —Proverbs 25:18

Don't you wish sometimes that the nose of those around you would grow—like Pinocchio—when they told a lie? Then, there would be no doubt.

It might just help you and me stay on the straight and narrow when it comes to telling lies, too.

We are so often unaware of how painful telling lies is to others, and the deep, longterm impact these lies can have upon all of our lives.

The Scripture above puts it into perspective for us, painting a very accurate word picture of the damage done.

But, do we ever learn the lesson God would have us to learn? And, what is that lesson?

Psalm 14:4 tells us, *"Will those who do evil never learn? They eat up my people like bread and wouldn't think of praying to the LORD.*

And, Psalm 130:4 says, *"But you offer forgiveness, that we might learn to fear you."*

Proverbs 24:26 says, *"An honest answer is like a kiss of friendship."*

And, Proverbs 2:7 tells us, *"He grants a treasure of common sense to the honest. He is a shield to those who walk with integrity."*

May our lips speak only what is true and honest today and every day.

SEPTEMBER 12

Quitter

"And have you forgotten the encouraging words God spoke to you as his children? He said, 'My child, don't make light of the Lord's discipline, and don't give up when he corrects you.'"
—Hebrews 12:5

Are you a quitter?

Maybe you grew up hearing the saying, "Quitters never win, and winners never quit."

I have to admit, when things become difficult in life, I have a tendency to want to throw in the towel, head for the hills, or run away from the world.

What about when things don't go right at work? Have you ever made a mistake that you felt your boss could never forgive?

Ecclesiastes 10:4 says, *"If your boss is angry at you, don't quit! A quiet spirit can overcome even great mistakes."*

In our Christian walk, God is showing us a new way to live every day, and He is renewing our spirits day by day so that we will not grow weary in the journey He has set before us.

2 Corinthians 4:1 tells us, *"Therefore, since God in his mercy has given us this new way, we never give up."*

2 Corinthians 4:16 says, *"That is why we never give up. Though our bodies are dying, our spirits are being renewed every day."*

May we remember God's wonderful protection of us as we consider Galatians 6:9, which says, *"So let's not get tired of doing what is good. At just the right time we will reap a harvest of blessing if we don't give up."*

SEPTEMBER 13

Put Me In, Coach

"Wait patiently for the Lord. Be brave and courageous. Yes, wait patiently for the Lord." — Psalm 27:14

There have been many times in life when I felt as though I was sitting on the sidelines while God called everyone else into action—except me.

Was I not good enough? I was always picked last in kickball, too.

Why wasn't He using me?

I just didn't understand—I *wanted* to be used by God!

Isn't that what He wanted, too?

God *does* want us to be willing—willing to do *whatever* He calls us to—even waiting.

The coach doesn't just throw the rookie into the game without any training. He tries to ensure that his player is in the perfect situation to succeed in the game.

So it is with our Heavenly Father. He prepares us. He doesn't just throw us in without any uniform or padding.

And, when we are truly being used by God, we are unaware of our impact, the Holy Spirit's impact, the way we are being used. That is not our chief concern. Our chief concern is obedience to our Coach.

The results are in His hands.

Are you tired of sitting on the sidelines? Tired of being the water boy/girl?

Perhaps that's exactly where God wants you.

And, your life may be changing every player on the team . . . while you're waiting.

SEPTEMBER 14

Walking On Water

"About three o'clock in the morning Jesus came toward them, walking on the water." — *Matthew 14:25*

It seems unreal to us . . . walking on water. But, why? Oh, we of little faith . . . How we limit our wonderful, merciful, loving Savior.

How He longs to do more than we could ever ask or imagine. But, God is not one to impose Himself upon us. He is beyond the perfect gentleman. And yet, the word *gentleman* is so very inadequate to describe Him.

He is beyond description. Do you long to know Him? *Really* know Him?

Peter longed to know Him. When He saw Jesus walking on the water, he wanted to believe. Matthew 14:28 tells us, *"Then Peter called to him, 'Lord, if it's really you, tell me to come to you, walking on the water.'"*

Peter was so much like you and I. Note the continuation of the story in Matthew 14:29-30, *"'Yes, come,' Jesus said. So Peter went over the side of the boat and walked on the water toward Jesus. But when he saw the strong wind and the waves, he was terrified and began to sink. 'Save me, Lord!' he shouted."*

Jesus did reach out and save Peter, just like He saves us. But, notice that Peter began to sink when he took his eyes off Jesus, and began to notice what was going on around him.

It is the same with us.

May we keep our eyes, our focus on Jesus, allowing Him to do infinitely more than walking on water.

SEPTEMBER 15

The Beauty Of Morning Prayer

"Before daybreak the next morning, Jesus got up and went out to an isolated place to pray."
—Mark 1:35

There is something beautiful and special about praying in the morning when we first awaken. It is honoring and obedient to give to God the first fruits of our day in this way.

You will also find, that as you make morning prayer a regular practice, your attitude will become more positive and hopeful.

The beauty of morning prayer also serves to establish your mindset for the day . . . on Christ.

When your mindset, your focus, is on Christ, sin takes a backseat. Saying "no" to wrong desires becomes second nature.

We should always pray. God's Word tells us in I Thessalonians 5:17 to, *"Never stop praying."* Bearing this in mind, we should both start and end our day in communion with the Father.

Psalm 5:3 says, *"Listen to my voice in the morning, Lord. Each morning I bring my requests to you and wait expectantly."*

Won't you join me in giving God the very best, the first fruits of our day?

SEPTEMBER 16

Purging The Evil

"Get out of my life, you evil-minded people, for I intend to obey the commands of my God."
—*Psalm 119:115*

Are you a purger or a hoarder?

When the closets get too full, and drawers begin to overflow, it is time to unload the items that are simply taking up space. If we don't remove these items, they become a hindrance. Purging can be difficult and time-consuming, but when the task is complete, there is great satisfaction.

But, what about people?

Do you hoard them?

Are there people in your life with divided loyalty?

Do you hold tightly to these people?

If so, these people will become a hindrance to you and your walk with Christ.

James 1:6b tells us, *"a person with divided loyalty is as unsettled as a wave of the sea that is blown and tossed by the wind."*

Ridding our lives of evil people is more difficult than clearing out closets. It is also infinitely more important.

Let us not forget that "bad company corrupts good character" (I Corinthians 15:33b), and may we purge the evil-minded people from our lives that we might obey the commands of our God.

SEPTEMBER 17

If At First You Don't Succeed . . .

"Commit your actions to the Lord, and your plans will succeed." —Proverbs 16:3

We've all heard the saying, "If at first you don't succeed, try, try again." But, what does the *Holy Bible* say?

Well, besides the passage of Scripture above, Proverbs 20:18 says, *"Plans succeed through good counsel; don't go to war without wise advice."*

Galatians 6:9 says, *"So let's not get tired of doing what is good. At just the right time we will reap a harvest of blessing if we don't give up."*

Hebrews 12:5 tells us, *"And have you forgotten the encouraging words God spoke to you as his children? He said, "My child, don't make light of the LORD's discipline, and don't give up when he corrects you."*

Proverbs 13:13 says, *"People who despise advice are asking for trouble; those who respect a command will succeed."*

And, Ecclesiastes 10:10 reminds us about the value of wisdom in succeeding, *"Using a dull ax requires great strength, so sharpen the blade. That's the value of wisdom; it helps you succeed."*

Clearly, through these verses and many more, the *Holy Bible* teaches us that there is more to success than merely trying over and over and not giving up. We must commit our plans to God, and we must give Him complete control of every area of our lives.

If at first you don't succeed, give it all to God. He turns messes into masterpieces.

SEPTEMBER 18

May I Help You

"Rescue the poor and helpless; deliver them from the grasp of evil people." —Psalm 82:4

Throughout the *Holy Bible*, Jesus commands us to help others. Yet, in this mixed-up me-centered world, how often do we really shift our focus from ourselves to those around us who need our help?

Galatians 6:1 tells us, *"Dear brothers and sisters, if another believer is overcome by some sin, you who are godly should gently and humbly help that person back onto the right path. And be careful not to fall into the same temptation yourself."*

And, what about the timing of our help? Do we respond immediately when we have the means to do so? Or, do we attempt to rationalize our delay?

Proverbs 3:28 reminds us, *"If you can help your neighbor now, don't say, 'Come back tomorrow, and then I'll help you.'"*

And, we should never turn a blind eye to those in need.

Deuteronomy 22:4 says, *"If you see that your neighbor's donkey or ox has collapsed on the road, do not look the other way. Go and help your neighbor get it back on its feet!"*

Let us pray and ask God to open our eyes and hearts to those in need of help today and every day.

SEPTEMBER 19

Clear

"My words are plain to anyone with understanding, clear to those with knowledge." — Proverbs 8:9

Our Heavenly Father wants the way of wisdom to be clear to us. He wants us to learn, and to see things plainly.

Psalm 119:130 tells us, *"The teaching of your word gives light, so even the simple can understand."*

God's Word, His wisdom makes things clear to us.

As we grow in wisdom, knowledge, and understanding, our daily life and the decisions God would have us to make become clear and uncluttered by the world around us. Growing deeper in our understanding of Him makes the chaos of life disappear.

Although many things in life and certain aspects of God's character are too grand, wonderful, and mysterious for us to understand, gaining a heart of wisdom will open our understanding to God's will for our lives on a daily basis.

As Isaiah 50:4 says, *"The Sovereign Lord has given me his words of wisdom, so that I know how to comfort the weary. Morning by morning he wakens me and opens my understanding to his will."*

May you spend time in God's Word so that you may grow in wisdom and knowledge, and may He open your understanding to His will.

SEPTEMBER 20

Shipwrecked

"Cling to your faith in Christ, and keep your conscience clear. For some people have deliberately violated their consciences; as a result, their faith has been shipwrecked." —I Timothy 1:19

There was a lot of talk about the Titanic before it set sail from Southampton, England en route to New York City on its maiden voyage—a lot of talk.

But, any ship captain can tell you that it is the storm that proves the seaworthiness of the ship.

What about you?

Are you just a lot of talk?

Or, are you a true follower of Christ?

Is your life full of hot air?

Or, is your faith real?

Life is full of storms. At times it seems they come one right after another . . . and, they never seem to stop.

Yet, if we cling to our faith in Christ and keep our consciences clear—through every storm in our life—we will prove the seaworthiness of our spiritual vessel.

Is your ship battered from the storms?

In the song, "The Anchor Holds" by Ray Boltz, one stanza says, "But it was in the night through the storms of my life. Oh, that's where God proved His love to me."

Do you have storms in your life today?

May you have faith in God. He will keep your life from becoming shipwrecked.

SEPTEMBER 21

Autumn Rain

"Rejoice, you people of Jerusalem! Rejoice in the Lord your God! For the rain he sends demonstrates his faithfulness. Once more the autumn rains will come, as well as the rains of spring." —Joel 2:23

It was the summer of 2011. Texas experienced the hottest June through August period of any U.S. state at any point in time on record.

The extreme heat and lack of rainfall sparked wildfires across the state. How we longed for relief from the hot and dry weather! Marquees and radio stations implored readers and listeners to pray for rain.

And, we did.

We prayed in the morning, we prayed throughout the day and into the night for God to send the refreshing autumn rain.

And, He did.

One day, it came . . . the autumn rain. Like a long, lost friend it came smiling on our yards, our gardens, and our sun-scorched homes. As in the days of Elijah in I Kings 18, the rain came.

Ezekiel 34:26 says, *"I will bless my people and their homes around my holy hill. And in the proper season I will send the showers they need. There will be showers of blessing."*

May we thank and praise our wonderful, merciful, generous, and loving Heavenly Father for showing us His blessing through the gift of autumn rain.

SEPTEMBER 22

The Valley Of Weeping

"When they walk through the Valley of Weeping, it will become a place of refreshing springs. The autumn rains will clothe it with blessings." —Psalm 84:6

Have you ever felt like David in Psalm 42:3, *"Day and night I have only tears for food..."*

It can feel as though your journey through the Valley of Weeping will never end.

But, God doesn't leave us there.

His Word promises that the same place we cried—that Valley of Weeping—will become a place of refreshing springs.

As God spoke through the prophet Isaiah to the Israelites in Isaiah 30:19, so he will do for you, *"O people of Zion, who live in Jerusalem, you will weep no more. He will be gracious if you ask for help. He will surely respond to the sound of your cries."*

Psalm 30:5 tells us, *"For his anger lasts only a moment, but his favor lasts a lifetime! Weeping may last through the night, but joy comes with the morning."*

Luke 6:21b says, *"God blesses you who weep now, for in due time you will laugh."*

May your time with God today remind you that the Valley of Weeping will become that place of refreshing springs as He proves His love for you.

SEPTEMBER 23

Worry Wart

"Don't worry about anything; instead, pray about everything. Tell God what you need, and thank him for all he has done." —Philippians 4:6

Are you a worry wart?

A worry wart is someone who worries about everything. But, this verse is telling us not to worry about anything. To please God, we must do the complete opposite.

Being a worry wart exhibits a lack of faith. It says, "I don't trust you to meet my needs, Lord."

But, if you think back over your life, and the times when you have needed God, the times when you have prayed earnestly and acted in obedience to Him . . . Has He not answered? Has He not proven Himself to you?

Have you praised Him for what He has done in your life? Have you thanked Him for the goodness and blessings He has given you?

Stop worrying and start praying.

Thank God for all that He has done.

Tell Him what you need.

And, just as in days past, He will answer.

He will be faithful to you.

May you stop being a worry wart and become a prayer warrior, instead.

You need never worry again.

SEPTEMBER 24

My Guide

"I will bless the Lord who guides me; even at night my heart instructs me. I know the Lord is always with me. I will not be shaken, for he is right beside me." —Psalm 16:7-8

In this journey called life, it is important to have the very best guide. This guide should know the destination very clearly.

Psalm 43:3 says, *"Send out your light and your truth; let them guide me. Let them lead me to your holy mountain, to the place where you live."*

And, Psalm 73:24 says, *"You guide me with your counsel, leading me to a glorious destiny."*

Our guide should also know the road well, including any and all pitfalls we may encounter along the way.

Psalm 32:8 tells us, *"The Lord says, 'I will guide you along the best pathway for your life. I will advise you and watch over you.'"*

Our guide should also go the distance, since the journey is long.

Psalm 48:14 reassures us, *"For that is what God is like. He is our God forever and ever, and he will guide us until we die."*

Our wonderful Lord guides us through wisdom, honesty, His Word, and His Holy Spirit.

"So I say, let the Holy Spirit guide your lives. Then you won't be doing what your sinful nature craves" (Galatians 5:16).

There is no better guide in all the world for this most important journey.

May you let Him be your guide every moment of every day.

SEPTEMBER 25

Enabler

"So we keep on praying for you, asking our God to enable you to live a life worthy of his call. May he give you the power to accomplish all the good things your faith prompts you to do."
—2 Thessalonians 1:11

When it comes to self-destructive behaviors, being an enabler is not a good thing.

Yet, when it comes to living the Christian life, there is nothing better than having one who enables us to live this life in a manner worthy of the One who called us.

That enabler is Christ—the One who called us.

We would self-destruct without *this* enabler.

He enables us to stand firm for Christ (2 Corinthians 1:21).

He enables us to be ministers of His new covenant (2 Corinthians 3:6).

He enables us to share in His inheritance (Colossians 1:12).

He enables us to live a life worthy of His call (2 Thessalonians 1:11).

He enables us to share His divine nature and escape the world's corruption (2 Peter 1:4).

He enables us to walk in victory (I John 4:4).

Praise His name!

He is the Great Enabler.

SEPTEMBER 26

His Sweet Fragrance

"But thank God! He has made us his captives and continues to lead us along in Christ's triumphal procession. Now he uses us to spread the knowledge of Christ everywhere, like a sweet perfume." —2 Corinthians 2:14

Chanel No. 5, Chloe, Beautiful, Obsession . . . these are just a few of the fragrances I smell each day as I enter the elevator each morning on the way to work.

One particular morning there was such a lovely, sweet fragrance in the elevator that I had to ask what it was. It was a plate of warm, fresh chocolate chip cookies, and I longed to follow the scent as it left the elevator.

That's how people should feel about the fragrance of Christ in us as it exudes through every pore of our being.

Yet, be forewarned. Not everyone finds the same fragrance appealing.

2 Corinthians 2:15-16 tells us, *"Our lives are a Christ-like fragrance rising up to God. But this fragrance is perceived differently by those who are being saved and by those who are perishing. To those who are perishing, we are a dreadful smell of death and doom. But to those who are being saved, we are a life-giving perfume. And who is adequate for such a task as this?"*

May God grant you the strength to wear the fragrance of Christ boldly—for those who may choose to receive Him.

SEPTEMBER 27

Body Building

"Their responsibility is to equip God's people to do his work and build up the church, the body of Christ." —Ephesians 4:12

"Put some muscle into it," the coach pushed.

"Come on! You can do it! You can do better than that this time!" he encouraged.

I never have been athletically inclined, but the coach was right. With God's help, I could do it—better. The pushing and the encouragement helped me to get into shape, and it felt great. All of the hard work was no fun, but once it was done, it was well worth the struggle.

Hebrews 12:11 says it like this, *"No discipline is enjoyable while it is happening—it's painful! But afterward there will be a peaceful harvest of right living for those who are trained in this way."*

If you serve in a leadership capacity in your church, you have the job of coach to those around you. It is your job to build the muscle up in your congregation—calling men and women to action—so that the body of Christ will not become flabby and out-of-shape.

Are you active in your local church?

Are you leading others to action?

Put some muscle in it!

Let's build up the body of Christ the way He intended.

SEPTEMBER 28

Rescue The Perishing

"Rescue others by snatching them from the flames of judgment. Show mercy to still others, but do so with great caution, hating the sins that contaminate their lives." —Jude 1:23

There is a wonderful old hymn written by Frances Jane "Fanny" Crosby in 1869, entitled, "Rescue the Perishing" in which the chorus goes like this:

> *Rescue the perishing, care for the dying,*
> *Snatch them in pity from sin and the grave;*
> *Weep o'er the erring one, lift up the fallen,*
> *Tell them of Jesus, the mighty to save.*

Though blind from the age of six weeks as the result of illness, Fanny Crosby penned over eight thousand hymns and numerous other poems.

Her life was the epitome of the verse above, although the method by which she rescued others was extraordinary. Her lifesaver of choice was the pen.

Fanny Crosby had an excellent memory, and a knack for positive, Spirit-filled writing that has encouraged people the world over for generations. She was grateful that God blessed her with blindness, and looked forward to the day her eyes would be opened to her Savior.

There are many dying in sin all around us today. Won't you snatch them in pity from sin and the grave?

May we rescue the perishing today and every day.

SEPTEMBER 29

Our Declaration Of Independence

"So Christ has truly set us free. Now make sure that you stay free, and don't get tied up again in slavery to the law." —Galatians 5:1

July 4, 1776, thirteen American colonies declared their independence from Great Britain and formed a new nation—the United States of America. Approximately twenty-five thousand Americans gave their lives so that the thirteen colonies could gain their freedom and independence as a sovereign nation—one nation under God, indivisible, with liberty and justice for all.

Those twenty-five thousand lives were given so that many in the future might have freedom—even though it happened long ago—before we were even a thought.

September 5, 1971, a five-year-old girl declared her independence from sin and the grave and began a new life—with Christ as her personal Savior. One perfect man gave His life so that this little girl could gain her freedom from the bondage of sin, hell and the grave to forge a new life—a life of faith, hope and love.

That one man who gave His life, did it so that all of us might have freedom—even though it happened long ago. But, in this case, we were always a thought.

We were His only thought.

He gave everything so that we might be declared independent and free to find real life in Him.

"For the Lord is the Spirit, and wherever the Spirit of the Lord is, there is freedom" (2 Corinthians 3:17).

"So if the Son sets you free, you are truly free" (John 8:36).

SEPTEMBER 30

Child Of The King

"Now you are no longer a slave but God's own child. And since you are his child, God has made you his heir." —Galatians 4:7

Bethany was a beautiful girl—shy and insecure, too.

Her single mother was busy working two jobs to make ends meet, and she never knew her father.

She had heard some stories. He was in prison. Made some bad choices. Some of the kids at school said mean things.

When Bethany was a teenager, her mother remarried. Her new step-father had two teenage daughters who treated Bethany as though she was their personal slave. They ordered her around, and said awful things to her about the father she had never known.

One day, a friend from school invited Bethany to church. There, she learned about another father she had never known—her Heavenly Father.

Bethany had a strong desire to get to know this father. She realized now that she was no longer a slave—she was God's own child. Bethany was a child of the King, with all the rights and benefits afforded her position.

Bethany discovered a love she had never known from her new adoptive father. She felt loved and cared for as never before. Bethany was now a child of the King.

Ephesians 1:5 says, *"God decided in advance to adopt us into his own family by bringing us to himself through Jesus Christ. This is what he wanted to do, and it gave him great pleasure."*

May you introduce someone to the King today.

OCTOBER 1

Training Wheels

"Solid food is for those who are mature, who through training have the skill to recognize the difference between right and wrong." —Hebrews 5:14

When my son, Dylan, was learning to ride his bicycle, he despised the training wheels and begged to have them removed. The problem was, he had not yet learned how to balance himself by steering. He needed the training wells to help him learn how to steer without falling over.

We went ahead and took the training wheels off for him, and it was painful to watch him fall time after time.

But, each time he fell, we were there to pick him up. Then, we encouraged him to use those training wheels again. This time, he did. And, he learned how to keep himself upright by steering.

In life, you and I need training wheels, too. Sometimes we despise the training, and just want to take our training wheels off.

But, we're not ready to ride yet. So, we fall over. And, each time we fall, our loving Heavenly Father is right there to help us up.

Oh, how it must hurt Him to watch us stubbornly refuse our training wheels.

Hebrews 12:11 tells us, *"No discipline is enjoyable while it is happening—it's painful! But afterward there will be a peaceful harvest of right living for those who are trained in this way."*

May you accept your training wheels today, and may you be ready to take them off when the time comes.

OCTOBER 2

Bedtime Stories

"Tell your children about it in the years to come, and let your children tell their children. Pass the story down from generation to generation." —Joel 1:3

Once upon a time . . .
    I have always loved making up bedtime stories for my children at night. They often give me an element or two to include in the story. "Tell a story about a purple frog this time!" Or, "Make it about a flying bear!"

We always find a way to incorporate all of their imaginative requests into the story, making it as fanciful and miraculous as possible.

The three chapters making up the Book of Joel tell a most miraculous bedtime story, too, and it isn't make-believe.

It starts with a rebellious people and a vicious attack by locusts with fangs, and teeth like lions! The locusts attack like a mighty army. The *Holy Bible* even tells us that they charge forward like warhorses, and they make a sound like the rumbling of chariots, like fire sweeping across a field of stubble (Joel 2:4-5).

The story goes on to tell us how the people pray and return to God, and He promises to restore them, to rescue all who call upon His name.

And, the ending is a happily ever after better than any fairy tale. It is an eternal blessing in heaven!

Once upon a time, there was a God who loved us. We sinned. He died. He arose. We repented. He forgave us.

And, one day, we will live happily ever after in heaven with Him.

OCTOBER 3

Early Retirement

"and they must retire at the age of fifty." —Numbers 8:25

We speak a great deal about retirement in the United States, often counting the years, the days until the blessed event. For many, it is thought of as the time they are accountable to no one—life is on their terms with no work required. They are on cruise control.

For the Levites serving in the Tabernacle during the days of Moses, service began at age twenty-five, with retirement at age fifty. After retirement, they were to assist their fellow Levites by serving as guards in the Tabernacle, but they were no longer to officiate in the service (Leviticus 8:26).

Service as a Tabernacle guard was very important. It was an honorable position that could be held only by a Levite. They handled the sacred vessels of the Tabernacle, that if mishandled, resulted in death. The Levite's role was that of a loyal, spiritual example throughout their lifetime.

This role didn't end with retirement at age fifty.

Your role doesn't end with retirement, either, regardless of the age.

People are still watching what you do, and they need you to be a loyal, spiritual example throughout your entire life.

Early retirement or not, your service to the Spirit lasts beyond your lifetime.

May you serve Him with every ounce of your being for every day that you have breath.

OCTOBER 4

Destined To Win

"You guide me with your counsel, leading me to a glorious destiny." —Psalm 73:24

I recall a difficult time in life in which I sought counsel from someone in my home church. Not knowing this individual very well, I sought this counsel solely based upon the position held within the church leadership.

Sadly, it didn't take a rocket scientist to realize it was not good counsel, and was probably the worst instruction I ever received.

Disappointed and disillusioned, I returned home and opened the *Holy Bible*. The words written there were perfect truth that overwhelmed me with the Holy Spirit's presence.

This was the counsel I should have sought in the first place. I was immediately encouraged, and after seeking God further in prayer, He provided me with a plan of action.

Jeremiah 29:11 tells us, *"'For I know the plans I have for you,' says the Lord. 'They are plans for good and not for disaster, to give you a future and a hope.'"*

Jeremiah wrote these words in a letter from Jerusalem to all those who had been exiled to Babylon by Nebuchadnezzar. They were to be exiled for seventy years, and these words were part of the beautiful promise, the hope, the blessing that God was sending to encourage them.

They were destined to win.

And, so are you.

OCTOBER 5

Bad Attitude

"You must have the same attitude that Christ Jesus had." —Philippians 2:5

While a student in college, a friend of mine was known for saying, "You have a B.A. on your forehead—bad attitude." She said this each time she encountered someone with a negative attitude.

Her bold statement had a tendency to jolt people into realizing just how unrealistically negative they were behaving.

Paul tells us we are not just to look out for "number one." We are to look out for the interests of others, and to have the same attitude as that of Christ Jesus.

What attitude was that?

Philippians 2 tells us about Jesus' attitude. He was unselfish, humble, and obedient to God. He didn't try to impress others. He thought of others as better than Himself, took an interest in others, and had the heart of a servant.

Jesus also did not cling to His divine position, but gave that up out of love for all mankind.

Do you have a B.A. on your forehead today?

May you replace it with the humble and loving attitude of Christ Jesus today.

OCTOBER 6

Self-Indulgence

"Do you like honey? Don't eat too much, or it will make you sick!" —Proverbs 25:16

God has blessed us with all manner of good things to enjoy on this earth. Our human, sinful nature being what it is, makes it easy to self-indulge.

But, we shouldn't self-indulge.

Self-indulgence is sin.

Proverbs 25:27 tells us, *"It's not good to eat too much honey, and it's not good to seek honors for yourself."*

Matthew 23:25 says, *"What sorrow awaits you teachers of religious law and you Pharisees. Hypocrites! For you are so careful to clean the outside of the cup and the dish, but inside you are filthy—full of greed and self-indulgence!"*

The problem with self-indulgence is that it is all about self. It forgets about everyone else. It is the opposite of altruism, and the opposite of what God's Word teaches us that life is all about.

If we want to be God's disciple, we must turn away from selfishness and self-indulgence.

In Luke 9:23, Jesus tells us, *"Then he said to the crowd, 'If any of you wants to be my follower, you must turn from your selfish ways, take up your cross daily, and follow me.'"*

OCTOBER 7

Beware Of The Dog

"Watch out for those dogs, those people who do evil, those mutilators who say you must be circumcised to be saved." —Philippians 3:2

I haven't seen a "beware of the dog" sign in quite some time. Perhaps we need a few more of them.

As a young child, I ventured into a yard in which there was a "beware of the dog" sign, but I didn't see the sign. I was bitten pretty badly.

The dogs that Paul is talking about in Philippians bite, too. They are vicious and evil. Paul warns us to watch out for them.

Jesus warned, *"Beware of false prophets who come disguised as harmless sheep but are really vicious wolves"* (Matthew 7:15).

These wolves and dogs practice evil, yet they cling to traditions that have no basis in the practice of holiness, righteousness, or salvation. They try to distract you with their traditions as a means of avoiding what God considers pure religion.

James 1:27 tells us what pure religion is, *"Pure and genuine religion in the sight of God the Father means caring for orphans and widows in their distress and refusing to let the world corrupt you."*

Beware of the dogs.

And, may you stay out of the yards where you might be bitten today.

OCTOBER 8

The Amazing Journey

"I have traveled on many long journeys. I have faced danger from rivers and from robbers. I have faced danger from my own people, the Jews, as well as from the Gentiles. I have faced danger in the cities, in the deserts, and on the seas. And I have faced danger from men who claim to be believers but are not." —2 Corinthians 11:26

When we accept Christ by faith as our Savior, our rescuer, our liberator—we begin an amazing journey with Him. He is our guide, and He takes us to places we never dreamed of visiting.

He leads us on some of the most difficult, heart-wrenching, painful journeys to the top of the highest mountains—eclipsing Sir Edmund Hillary's expedition to the summit of Mount Everest—filling us with indescribable joy, awe, and wonder.

He directs us through treacherous and often frightening passageways to discover beauty and new worlds we never imagined—more awesome than Christopher Columbus.

Along this journey it is required that we trust Him . . . completely.

It is required that we lean on Him . . . fully.

He alone knows the way.

He has all the supplies for the journey.

He is all we will ever need.

Psalm 34:9 tells us, *"Fear the LORD, you his godly people, for those who fear him will have all they need."*

May we trust absolutely in our Guide, and continue our amazing journey with Him.

OCTOBER 9

Home Improvement

"I know all the things you do. I have seen your love, your faith, your service, and your patient endurance. And I can see your constant improvement in all these things." —Revelation 2:19

Looking around my house as I sit on the sofa typing these words, I see so many things in need of improvement. There are the spots on the ceiling that need painting. The carpet needs stretching, the cabinets need to be refinished, and the list could go on and on.

And, then there is the foundation. It has been shifting for years. We have been putting off this repair because it is so costly. Yet, it will be more costly if we wait too long. No one really sees the small cracks or the doors that stick. Or, do they?

It is a lot like my heart.

There are so many areas of my heart that are in need of improvement. My carnal nature wants to focus on all of the improvements needed on the outside of me and my home, rather than the inside.

But, the inside is what is most critical.

It is that foundation that has been shifting for years that effects everything else. I put off the realignment of my heart because it is costly, too. Yet, it will be more costly if I wait too long. Does anyone really see it? Do they see the cracks? What about the doors that don't close properly?

How about you? Are you in need of some heart improvement? Has your foundation been shifting for years, too?

Don't wait too long to get things realigned.

It will be more costly if you wait.

OCTOBER 10

Speech Problems

"Don't use foul or abusive language. Let everything you say be good and helpful, so that your words will be an encouragement to those who hear them." —Ephesians 4:29

Do you have a speech problem?

Perhaps you don't use profane speech or take God's name in vain, but what about the way you speak about others?

Matthew 5:22b-23 says, *"If you call someone an idiot, you are in danger of being brought before the court. And if you curse someone, you are in danger of the fires of hell."*

James 3:9-10 talks about the evil from our tongues when it says, *"Sometimes it praises our Lord and Father, and sometimes it curses those who have been made in the image of God. And so blessing and cursing come pouring out of the same mouth. Surely, my brothers and sisters, this is not right!"*

And, what about the manner in which we speak about those who serve in public office. We may not always agree with how things are being done on our behalf, but note what Scripture says in Acts 23:5b, *"for the Scriptures say, 'You must not speak evil of any of your rulers.'"*

Let us remember the words of Proverbs 15:28, which says, *"The heart of the godly thinks carefully before speaking; the mouth of the wicked overflows with evil words."*

And, may we also remember the words of I Peter 3:10, *"For the Scriptures say, "If you want to enjoy life and see many happy days, keep your tongue from speaking evil and your lips from telling lies."*

OCTOBER 11

The Green-Eyed Monster

"Anger is cruel, and wrath is like a flood, but jealousy is even more dangerous." —Proverbs 27:4

God's Word speaks a great deal about jealousy. It was Cain's jealousy that caused him to kill his brother, Abel, in Genesis 4. Rachel was jealous of Leah because she was unable to provide Jacob with children as easily as Leah (Genesis 30). Joseph's brothers were jealous of him, and sold him into slavery (Genesis 37).

And, the list goes on.

Scripture even tells us in Exodus 34:14, *"You must worship no other gods, for the Lord, whose very name is Jealous, is a God who is jealous about his relationship with you."*

So, what do we do to overcome that green-eyed monster we call, jealousy?

Clearly, jealousy is the result of being controlled by our sin nature.

James 3:15 tells us, *"For jealousy and selfishness are not God's kind of wisdom. Such things are earthly, unspiritual, and demonic."*

If our lives are filled with the love of Christ, we will be happy for the successes of others, and jealousy will not control our lives (I Corinthians 13:4).

"Let us not become conceited, or provoke one another, or be jealous of one another" (Galatians 5:26).

OCTOBER 12

Peace Like A River

"Oh, that you had listened to my commands! Then you would have had peace flowing like a gentle river and righteousness rolling over you like waves in the sea." —Isaiah 48:18

The term *shalom* in the Hebrew, translated *peace*, conveys with it so much more meaning than the American word, *peace*. It is the idea or feeling of contentment and completeness; of having health, wholeness, and harmony. The term carries with it a great deal of positive emotion, and is used as both a greeting and a farewell.

The word *peace* is used three hundred sixty-two times in the New Living Translation of the *Holy Bible*.

Do you long to have peace flowing like a gentle river and righteousness rolling over you like waves in the sea?

The *Holy Bible* tells us how this can be achieved.

Job 22:21 tells us, *"Submit to God, and you will have peace; then things will go well for you."*

Psalm 119:165 says, *"Those who love your instructions have great peace and do not stumble."*

Are you still trying to take care of things, handle things, fix things on your own? Bring them all to the feet of Jesus in submission and obedience to His will and His commands.

"I pray that God, the source of hope, will fill you completely with joy and peace because you trust in him. Then you will overflow with confident hope through the power of the Holy Spirit" (Romans 15:13).

OCTOBER 13

Impenetrably Safe

"Keep me safe, O God, for I have come to you for refuge." —Psalm 16:1

The United States Bullion Depository at Fort Knox has what is considered to be the most impenetrable bank vault, or safe, in the world. The outside perimeter is a solid granite wall.

Next, there are squadrons of machine gun-wielding military guards.

Then, there is a twenty-two ton vault door that is held shut by a lock so intricate it requires a ten-person team to open it. It would be very difficult to get through that door.

In many ways, I think of God as an impenetrable safe, like Fort Knox, only better.

His walls of protection are thicker than granite. Proverbs 18:10 tells us, *"The name of the Lord is a strong fortress; the godly run to him and are safe."*

He has angels more powerful than machine gun-wielding guards. *"For he will order his angels to protect you wherever you go"* (Psalm 91:11).

With regard to the vault door, Scripture tells us, *"When he opens doors, no one will be able to close them; when he closes doors, no one will be able to open them"* (Isaiah 22:22b).

And, He values us more than all the gold in Fort Knox (Mark 8:37).

When we run to Him for refuge, there isn't anyone who could get through that door without His permission.

May you rest safely in the impenetrable strength of the Heavenly Father's care.

OCTOBER 14

My Superhero

"I said to the Lord, 'You are my Master! Every good thing I have comes from you.' The godly people in the land are my true heroes! I take pleasure in them! Troubles multiply for those who chase after other gods. I will not take part in their sacrifices of blood or even speak the names of their gods." —Psalm 16:2-4

Who doesn't love a hero? I still remember enjoying Underdog, Mighty Mouse, Batman, and other heroes I watched as a child. I cheered as they rescued the damsel in distress and destroyed the villain. It was good vs. evil, and good always won! There was a special comfort in knowing that good would triumph in the end.

There is a special comfort in knowing that in the real-life battle of good vs. evil, good will triumph in the end, too.

Unlike the cartoons, there are battles and skirmishes in real life that evil wins. But, God's Word reminds us in 1 John 5:4, *"For every child of God defeats this evil world, and we achieve this victory through our faith."*

David experienced this glorious promise of victory in his life. He knew the greatest superhero of all time. And, David took great pleasure in the faithfulness and love of God who provided him with a wonderful life on this earth, as well as in the life to come.

Because God enables us to defeat this evil world, He far surpasses any hero. May we remember the words of Isaiah 42:13, *"The Lord will march forth like a mighty hero; he will come out like a warrior, full of fury. He will shout his battle cry and crush all his enemies."*

Who could ask for a better superhero?

OCTOBER 15

The Reading Of The Will

"Lord, you alone are my inheritance, my cup of blessing. You guard all that is mine. The land you have given me is a pleasant land. What a wonderful inheritance!" —Psalm 16:5-6

The family plodded into the room, single-file. It was a somber occasion.

It was the reading of the will, Louise's will.

They all loved Louise, but the feeling was not mutual, at least not toward one of them, Charles. Charles was Louise's eldest son. The two had a falling out a few years before when he married a Jewish Christian girl, against Louise's wishes. Louise vowed to write Charles out of the will if he married her.

And, she did.

But, Charles harbored no ill feelings toward his mother. He loved her very much and honored her, but he also knew he must honor and obey God when the two were at odds.

Charles knew, like David, that his real inheritance, his cup of blessing was in God alone. God had given him a pleasant life, and an eternal inheritance that no one could take away. He would never be written out of God's will.

Revelation 3:5 tells us, *"All who are victorious will be clothed in white. I will never erase their names from the Book of Life, but I will announce before my Father and his angels that they are mine."*

In spite of his mother's action, Charles was joyful in the realization that God had blessed him with a truly wonderful life.

Are you?

OCTOBER 16

My Forever Joy

"No wonder my heart is glad, and I rejoice. My body rests in safety. For you will not leave my soul among the dead or allow your holy one to rot in the grave. You will show me the way of life, granting me the joy of your presence and the pleasures of living with you forever." —Psalm 16:9-11

Can you feel the exuberance David has for his relationship with God? He is consumed with an awe, a joy, a reverence for his Savior, his Great Master, his Abba Father.

He cannot help but rejoice!

How about you?

I am reminded of the story in 2 Samuel 6 when David moves the Ark of the Covenant to Jerusalem, and there is a great celebration.

The Scripture tells us in 2 Samuel 6:14, *"And David danced before the LORD with all his might, wearing a priestly garment."*

When his wife, Michal (Saul's daughter), is disgusted by his behavior before the servant girls, 2 Samuel 6:21-22a tells us, *"David retorted to Michal, 'I was dancing before the LORD, who chose me above your father and all his family! He appointed me as the leader of Israel, the people of the LORD, so I celebrate before the LORD. Yes, and I am willing to look even more foolish than this, even to be humiliated in my own eyes!'"*

David knows what it means to rejoice in the presence of God. He knows the joy and the pleasure of living with his Savior, and looks forward to rejoicing in His presence forever.

He is our forever joy!

OCTOBER 17

The Wonder Of It All

"Those who live at the ends of the earth stand in awe of your wonders. From where the sun rises to where it sets, you inspire shouts of joy." —Psalm 65:8

The colors in the autumn sky at daybreak and sunset are amazing. Have you stopped long enough to enjoy them lately?

God's paintbrush is beyond inspiring, isn't it? When I look at all that God has created in nature—from the mountains and forests, to the valleys and beaches, and everything in between—I can't help but smile and my heart swells with joy.

It is a picture of His love for us in the richest of beauties.

Then, there are the glorious sounds of the nature around us. The chirping birds, crickets, cicadas, and croaking frogs are all a reflection of God's peace and sovereignty in the world around us.

The smells, too, serve to awaken our spirits to His, and invite us to commune with Him.

And the humidity or dryness in the air envelopes our bodies as nature's soft hug from God.

May you shout for joy to God as you embrace the wonder that He has created all around you. May all He has created sing His praise!

OCTOBER 18

R-E-S-P-E-C-T

"Respect everyone, and love your Christian brothers and sisters. Fear God, and respect the king." —I Peter 2:17

The word *respect* means, to admire someone deeply based upon their abilities, qualities or achievements.[5]

With this definition in mind, one is obliged to earn the privilege of respect.

So, how can we possibly respect everyone? There are some people that behave in such a manner as to not *deserve* our respect, aren't there?

C. H. Spurgeon said of this passage of Scripture, that "whatever his condition may be, we are to honor the manhood," the brotherhood of all people.

The use of the word *respect* here carries with it the idea that all people are to be valued, to be treated with dignity because God created all of us with qualities that are valuable.

And, what about the king?

We all face the temptation of speaking disrespectfully about our government leadership—especially when our choice for leadership does not hold the current office.

But, this verse reminds us that we should show honor and respect for all individuals in positions of authority over us. We should honor and respect them for the position they hold, as well as for their value and worth as God's creation.

May you look at those around you a bit differently, seeing them as valuable today and every day.

---

[5] The Merriam-Webster Dictionary, 2012.

OCTOBER 19

Temper Temper

"Stop being angry! Turn from your rage! Do not lose your temper— it only leads to harm."
—Psalm 37:8

Are you an angry person?
Is your rage hair-trigger ready?
What do others say about you with regard to emotional self-control?
The emotion of anger is a normal, natural healthy emotion. We all feel it at times, as Jesus did (Mark 10:14; Mark 11:15-16; John 2:15; John 11:33-38).
But, Scripture tells us that it is what we do with the emotion that causes the trouble.
Ephesians 4:26-27 tells us, *"And 'don't sin by letting anger control you.' Don't let the sun go down while you are still angry, for anger gives a foothold to the devil."*
Proverbs 15:18 says, *"A hot-tempered person starts fights; a cool-tempered person stops them."*
Proverbs 19:11 reminds us, *"Sensible people control their temper; they earn respect by overlooking wrongs."*
The *Holy Bible* also warns us not to associate with angry people in Proverbs 22:24-25, which says, *"Don't befriend angry people or associate with hot-tempered people, or you will learn to be like them and endanger your soul."*
May the Lord guard your soul and enable you to control your temper so that you will not be labeled a fool (Ecclesiastes 7:9).

OCTOBER 20

Haste Makes Waste

"Enthusiasm without knowledge is no good; haste makes mistakes." —Proverbs 19:2

Are you the type of person who is the king or queen of getting excited about new ideas? Do you jump on the bandwagon of things you know very little about?

There is nothing wrong with enthusiasm in and of itself. But, enthusiasm needs to have the proper direction. It must be tempered with the proper knowledge, understanding, and it must be preceded by the proper preparation. Haste is the idea of hurrying with a lack of adequate groundwork and understanding.

The *Holy Bible* speaks a great deal about preparation.

Proverbs 24:27 tells us, *"Do your planning and prepare your fields before building your house."*

We are to prepare.

In the Parable of the Ten Bridesmaids, we read in Matthew25 that five of the bridesmaids were wise, preparing their lamps for the long night, and five were foolish—they did not prepare. In their haste, they missed the marriage feast. It is a reminder that we will miss the marriage supper of the lamb if we are not prepared for Jesus' return.

Jesus tells us in Hebrews 11:16 that He has prepared a city for us—a heavenly homeland. It is a better place than we have ever known.

May we follow our Heavenly Father's example by preparing properly in our every endeavor that we may bring glory and honor to Him in all our hands find to do.

OCTOBER 21

Leaving A Legacy

"The wise inherit honor, but fools are put to shame!" —Proverbs 3:35

You are never too young to consider the legacy that your life will leave to those who come after you. The choices you make each and every day will have an eternal impact on generations to come.

Too many look at the dawning of each day in a foolhardy manner, but God's Word encourages us in I Thessalonians 5:8, *"But let us who live in the light be clearheaded, protected by the armor of faith and love, and wearing as our helmet the confidence of our salvation."*

So often we are unaware of the consequences of our actions—both good and bad.

I Corinthians 6:9-10 tells us, *"Don't you realize that those who do wrong will not inherit the Kingdom of God? Don't fool yourselves. Those who indulge in sexual sin, or who worship idols, or commit adultery, or are male prostitutes, or practice homosexuality, or are thieves, or greedy people, or drunkards, or are abusive, or cheat people—none of these will inherit the Kingdom of God."*

Conversely, Psalm 37:18 says, *"Day by day the LORD takes care of the innocent, and they will receive an inheritance that lasts forever."*

May you choose to live a life of faithfulness and obedience to Christ, understanding the sober reality of your eternal legacy.

OCTOBER 22

My Forever Love

"Prophecy and speaking in unknown languages and special knowledge will become useless. But love will last forever!" —I Corinthians 13:8

We can define love in one very complex word: God.

I John 4:8 tells us, *"But anyone who does not love does not know God, for God is love."*

God is the very definition of love.

He will last forever.

The gift of His love will last forever, too.

I Corinthians 13:4-7 tells us the characteristics of love. It says, *"Love is patient and kind. Love is not jealous or boastful or proud or rude. It does not demand its own way. It is not irritable, and it keeps no record of being wronged. It does not rejoice about injustice but rejoices whenever the truth wins out. Love never gives up, never loses faith, is always hopeful, and endures through every circumstance."*

That is love.

And, that is God.

He is not a fleeting, superficial love.

God is love that lasts forever.

"Let all who fear the Lord *repeat: 'His faithful love endures forever'"* (Psalm 118:4).

He is forever love.

OCTOBER 23

Fraidy Cat

"But when I am afraid, I will put my trust in you." —Psalm 56:3

Are you a fraidy cat?

When I was a little girl, I was quite the fraidy cat. At night, I would check in the closet before getting into bed. In the bathroom, I would check behind the shower curtain to make sure the boogie man wasn't there, and as I returned to my bed, I would get a running start and leap into the bed—just in case the boogie man was hiding under my bed, ready to grab my feet.

And, there were the calls for Momma in the middle of the night because of a shadow, a bad dream, or a scary thought. She always came, patiently, and reminded me of Psalm 56:3. Then, she would comfort me, and sing me back to sleep.

As an adult, the fears I have faced have been different than the non-existent boogie man behind the shower curtain and under the bed.

And, although I can't call to Momma in the middle of the night to comfort me anymore, I can call to my Heavenly Father, as Psalm 23:4 tells me, *"Even when I walk through the darkest valley, I will not be afraid, for you are close beside me. Your rod and your staff protect and comfort me."*

He even dries my tears (Revelation 21:4), calms my fears, and He rejoices over me with joyful singing (Zephaniah 3:17).

How could we ask for anything more?

OCTOBER 24

Fear The Lord

"Fear of the Lord is the foundation of true wisdom. All who obey his commandments will grow in wisdom. Praise him forever!" —Psalm 111:10

As a child growing up, my siblings and I always had a healthy fear of our father.

I can remember vividly the sound of his size ten black dress shoes as they briskly marched across the wood floor of the hallway toward the bedroom door where my sister and I slept. He would open the door, checking to see if we were asleep, and then continue on to the room he shared with my mother.

I was not one to suck my thumb, but was in the habit of placing two favorite fingers in my mouth as a comfort on a regular basis—for which habit my father promised a spanking when caught.

Just as I was drifting off to sleep—fingers in mouth—fear gripped my heart upon hearing those size ten black shoes approach the door. That healthy fear wrought obedience, and I removed the fingers from my mouth, burying my moist hand beneath the covers and vowing in my heart to never disobey my father again.

A healthy fear of the Lord draws us to obedience and teaches us wisdom. When we continue in this reverential fear, we will continue in obedience to God, and we will see the work of His mighty hand, increasing our faith, our hope, our devotion, and wisdom's foundation will grow.

"Fear of the LORD is the foundation of wisdom. Knowledge of the Holy One results in good judgment" (Proverbs 9:10).

OCTOBER 25

Terrifying Times

"There will be great earthquakes, and there will be famines and plagues in many lands, and there will be terrifying things and great miraculous signs from heaven." —Luke 21:11

Though the timing of earth's end remains a mystery, there is much that Scripture tells us about these terrifying times ahead.

Matthew 24, Luke 21:5-36, Daniel 7:13; 9:27; 11:31; 12:11, Isaiah 13:10; 34:4, and Joel 2:10 all deal with the end times, in addition to the Book of Revelation. They each describe vivid and dreadful events together with the warning and admonition to be always ready for Christ's return.

Our Heavenly Father has lovingly provided the signs that we may be always ready for His return.

Make no mistake, many will be deceived and fall away from the faith (Matthew 24:11). Christians all over the world will be hated and persecuted because of their beliefs (Matthew 24:9). The Parable of the Ten Virgins speaks of His return (Matthew 25:1-13).

Yet, if we are diligent to listen and heed the many warnings of Christ in Scripture, and to endure this time of persecution, we can be ready when Christ returns.

Matthew 24:13 encourages us, *"But the one who endures to the end will be saved."*

Are you ready for Christ if He were to return today?

May we live each and every moment of each and every day as though the Master were coming immediately to take us home.

OCTOBER 26

Disguised

"These people are false apostles. They are deceitful workers who disguise themselves as apostles of Christ. But I am not surprised! Even Satan disguises himself as an angel of light."
—*2 Corinthians 11:13-14*

Sometimes life can seem like a perpetual masquerade party. Just when you're getting to know someone, you find out they are not who they claimed to be at all.

And, what about those people that you've known for years. One day, you wake up and realize they are completely different people, with entirely different motives, than they led you to believe they were. They claim to be Christians, but their walk doesn't match their talk one iota.

God's Word helps us to distinguish between real and disguised Christians. I John 3:10 tells us, "So now we can tell who are children of God and who are children of the devil. Anyone who does not live righteously and does not love other believers does not belong to God."

Matthew 7:15 reminds us, *"Beware of false prophets who come disguised as harmless sheep but are really vicious wolves."* Verse 20 says, *"Yes, just as you can identify a tree by its fruit, so you can identify people by their actions."*

May we be mindful of the many who are masquerading as God's children around us. May we examine their fruit.

And, may we trust the Holy Spirit to shepherd us from the many disguised wolves in the world around us.

OCTOBER 27

God's Little Surprises

"Around midnight Boaz suddenly woke up and turned over. He was surprised to find a woman lying at his feet!" —Ruth 3:8

Our wonderful Heavenly Father is full of surprises. Imagine the surprise of Abraham and Sarah when Isaac was born. Abraham was one hundred years old, and Sarah ninety (Genesis 21:1-5)! The name, Isaac, means *laughter*. His birth was such a surprise it brought laughter to the family.

If we consider Jesus' ministry on earth, we find that nearly everything Jesus did was a surprise to those around Him. He did the unexpected . . . the amazing.

And, He still does.

Have you paid attention recently to His surprising work in your life?

Have you seen the surprising things He has done in the lives of those around you?

Some surprises that come our way may not seem to us to be good things at the time they occur, but remember Romans 8:28, *"And we know that God causes everything to work together for the good of those who love God and are called according to his purpose for them."*

May you open your eyes and praise God today and every day for His big and little surprises happening all around you.

Perhaps He has a surprise for you today.

OCTOBER 28

My Beautiful Savior

"His Spirit made the heavens beautiful, and his power pierced the gliding serpent." — Job 26:13

Everything our glorious Savior does is beautiful, glorious, magnificent, awe-inspiring.

While gazing at the faces of my children sleeping, I am overwhelmed with the beauty that God creates. He has made each of us in His own image (Genesis 1:27), and He makes everything beautiful for its own time (Ecclesiastes 3:11).

All that God touches is filled with His beauty and splendor.

Have you watched the sunset with nothing on your mind except God? I challenge you to do it soon. Step outside and erase the daily to-do list from your mind. Face the sun as it is setting, and simply capture some of the beauty that is Christ for your heart, mind, and soul.

His beauty changes us.

Daily He changes us.

"And now, dear brothers and sisters, one final thing. Fix your thoughts on what is true, and honorable, and right, and pure, and lovely, and admirable. Think about things that are excellent and worthy of praise" (Philippians 4:8).

Focus your eyes on the beauty that is God.

May His beauty make you beautiful, too.

OCTOBER 29

Homecoming

"Look and see, for everyone is coming home! Your sons are coming from distant lands; your little daughters will be carried home." —Isaiah 60:4

"*So he returned home to his father. And while he was still a long way off, his father saw him coming. Filled with love and compassion, he ran to his son, embraced him, and kissed him*" (Luke 15:20).

It is a beautiful scene, isn't it?

The prodigal son leaves home and foolishly squanders the family fortune. Then, he returns home and is met by his father's loving embrace. It is a beautiful story of redemption and forgiveness.

And, what about you?

Perhaps you haven't wandered far from home. Maybe you've just gone around the corner, but you're out of fellowship with the Father—and you know it.

No matter how far we wander off, whether to a foreign country or just around the corner, our Heavenly Father wants us to come home.

Filled with compassion, He will run to us, embrace us, and kiss us.

And, that's not all.

One day we will take part in the ultimate Homecoming in glory with Him.

OCTOBER 30

Storm Coming

"As I looked, I saw a great storm coming from the north, driving before it a huge cloud that flashed with lightning and shone with brilliant light. There was fire inside the cloud, and in the middle of the fire glowed something like gleaming amber." —Ezekiel 1:4

Living in the storm-prone Texas Gulf Coast, our family has *hunkered down* for many a great storm. We've watched as the massive, dark clouds fill the sky with a deep, ominous darkness before a hurricane. The depth of darkness is so great that the flashes of lightning radiate through the cavernous night with the intensity of fire.

But, there is a storm coming unlike anything man has ever known or will ever experience again.

The *Holy Bible* tells us about this coming storm. Joel 2:2 tells us it is, *"It is a day of darkness and gloom, a day of thick clouds and deep blackness. Suddenly, like dawn spreading across the mountains, a great and mighty army appears. Nothing like it has been seen before or will ever be seen again."*

Revelation 1:7 says, *"Look! He comes with the clouds of heaven. And everyone will see him—even those who pierced him. And all the nations of the world will mourn for him. Yes! Amen!"*

Revelation 14:15 says, *"Then another angel came from the Temple and shouted to the one sitting on the cloud, 'Swing the sickle, for the time of harvest has come; the crop on earth is ripe.'"*

Just as we prepare for hurricane season and the other storm seasons of life, may we prepare for this—most important—storm coming.

OCTOBER 31

Trick Or Truth

"We reject all shameful deeds and underhanded methods. We don't try to trick anyone or distort the word of God. We tell the truth before God, and all who are honest know this."
—*2 Corinthians 4:2*

Have you ever known someone who lied to you, and then when confronted with their lie, they responded, "Come on, you know I was only kidding!"

But, in reality, what they did was deceitful, and they clearly had intent to trick or mislead you. They are merely trying to cover it up because they know the damage they have inflicted.

The *Holy Bible* talks about people who do such things.

Proverbs 26:18-19 says, *"Just as damaging as a madman shooting a deadly weapon is someone who lies to a friend and then says, 'I was only joking.'"*

Proverbs 12:22 tells us, *"The LORD detests lying lips, but he delights in those who tell the truth."*

Proverbs 16:13 encourages us with these words, *"The king is pleased with words from righteous lips; he loves those who speak honestly."*

I do, too. Don't you?

No one enjoys the mockery of having a friend lie to them, and then turn around and say they were just kidding.

"Instead, we will speak the truth in love, growing in every way more and more like Christ, who is the head of his body, the church" (Ephesians 4:15).

NOVEMBER 1

A Slice Of Humble Pie

"True humility and the fear of the Lord lead to riches, honor, and long life." —Proverbs 22:4

Have you ever eaten humble pie? I'm afraid over the past few decades I've eaten enough slices of humble pie to equal more than enough pies for our nation's Thanksgiving.

The *Holy Bible* tells us in Numbers 12:3 that Moses was more humble than any other person on earth. God was able to use Moses, and also to bless him with riches, honor, and long life because of his humility.

If we want to be used by God and have His power flow through us, we must first humble ourselves—die to self.

James 4:10 tells us, *"Humble yourselves before the Lord, and he will lift you up in honor."*

Ephesians 4:2 encourages us with these words, *"Always be humble and gentle. Be patient with each other, making allowance for each other's faults because of your love."*

May we commit to true humility today and every day, that we may be used by God, our Father.

NOVEMBER 2

Joy And Thanksgiving

"For the Lord shall comfort Israel again and have pity on her ruins. Her desert will blossom like Eden, her barren wilderness like the garden of the Lord. Joy and gladness will be found there. Songs of thanksgiving will fill the air." —Isaiah 51:3

Isaiah 51 is a wonderful passage reminding us of God's infinite mercy, power and love for us. He reminds us to trust in Him at all times, and proclaims that the day of victory will once again return in our lives!

Just as God restored the people of Israel to a place of prominence in the promised land, and transformed their many years of wandering in the wilderness to living in the garden of the Lord, so He can comfort you and restore you.

Are you experiencing difficulty in your life right now? Trust in the Lord and in the power of His might, and remember that you will again blossom! Joy and gladness will be yours once again, and songs of thanksgiving will fill the air surrounding you, but you must first repent and seek Him with all of your being—everything that you have and everything that you are.

May you thank Him for what He has done, and for what He is about to do in and through your life as you commit wholly to Him.

This is my prayer for you, and may you have the best day you've ever had in your life.

NOVEMBER 3

Can Doesn't Mean Should

"You say, 'I am allowed to do anything'—but not everything is good for you. You say, 'I am allowed to do anything'—but not everything is beneficial." —I Corinthians 10:23

There are many instances in life in which God's grace makes things permissible for us, but that does not mean that we *should* do everything that is allowed.

There is a wonderful illustration of this principle in the Old Testament when King Saul, jealous of the newly anointed and soon-to-be King David, was desperately trying to kill David. God allowed David the opportunity to take King Saul's life on two separate occasions, yet David chose not to kill Saul, stating, *"'The Lord knows I shouldn't have done that to my lord the king,' he said to his men. 'The Lord forbid that I should do this to my lord the king and attack the Lord's anointed one, for the Lord himself has chosen him.' So David restrained his men and did not let them kill Saul"* (I Samuel 24:6-7).

Romans 14 tells us that we are to seek peace with regard to the things that are permissible for us. If one person believes it is wrong to drink alcohol, and you do not, then for the sake of the one who believes it is wrong, you should not drink it.

Romans 14:15 says this, *"And if another believer is distressed by what you eat, you are not acting in love if you eat it."*

We are to seek love and peace in all we do, and consider the needs of others above our own. May we remember this truth today and every day.

NOVEMBER 4

The Inside Scoop

"Each heart knows its own bitterness, and no one else can fully share its joy." —Isaiah 14:10

Do you have struggles you can't really share with anyone else? Struggles that you feel no one understands?

There is One who understands.

He knows the internal battles you face every day. He knows your struggles, and He has the complete 411 on you.

David was the King of Israel, yet he felt no one understood or cared about him. In Psalm 142:4 he wrote, *"I look for someone to come and help me, but no one gives me a passing thought! No one will help me; no one cares a bit what happens to me."*

But again, there is One with the inside scoop on all of us. We can take our every struggle to Him—regardless of whether anyone else on the planet understands or not.

I Peter 5:7 tells us, *"Give all your worries and cares to God, for he cares about you."*

He has the inside scoop on you.

He understands.

He sees.

He cares.

He loves.

And, He has the ability to effect change like no one else.

May you find ultimate fulfillment and understanding through a deeper, more personal relationship with Christ today.

NOVEMBER 5

Misplaced Anger

"People ruin their lives by their own foolishness and then are angry at the Lord." — *Proverbs 19:3*

Do you ever become angry at God or others because of your own foolish behavior?

This response is sin.

Remember that James 1:20 tells us, *"Human anger does not produce the righteousness God desires."* The word "human" in this passage is referring to the imperfect, temperamental rage born out of our own selfish frustration at not having our own way about things. It is not referring to the righteous indignation of God.

Instead of becoming angry at God, we should instead seek Him more, and ask of Him what it is that He wishes us to learn from the difficult circumstance we find ourselves in the midst of.

Our thoughts should also be those of humility and gratitude at the wonder that God loves us so very intensely and passionately as to teach us, to draw us more deeply into the knowledge of who He is.

He desires that we walk with Him.

He desires that we come away with Him.

May we forsake our anger for a grateful and humble heart which seeks to be one with the Father above all else.

NOVEMBER 6

Out Of No Way

"For I am about to do something new. See, I have already begun! Do you not see it? I will make a pathway through the wilderness. I will create rivers in the dry wasteland." —Isaiah 43:19

God is the Master of making a way where there is no way. Where our human sight ends, God's divine power begins.

The *Holy Bible* tells us in 2 Corinthians 5:7, *"For we live by believing and not by seeing."*

Remember the way that God made for the Israelites to cross the Red Sea on dry ground.

Remember how God made a way of survival for Shadrach, Meshach, and Abednego when they were thrown into the fiery furnace.

Remember how God saved Daniel when he was thrown into the lion's den.

Remember Jesus bringing Lazarus back to life after he had been dead for four days.

I remember God making a way for me to attend college at the age of sixteen, and miraculously managing every last detail in each day that followed.

Has God made a way out of no way for you?

Do you need Him to make a way out of no way for you?

Perhaps you can't see the way that God has prepared before you. May we seek Him and trust that He will make a way for us and show us the way to go—now and always.

NOVEMBER 7

Godly Obstacles

"If righteous people turn away from their righteous behavior and ignore the obstacles I put in their way, they will die. And if you do not warn them, they will die in their sins. None of their righteous acts will be remembered, and I will hold you responsible for their deaths."
—*Ezekiel 3:20*

Do you ever ask God to help you to overcome temptations in your life?

There are areas of weakness in each of our lives in which Satan often wins the victory. Yet, God's Word reminds us in 1 Corinthians 10:13, *"The temptations in your life are no different from what others experience. And God is faithful. He will not allow the temptation to be more than you can stand. When you are tempted, he will show you a way out so that you can endure."*

That "way out" often comes in the form of an obstacle or a road block that God puts before us. When confronted with this obstacle, we have the choice to recognize it for the godly "way out" that it is, or we can bulldoze right through God's road block into sin.

It's your choice.

And, it's mine.

So, what will you do today when you encounter that temptation?

May we remember the words Jesus gave us as an example to follow in The Lord's Prayer, *"And don't let us yield to temptation, but rescue us from the evil one"* (Matthew 6:13).

May we determine to choose right at every opportunity today and every day.

NOVEMBER 8

Moral Decay

"For the Lord brought Judah low because of Ahaz king of Israel, for he had encouraged moral decline in Judah and had been continually unfaithful to the Lord." —2 Chronicles 28:19

God's moral standard is evaporating everywhere around us. Moral decay is in our schools, on television, in our neighborhoods, in our government, and sadly, it is in our churches, too.

These aren't warm and fuzzy thoughts, but they are real, and we can't ignore them.

In the passage above, King Ahaz did not follow after God as his father, David, had. Because of his rebellion and disobedience, his country, Judah, was defeated by Syria and Israel. The *Holy Bible* tells us there was a great slaughter, and two hundred thousand women and children were taken captive.

Sadly, King Ahaz only grew more wicked and disobedient, resulting in his death.

The same thing is happening around us each and every day. Despite harsh consequences, people continue in sin, becoming worse and worse—often because of the silence of godly men and women.

How long will we sit silently, allowing moral decay to continue around us? How long will we accept *the little things* that are wrong, allowing them to continue without taking a stand?

May God convict us of our sin and disobedience, may we speak up for the sake of Christ, and may His love spur us on in faithful service.

NOVEMBER 9

A Thankful Heart

"Devote yourselves to prayer with an alert mind and a thankful heart." —Colossians 4:2

The attitude with which we approach the throne of God in prayer often has a direct impact on the outcome of our prayer time.

Being thankful is key.

A grateful attitude is a display of faith. It tells God that we completely trust His sovereign authority working in and through our lives. It says, "I know that You have the best possible outcome in your complete control, Lord."

A thankful heart unlocks the power of faith, enabling God to act. It relinquishes our will freely to the will of God.

Do you have a thankful heart?

Philippians 4:6 says, *"Don't worry about anything; instead, pray about everything. Tell God what you need, and thank him for all he has done."*

Our state of mind is also important.

We must be alert. An alert mind helps to guard against temptation, as Jesus reminded the disciples in Luke 22:46, *"'Why are you sleeping?' he asked them. 'Get up and pray, so that you will not give in to temptation.'"*

An alert mind also enables a thankful heart.

May we heed the words of Colossians 4:2, coming before our Heavenly Father in prayer always with an alert mind and thankful heart.

NOVEMBER 10

Can't Never Could Do Nothin'

"For I can do everything through Christ, who gives me strength." —Philippians 4:13

When I was a little girl, my father would often ask me to do challenging things, to which I would respond, "I can't, Daddy."

Daddy would then respond with, "Can't never could do nothin'." Then, he would smile and say, *"I can do everything through Christ, who gives me strength."*

He would then, lovingly, guide me back to the task at hand, instruct me once again, and stand back while the work was completed.

What about you?

Is God asking you to do something today?

Have you resigned yourself to defeat, saying, "I can't, Father!"

May I remind you that if God has called you to a task, He has equipped you, too.

We must remain attached to God, our power source, in order to accomplish the tasks He has set before us.

As John 15:5 points out, *"Yes, I am the vine; you are the branches. Those who remain in me, and I in them, will produce much fruit. For apart from me you can do nothing."*

Today, may you grasp the reality that we serve a *can-do* God—a God of infinite possibilities. And, may it be the best day you've ever had in your life.

NOVEMBER 11

Ready To Save

"Mounted on a mighty angelic being, he flew, soaring on the wings of the wind." — Psalm 18:10

Have you ever longed for God to come riding in on a white horse to save the day?

In this verse, we see that He did even better for David—He flew in!

Psalm 18 is a beautiful song written by David in thanksgiving to God for coming to his rescue. God flew on a mighty angelic being, soaring on the wings of the wind.

Revelation 6:2 tells us about the rider on the white horse, too, when it says, "I looked up and saw a white horse standing there. Its rider carried a bow, and a crown was placed on his head. He rode out to win many battles and gain the victory."

Our Savior is ready to save more than just the day—He is ready to gain the ultimate victory in your life and in mine. He stands ready to conquer sin and death.

But, we must exercise our free will inviting Him to do this in our lives.

I Corinthians 15:57 tells us, *"But thank God! He gives us victory over sin and death through our Lord Jesus Christ."*

Give your burdens and temptations to the Lord, and allow Him to give you victory in every area of your life.

He is ready to save.

NOVEMBER 12

No Tolerance

"O God, you take no pleasure in wickedness; you cannot tolerate the sins of the wicked."
—*Psalm 5:4*

There are many today who preach tolerance of sin in the name of acceptance and progress. Yet, God says something different.

Though we often have difficulty distinguishing between the people and their sin, God does not. He will never stop loving us, and He will never stop hating our sin.

We know that God sees every sin (Jeremiah 16:17), and we also know that His children do not make a practice of continuing in sin (I John 5:18).

Continuing purposefully in sin is the definition of wickedness.

2 Peter 2:9 provides a comfort for us when it says, *"So you see, the Lord knows how to rescue godly people from their trials, even while keeping the wicked under punishment until the day of final judgment."*

And, we should detest sin, as our Heavenly Father does.

Will you raise your own standard?

Will you choose to find sin unacceptable while still loving others with every ounce of your being?

May we follow the example of Christ as we never stop loving others, and never stop hating sin.

NOVEMBER 13

An Opened Mind

"Then he opened their minds to understand the Scriptures." —Luke 24:45

As a freshman attending a Christian university, there was one particular professor I had who was very streetwise, and determined to educate his sheltered students in the ways of the world. He spoke incessantly about our need to have an open mind and not simply accept anything and everything we had been fed by our parents.

His words were threatening to me, as I had valued my upbringing. My parents had introduced me to Christ, with whom I had a close, personal relationship. I wanted my mind to remain closed to any idea that was contrary to Scripture.

Yet, over time, I realized the need for my mind to be opened—by Christ.

There are so many things in Scripture that I do not understand fully, but if I will seek Him above all else, and allow Him to open my mind, the Scriptures will become clear to me and I will grow in my walk with Christ.

"For everyone who asks, receives. Everyone who seeks, finds. And to everyone who knocks, the door will be opened" (Matthew 7:8).

Proverbs 3:13 says, *"Joyful is the person who finds wisdom, the one who gains understanding."*

May we ask God to open our hearts and minds to reveal the truth in His Word today.

NOVEMBER 14

Hard Times Come

"People can never predict when hard times might come. Like fish in a net or birds in a trap, people are caught by sudden tragedy." —*Ecclesiastes 9:12*

If you have lived for any length of time, there is a high probability that you have faced some difficulty in your life. This verse reminds us that we can never predict when sudden tragedy might strike us. But, what do we do when we encounter these hard times? What else does the *Holy Bible* say about hard times and tragedies?

First, we are to pray.

James 5:13 says, *"Are any of you suffering hardships? You should pray. Are any of you happy? You should sing praises."* And, I Thessalonians 5:17 tells us, *"Never stop praying."*

Next, we are to rejoice.

Romans 12:12 tells us to, *"Rejoice in our confident hope. Be patient in trouble, and keep on praying."* Philippians 4:4 says, *"Always be full of joy in the Lord. I say it again—rejoice!"*

And finally, we must believe.

In Mark 11:24, Jesus said, *"I tell you, you can pray for anything, and if you believe that you've received it, it will be yours."* Hebrews 11:6 tells us, *"And it is impossible to please God without faith. Anyone who wants to come to him must believe that God exists and that he rewards those who sincerely seek him."*

May we always pray, rejoice, and believe when hard times come, knowing that God still has ultimate control of all things.

NOVEMBER 15

Internal Cleansing

"You blind Pharisee! First wash the inside of the cup and the dish, and then the outside will become clean, too." —Matthew 23:26

We live in a vain world where outward appearance is often valued much higher than the inside. We spend hundreds of dollars on just the right clothes, hair, make-up, accessories, cars, and homes.

But, why do we do that when we know that it is the inside of man—the heart—that is most important?

It is often difficult for us to distinguish the condition of a man's heart when we have not known them long enough to see the fruit of their life. We are anxious to pass judgment about character based on face value, just as Samuel was when finding a king over Israel to replace Saul.

I Samuel 16:7 tells us, *"But the LORD said to Samuel, 'Don't judge by his appearance or height, for I have rejected him. The LORD doesn't see things the way you see them. People judge by outward appearance, but the LORD looks at the heart.'"*

I Peter 3:3-4 says, *"Don't be concerned about the outward beauty of fancy hairstyles, expensive jewelry, or beautiful clothes. You should clothe yourselves instead with the beauty that comes from within, the unfading beauty of a gentle and quiet spirit, which is so precious to God."*

It's tempting to pretty up our outward appearance, neglecting our heart. But, God looks at our hearts. And, eventually others see what is really in our hearts, too.

May we cleanse our hearts—not just our bodies—knowing the internal beauty of God will shine through us to make us outwardly beautiful—without the extra expense.

NOVEMBER 16

Cornucopia Of Love

"Let them praise the Lord for his great love and for the wonderful things he has done for them."
—Psalm 107:31

The cornucopia is a symbol of God's bounty and blessing, an abundance of God's provision, and a reason for thanksgiving and celebration.

It is at this time of year and all year 'round that we should thank and praise Him for the gifts of abundance He showers upon us constantly, and most of all, for the profound and immeasurable love He has for each of us.

God shows this love to us in so many different ways. Undoubtedly, the greatest demonstration of God's love for us was in the death of His son, Jesus, as Romans 5:8 reminds us, *"But God showed his great love for us by sending Christ to die for us while we were still sinners."*

If that isn't mind-blowing enough, He daily showers His unfailing love on us by providing for us, by forgiving us daily, and by showering us with His grace.

Knowing this, how can we not pour out the same cornucopia of love on everyone we meet? Let us do this as an expression of our love and thanksgiving to Christ.

I Peter 1:22 tells us, *"You were cleansed from your sins when you obeyed the truth, so now you must show sincere love to each other as brothers and sisters. Love each other deeply with all your heart."*

May we share the bounty of God's love with everyone we meet today and always.

NOVEMBER 17

Abundant Harvest

"The seed that fell on good soil represents those who truly hear and understand God's word and produce a harvest of thirty, sixty, or even a hundred times as much as had been planted!"
—Matthew 13:23

How is your crop looking?

Is your life producing a hundred times the seed that was planted there?

Or, has there been a drought in your life? Pestilence?

If your life is producing an abundant harvest for Christ, praise Him for His blessing in your life and the lives of those He's touched through you.

If there is a famine in the land or the harvest is lacking, ask God what it is that is keeping you from truly hearing and understanding His Word.

Perhaps your roots have not grown deep enough into His Word. Or, maybe the difficulties of life or the cares of this world are suffocating any harvest your life may produce.

Whatever the problem, take it to the Lord and ask Him to give you ears to hear that you might listen and understand.

For those who listen to His teaching, more understanding will be given, and they will have an abundance of knowledge (Matthew 13:12), and a harvest beyond imagination.

NOVEMBER 18

Carried Away

"I am warning you ahead of time, dear friends. Be on guard so that you will not be carried away by the errors of these wicked people and lose your own secure footing." —2 Peter 3:17

Oh, how quickly and easily we fall. If we learn anything at all from the Old Testament with regard to the Israelites, it is how quickly and easily they wandered away from God.

We are no different than the Israelites in the Old Testament. We must be always on guard to avoid the same fate.

In Matthew 26:41, Jesus reminds us, *"Keep watch and pray, so that you will not give in to temptation. For the spirit is willing, but the body is weak!"*

Consider Peter who adamantly told his Savior that even if he had to die with Him, he would never deny Him. Yet, before the next morning, he had denied Christ three times—even using profanity in fierce deprecation of his Lord.

You can probably recall a similar situation in your own life.

Oh, that we would heed our Savior's loving warning.

Let us watch and pray lest we fall into temptation and sin.

And, let us praise Him, and spend time dwelling on His goodness which leads us to repentance and a healthy, reverential fear of our Maker, lest we be carried away and lose our secure footing.

NOVEMBER 19

The Grateful Dead

"But those who die in the Lord will live; their bodies will rise again! Those who sleep in the earth will rise up and sing for joy! For your life-giving light will fall like dew on your people in the place of the dead!" —Isaiah 26:19

Death is a glorious event when we have a close, personal relationship with God. I Corinthians 15 talks about this principle in great detail. My favorite verse in this passage is I Corinthians 15:55, which says, *"O death, where is your victory? O death, where is your sting?"*

When we have a close relationship with Christ, the sting of death—its victory—is removed. The sting has been removed by the salvation we receive through Christ's death on the cross.

How grateful I am to receive victory over sin and death through Jesus Christ!

Psalm 116:15 says, *"Precious in the sight of the Lord is the death of His saints"* (NKJV).

How about you?

Do you look forward with expectation to this transition in your life with Christ?

Or, do you allow the mystery surrounding this future experience to overwhelm you?

Isaiah 57:2 tells us, *"For those who follow godly paths will rest in peace when they die."*

NOVEMBER 20

Forbidden Fruit

"But the Lord God warned him, 'You may freely eat the fruit of every tree in the garden—except the tree of the knowledge of good and evil. If you eat its fruit, you are sure to die.'"
—*Genesis 2:16-17*

"*Every tree in the garden—except . . .*" Except . . . Why is it that our sinful human nature finds the forbidden fruit sweeter than the rest?

We look longingly and lustfully at what we cannot have when we are dominated by our sin nature.

James 4:2-3 addresses this issue head on. It says, *"You want what you don't have, so you scheme and kill to get it. You are jealous of what others have, but you can't get it, so you fight and wage war to take it away from them. Yet you don't have what you want because you don't ask God for it. And even when you ask, you don't get it because your motives are all wrong—you want only what will give you pleasure."*

Pleasure . . .

I John 2:16 says, *"For the world offers only a craving for physical pleasure, a craving for everything we see, and pride in our achievements and possessions. These are not from the Father, but are from this world."*

This doesn't mean that we should never have any enjoyment. But, it does mean we shouldn't be consumed with our own selfish desires. God wants us to desire Him.

"Seek the Kingdom of God above all else, and live righteously, and he will give you everything you need" (Matthew 6:33).

NOVEMBER 21

Truly Unlimited Data

"I pray that from his glorious, unlimited resources he will empower you with inner strength through his Spirit." —Ephesians 3:16

My cellular telephone has limited data. There are times when I would really like to use the data-dependent features on my phone, but due to data and budget constraints, I don't.

But, I don't need a data plan to access God. He is available twenty four hours a day, seven days a week. He is always there, and His resources are beyond anything we could ever imagine.

I often see the resources entrusted to me as very limited. But, when our resources are committed to God, there is nothing that they cannot accomplish for His purposes. He has an infinite supply of all good things.

Romans 11:33 says, *"Oh, how great are God's riches and wisdom and knowledge! How impossible it is for us to understand his decisions and his ways!"*

Philippians 4:19 continues this promise with, *"And this same God who takes care of me will supply all your needs from his glorious riches, which have been given to us in Christ Jesus."*

Do you need the Holy Spirit to empower you with inner strength?

Seek God—the source of all power and all good things.

He is always with us.

That's truly unlimited data.

NOVEMBER 22

Suffering Servant

"In all their suffering he also suffered, and he personally rescued them. In his love and mercy he redeemed them. He lifted them up and carried them through all the years." —Isaiah 63:9

In the Old Testament, we read the account of God personally rescuing the Israelites from their captivity in Egypt. Their suffering caused Him to suffer, and so He carried them through the wilderness as they wandered for forty years—and wandered away from Him.

Jesus Christ personally rescues sinners—both the living and those yet to be born—through His suffering and death on the cross.

And, He continues to carry us each and every day, suffering as we suffer, and redeeming us because of His great love and mercy.

He is the King who rules from the position of a servant, and He bears all of our burdens.

Philippians 2:6-8 says, *"Though he was God, he did not think of equality with God as something to cling to. Instead, he gave up his divine privileges; he took the humble position of a slave and was born as a human being. When he appeared in human form, he humbled himself in obedience to God and died a criminal's death on a cross."*

May we learn what it is to suffer with Him, to experience the mighty power that raised Him from the dead (Philippians 3:10-11). And, may we learn that to be greatest of all in His Kingdom, we must be servant of all (Mark 9:35).

NOVEMBER 23

A Thanksgiving Feast

"Then Jesus took the loaves, gave thanks to God, and distributed them to the people. Afterward he did the same with the fish. And they all ate as much as they wanted." —John 6:11

At Thanksgiving time, many people remember America's first Thanksgiving between the pilgrims and the Indians—a wonderful time in the history of our country. There was so much to be thankful for then, and there is so much to be thankful for now.

But, I am also reminded of a different Thanksgiving feast. The Thanksgiving meal that comes to my mind is found in John 6:1-12. Verse 2 says, *"And a huge crowd, many of them pilgrims on their way to Jerusalem for the annual Passover celebration, were following him wherever he went, to watch him heal the sick."*

These pilgrims were seeking a new life, too. And, although they feasted on five loaves of bread and two small fish rather than turkey and dressing, they were every bit as thankful. By the time the meal was over, these pilgrims realized they had found the Savior—Jesus.

Have you found the Savior? If so, you have so very much to be thankful for! Life with Christ is a constant blessing!

"For the despondent, every day brings trouble; for the happy heart, life is a continual feast" (Proverbs 15:15).

If you haven't found Christ, I pray that you will find Him today. And, if you *have* found Christ, I pray that you will share your feast with someone else this Thanksgiving.

May this be the best Thanksgiving you've ever had in your life.

NOVEMBER 24

Lemon Drops And Gopher Holes

"Yes, you have been with me from birth; from my mother's womb you have cared for me. No wonder I am always praising you!" —Psalm 71:6

I still recall vividly the day of my salvation, although I was only five years old. My mother had given me the usual lemon drops to minimize fidgeting and chatter in church, and I had put my head down in her lap as the sermon began. Mother rubbed my head gently, and I usually fell fast asleep.

Daddy was the pastor, and it was easy to tell when the invitation time was nearing on any given Sunday, as the volume and voracity of his speech would increase dramatically. I was often startled awake, popping my head up from the pew like a gopher roused from its hole.

But, this particular Sunday was different. There was no napping in Mother's lap, even though my head was down. I heard every word my father said; although, I couldn't recall a single one. The words went straight to my heart—convicting me of my sin and need for Him.

I was overwhelmed with God's love for me, His care of me, and my need for Him, and I accepted Him as my Savior.

Perhaps your story is similar, or maybe it is quite different from mine. In either case, our loving Heavenly Father has been with us, caring for us and preparing us from our mother's womb.

May we spend this day and every day with an overwhelming attitude of thanksgiving and praise for the one who loves and cares for us more than anyone else, more than we can ever possibly imagine.

NOVEMBER 25

Ambassador Of Thanksgiving

"And whatever you do or say, do it as a representative of the Lord Jesus, giving thanks through him to God the Father." —Colossians 3:17

Whether you recognize it or not, you are an ambassador for Christ. You have been an ambassador since the day you accepted Him into your life.

On that day and thereafter, people have been watching you. They have been watching everything you say and everything you do. And, all of those things that you say and do are influencing the future actions of the ones who have been watching you.

It is a big responsibility, being a Christian.

Are you taking it seriously?

Or, when you fall, do you say, "Cut me some slack! I'm human!"

This kind of response is simply an excuse to sin.

Ephesians 5:6 warns us, *"Don't be fooled by those who try to excuse these sins, for the anger of God will fall on all who disobey him."*

May we take our responsibility seriously, realizing we are God's Ambassador, revealing a heart of thanksgiving in everything that we say and do.

NOVEMBER 26

A.m. Vs. F.m.

"Then a cloud overshadowed them, and a voice from the cloud said, 'This is my dearly loved Son. Listen to him.'" —Mark 9:7

There are two different frequencies I can tune my heart and mind to listen to in this world: *a.m.*, that is, the voices that are *against me*; and, *f.m.*, the voices that are *for me*.

Which frequency are you listening to?

I've noticed on my radio that *a.m.* radio stations have more static than *f.m.* stations. It is also harder to get a clear, uninterrupted signal on *a.m.*

It is the same with the voices in life.

The *a.m.* voices in this world are muddled and confusing. They give no clear direction, and they point us in the pathway of defeat. These voices also lead us into temptation and sin. They take a small truth and wrap it up in a great big lie.

On the other side, the *f.m.* voices are clear, fresh, unmuddled, and filled with God's positive and encouraging truth. When we are attuned to the voice of our Heavenly Father, there is no static. He comes in loud and clear.

John 5:25 says, *"And I assure you that the time is coming, indeed it's here now, when the dead will hear my voice—the voice of the Son of God. And those who listen will live."*

Which frequency are you tuned into today?

"What shall we say about such wonderful things as these? If God is for us, who can ever be against us" (Romans 8:31)?

NOVEMBER 27

Mind Your Own Business

"Make it your goal to live a quiet life, minding your own business and working with your hands, just as we instructed you before." —I Thessalonians 4:11

Are you a busybody?

Do you have difficulty minding your own business?

Perhaps you have a desire to control things that are out of your control.

Often, out of a desire to control situations and people, we meddle where we don't belong.

Have you ever done that?

Perhaps you see it as just trying to help.

While there are definitely times where our help and input are needed and desired, meddling is distinctly different. It is imposing our way on others where it doesn't belong.

When we meddle in other people's affairs, we are really usurping God's authority in our life as well as theirs.

Daniel 2:21 reminds us, *"He controls the course of world events; he removes kings and sets up other kings. He gives wisdom to the wise and knowledge to the scholars."*

But, when we allow the Holy Spirit to control us, we have no need to control others or meddle where we don't belong.

May we learn to mind the business of God and allow Him to have complete control of all things.

NOVEMBER 28

House Of Hypocrites

"He said to them, 'The Scriptures declare, My Temple will be called a house of prayer,' but you have turned it into a den of thieves!" —Matthew 21:13

Is the church you attend a house of prayer? Or, is it more like a house of hypocrites? Certainly, none of us has obtained perfection, but what is the overwhelming influence in your congregation?

In Matthew 23, Jesus addressed the religious leaders about their hypocrisy at length. He called them blind guides, blind fools, hypocrites, snakes, and sons of vipers. He said everything they did was for show. There was no sugarcoating here.

Matthew 23:15 says, *"What sorrow awaits you teachers of religious law and you Pharisees. Hypocrites! For you cross land and sea to make one convert, and then you turn that person into twice the child of hell you yourselves are!"*

Christ reminded the religious leaders that they were ignoring the more important aspects of Christianity—justice, mercy, faith, purity—for the sake of burdening converts with the letter of the law, down to the smallest detail.

Does this sound like your congregation?

If so, what do you do?

Jesus sent prophets, wise men, and teachers of the law to bring needed change, but they were killed, flogged, and chased from city to city.

May we pray for God to convict us of sin and bring revival to our churches, that we may be catalysts for change in obedience to the will of our Heavenly Father.

NOVEMBER 29

We Gather Together

"For where two or three gather together as my followers, I am there among them." — Matthew 18:20

What an awesome promise to know that when we gather together as followers of Christ, He is in our midst.

He knows why we are gathering.

He knows the need.

And, He responds.

He goes beyond our need.

Matthew 18:19 says, *"I also tell you this: If two of you agree here on earth concerning anything you ask, my Father in heaven will do it for you."*

That is an amazing promise.

Considering this promise, as His followers, we should gather together frequently.

Hebrews 10:25 reminds us of our need to be together as God's children when it says, *"And let us not neglect our meeting together, as some people do, but encourage one another, especially now that the day of his return is drawing near."*

May we never forget nor neglect the unity that we have as we gather together as followers of Christ Jesus our Lord.

NOVEMBER 30

Remember

"He took some bread and gave thanks to God for it. Then he broke it in pieces and gave it to the disciples, saying, 'This is my body, which is given for you. Do this to remember me.'"
—Luke 22:19

Do you remember what Christ has done for you?
Do you remember the price He paid for your sins?
He gave His life.
He gave His perfect, sinless life.
He gave it for your sin and for mine.
Do you remember this beautiful, generous gift that was lavished upon you, every time you break bread?
What else has Christ done for you?
Do you remember all of the blessings He has so richly and generously provided?
How often do you recall His love for you?
How often do you allow Him to use this remembrance to change your heart, and in turn, your attitude?
2 Timothy 2:8 tells us, *"Always remember that Jesus Christ, a descendant of King David, was raised from the dead. This is the Good News I preach."*
Always remember.
May we choose to remember the sacrifice, the death, the burial, and the resurrection of our perfect, loving Heavenly Father not only at times of communion, but always.

DECEMBER 1

Forget

"But forget all that—it is nothing compared to what I am going to do." —Isaiah 43:18

Do you have a difficult time letting go of painful past events?

Often our recollection of the past inhibits and limits our faith regarding God's ability to accomplish great things in the future. We must remember that God's ability to accomplish new things, great things, things never seen before, is infinite. And, we must forget the things that limit His power to work within us.

Ephesians 3:20 tells us, *"Now all glory to God, who is able, through his mighty power at work within us, to accomplish infinitely more than we might ask or think."*

We must learn to forget the things that have the potential to limit God's power within our lives.

Paul talked about the importance of this in Philippians 3:13b-14, when he said, *"but I focus on this one thing: Forgetting the past and looking forward to what lies ahead, I press on to reach the end of the race and receive the heavenly prize for which God, through Christ Jesus, is calling us."*

A runner doesn't look back when running a race. He looks forward to the goal.

May we look forward each day to fulfilling the goal of living for Christ with every ounce of our being each and every day.

DECEMBER 2

Be Strong In The Lord

"A final word: Be strong in the Lord and in his mighty power." —Ephesians 6:10

We have a wonderful opportunity as followers of Christ to depend upon Him for our strength. Our human strength cannot compare to the infinite strength available to us when we rely upon Him.

2 Corinthians 12:9 says, *"Each time he said, 'My grace is all you need. My power works best in weakness.' So now I am glad to boast about my weaknesses, so that the power of Christ can work through me."*

Do you ever feel as though your strength has failed and you cannot go one step further?

God's strength is perfect when our strength is gone.

Psalm 18:32 tells us, *"God arms me with strength, and he makes my way perfect."*

And, His strength never fails.

I Peter 4:19 says, *"So if you are suffering in a manner that pleases God, keep on doing what is right, and trust your lives to the God who created you, for he will never fail you."*

May the Holy Spirit fill you with His strength throughout every day of your life.

"He will keep you strong to the end so that you will be free from all blame on the day when our Lord Jesus Christ returns" (I Corinthians 1:8).

DECEMBER 3

Quiet, Please

"Teach me, and I will keep quiet. Show me what I have done wrong." —Job 6:24

Do you talk too much? Proverbs 10:19 says, *"Too much talk leads to sin. Be sensible and keep your mouth shut."*

Or, are you a good listener? Proverbs 12:15 tells us, *"Fools think their own way is right, but the wise listen to others."*

Perhaps you know someone who talks too much, and just can't seem to reign in their tongue.

The *Holy Bible* talks a great deal about the importance of being quiet. Many times we are so busy running our minds and mouths that we miss the blessings God is trying to bestow upon us.

That was the case in Deuteronomy 27 as Moses and the Levitical priests were giving the Israelites instruction regarding the blessing they were about to receive. They were about to enter the land flowing with milk and honey that God had promised them.

Yet, Deuteronomy 27:9 tells us, *"Then Moses and the Levitical priests addressed all Israel as follows: 'O Israel, be quiet and listen! Today you have become the people of the LORD your God.'"*

Israel was having trouble keeping quiet long enough to receive the promised blessing. What about you?

Are you so busy figuring things out and running your mouth that you fail to hear or receive the blessing of the Lord?

"Let all that I am wait quietly before God, for my hope is in him" (Psalm 62:5).

DECEMBER 4

The Antidote

"These miraculous signs will accompany those who believe: They will cast out demons in my name, and they will speak in new languages. They will be able to handle snakes with safety, and if they drink anything poisonous, it won't hurt them. They will be able to place their hands on the sick, and they will be healed." —Mark 16:17-18

When doctors treat a person bitten by a poisonous snake, they need the anti-venom, the antidote, to most effectively cancel out the effects of the poison. Without this antidote, the poison will ravage the body, destroying vital systems, often leading to the person's death.

If we have Christ in our lives, He is our antidote against the damaging effects of sin. Without Him in our lives, sin's destructive power will ravage our lives, leading to our ultimate destruction and death.

With Him, sin has no power over us.

I Corinthians 15:56-57 tells us, *"For sin is the sting that results in death, and the law gives sin its power. But thank God! He gives us victory over sin and death through our Lord Jesus Christ."*

If you, having the antidote, knew someone who had been bitten by a poisonous snake, wouldn't you share the antidote with them?

May you take up your cross and allow the Spirit to control your mind, will, and emotions today. And, may you share Christ, the antidote, with someone you meet today.

DECEMBER 5

Moral Cancer

"When there is moral rot within a nation, its government topples easily. But wise and knowledgeable leaders bring stability." —Proverbs 28:2

It is often espoused by doctors that too much sugar in the diet is not good for the human body. This same sugar that tastes so sweet and scrumptious, also causes tooth decay, as well as body decay by feeding the growth of cancer cells.

Proverbs 25:16 says, *"Do you like honey? Don't eat too much, or it will make you sick!"*

Sugarcoating sin does the same thing to our moral bodies. It causes our morals, our values, to decay, to rot. It waters down our convictions and destroys our moral compass.

When we say, "That's not so bad. What are you getting so upset about?" and "Everyone does it," we are sugarcoating sin.

When we go along with things that the *Holy Bible* tells us are unacceptable, we are sugarcoating sin.

When we refuse to speak up in the face of injustice and wrong, we are sugarcoating sin.

May we heed the words of Ephesians 5:5-7 which tells us, *"You can be sure that no immoral, impure, or greedy person will inherit the Kingdom of Christ and of God. For a greedy person is an idolater, worshiping the things of this world. Don't be fooled by those who try to excuse these sins, for the anger of God will fall on all who disobey him. Don't participate in the things these people do."*

May we focus our lives on seeking God with every ounce of our being so that we can avoid moral decay.

DECEMBER 6

More Of Him

"He must become greater and greater, and I must become less and less." —John 3:30

John the Baptist came to prepare the way for the Messiah. In Matthew 3:11, he tells us, *"I baptize with water those who repent of their sins and turn to God. But someone is coming soon who is greater than I am—so much greater that I'm not worthy even to be his slave and carry his sandals. He will baptize you with the Holy Spirit and with fire."*

John the Baptist understood his purpose.

He was a vessel.

John the Baptist knew that it wasn't all about him.

It was all about Jesus, and he took the task set before him seriously.

When those who were followers of John the Baptist recognized that Jesus, the Messiah, was gaining recognition, their selfish, me-first attitude became concerned and somewhat jealous.

But, John the Baptist was quick to set them straight.

John 3:28-29 tells us, *"You yourselves know how plainly I told you, 'I am not the Messiah. I am only here to prepare the way for him.' It is the bridegroom who marries the bride, and the best man is simply glad to stand with him and hear his vows. Therefore, I am filled with joy at his success."*

We are to be His vessel, too.

Have you asked Him to fill your vessel today?

DECEMBER 7

Identity Crisis

"Once you had no identity as a people; now you are God's people. Once you received no mercy; now you have received God's mercy." —I Peter 2:10

Who or what do you identify with? Is your identity wrapped up in a job? Your family? A club? An accomplishment? A certain group of people?

Where do you find your identity?

When God is our Savior, we receive a new identity. That identity is in Him. Everything we have and are, everything we do, our very being identifies with God.

Having our identity in Christ changes the way we live, too.

Matthew 7:20 tells us, *"Yes, just as you can identify a tree by its fruit, so you can identify people by their actions."*

And, Ecclesiastes 10:3 says, *"You can identify fools just by the way they walk down the street!"*

Often we face identity crises when we identify with and associate our value, our very worth with people and things other than Christ.

We are His people.

May we remember and heed the words of Psalm 100:3 which says, *"Acknowledge that the LORD is God! He made us, and we are his. We are his people, the sheep of his pasture."*

May you find your identity in Christ today.

DECEMBER 8

Ready Or Not

"Look, I will come as unexpectedly as a thief! Blessed are all who are watching for me, who keep their clothing ready so they will not have to walk around naked and ashamed." — Revelation 16:15

As a child, I always loved playing *Hide and Go Seek*. There was something about the familiar call of, "Ready or not, here I come" that always made my heartbeat quicken.

The thought of Christ's return, and the angels mighty trumpet blast, makes my heartbeat quicken so much more.

The *Holy Bible* tells us that no man knows the day or the hour of God's return—not the angels in heaven or even the Son. Only the Father knows (Matthew 24:36).

And, we are to make ready.

We are to be ready always for His return.

Matthew 25 tells us in the Parable of the Ten Virgins that five were wise, having enough oil when the bridegroom was delayed; and, five were foolish, as they did not have enough oil when the bridegroom was delayed in his return.

In this parable, the bridegroom represents Christ, we are the virgins, and the oil represents salvation. We cannot give salvation to others, nor can they receive it from us.

Salvation comes from God. Accepting this gift from Him and continuing to seek Him for all of our days is the only way to be ready for His return.

Ready or not, He will come.

May He find us all ready when He returns.

DECEMBER 9

Tree Of Life

"The seeds of good deeds become a tree of life; a wise person wins friends." —Proverbs 11:30

What kind of seed are you planting today? Are you sowing good deeds that will sprout and grow into a tree of life?

Or, are you planting seeds of strife that grow into discord and trouble?

The *Holy Bible* tells us in Hosea 10:12, *"I said, 'Plant the good seeds of righteousness, and you will harvest a crop of love. Plow up the hard ground of your hearts, for now is the time to seek the L*ORD*, that he may come and shower righteousness upon you.'"*

Each day, we are surrounded with opportunities to sow love, righteousness, and good deeds all around us. These opportunities are as simple as smiling and sharing a positive word with others. And, they are as complex as selling all we have and uprooting our family to meet the needs of others that God has placed upon our heart.

Planting a tree of life often requires us to step outside of our comfort zone, but that zone will soon become comfortable, as we allow the Holy Spirit to work within our heart, filling us with His gentle, generous, and loving nature.

What kind of tree will you plant today?

DECEMBER 10

Those Were The Days

"Those were the days when I went to the city gate and took my place among the honored leaders. The young stepped aside when they saw me, and even the aged rose in respect at my coming." —Job 29:7-8

Ah, the good ol' days... Do you ever allow your memory to languish in pleasurable thoughts of days gone by?

Job did. "Those were the days," he says.

Yet, the place that he finds himself in this passage of Scripture is far from the place he desires to be. His heart longs to return to the place of God's favor. He can't understand why he finds himself in this place of utter despair, and he desperately seeks the glory of days gone by.

The Israelites longed for "the good ol' days," too. But, for them, the good ol' days meant slavery in Egypt. Their new-found freedom of wandering in the wilderness left them desperate to return to the days of that which was familiar to them.

Do you ever feel like that?

Do you long for days gone by?

Isaiah 43 reminds us that God goes with us through every circumstance. He is always with us.

Just as God had a wonderful plan and restoration for Job and for the Israelites, He has a magnificent plan for you.

"The LORD will work out his plans for my life—for your faithful love, O LORD, endures forever. Don't abandon me, for you made me" (Psalm 138:8).

DECEMBER 11

The Tempter's Snare

"What sorrow awaits the world, because it tempts people to sin. Temptations are inevitable, but what sorrow awaits the person who does the tempting." —Matthew 18:7

Since the beginning of time, there have been temptations. Adam and Eve experienced temptation.

They fell.

There are countless examples of those who have fallen victim to the temptations they faced. But, what about those who have withstood temptation? There is Joseph, Daniel, Job, and the best example of all—the only example of perfection—Jesus.

I Corinthians 10:13 reminds us, *"The temptations in your life are no different from what others experience. And God is faithful. He will not allow the temptation to be more than you can stand. When you are tempted, he will show you a way out so that you can endure."*

It is bad enough when we yield to temptation, but Matthew 18:7 warns us of the sorrow that awaits us for tempting others to sin. It says, *"What sorrow awaits the world, because it tempts people to sin. Temptations are inevitable, but what sorrow awaits the person who does the tempting."*

Are you guilty of leading others into sin?

In the Old Testament, such rebellion was punishable by death (Deuteronomy 13:5).

May we pray that the Spirit would control our mind, leading to life and peace that we may avoid the tempter's snare.

DECEMBER 12

Joy Ahead

"So be truly glad. There is wonderful joy ahead, even though you have to endure many trials for a little while." —I Peter 1:6

Life can be full of trials and suffering. But, what a glorious promise God gives us in His Word.

I Peter 1:3b-5 tells us, *"Now we live with great expectation, and we have a priceless inheritance—an inheritance that is kept in heaven for you, pure and undefiled, beyond the reach of change and decay. And through your faith, God is protecting you by his power until you receive this salvation, which is ready to be revealed on the last day for all to see."*

There is a coming joy. It is found at the end of our journey, if we journey with Christ. Our joy is in who is waiting for us at the end.

But, there is also joy in the journey, itself.

Do you know what I mean?

The difficulties and trials of life are an opportunity for joy. James 1:2-4 tells us, *"Dear brothers and sisters, when troubles come your way, consider it an opportunity for great joy. For you know that when your faith is tested, your endurance has a chance to grow. So let it grow, for when your endurance is fully developed, you will be perfect and complete, needing nothing."*

Philippians 4:4 tells us, *"Always be full of joy in the Lord. I say it again—rejoice!"*

May we look forward with great anticipation to the coming joy.

DECEMBER 13

Help, I've Fallen

"The Lord helps the fallen and lifts those bent beneath their loads." —Psalm 145:14

Have you ever felt as though you've fallen so far that you're out of God's reach? Guess what?

You're never out of His reach.

Psalm 18:16 says, *"He reached down from heaven and rescued me; he drew me out of deep waters."*

Isaiah 59:1 says, *"Listen! The LORD's arm is not too weak to save you, nor is his ear too deaf to hear you call."*

When we are bent beneath our load, God is there to help us.

In Matthew 11:30, Jesus tells us, *"For my yoke is easy to bear, and the burden I give you is light."*

Many times the reason for our struggle is our own attempt to do things on our own—our way. We make things harder for ourselves than they need to be or ought to be, and we wind up falling off the path that God intends for us to follow. When we realize how far away from Him we've gotten, we often become discouraged.

Take heart.

Isaiah 41:10 says, *"Don't be afraid, for I am with you. Don't be discouraged, for I am your God. I will strengthen you and help you. I will hold you up with my victorious right hand."*

You can never fall so far that God can't lift you up.

DECEMBER 14

I Can Begin Again

"But the jar he was making did not turn out as he had hoped, so he crushed it into a lump of clay again and started over." —Jeremiah 18:4

Have you ever felt as though your life was not turning out quite as God's perfect plan would have it to?

Me, too.

Yet, we are all formed by His hand. Our Lord is the potter, and we are His clay (Isaiah 64:8). And, we must never argue with our Creator, as Isaiah 45:9 warns us, *"What sorrow awaits those who argue with their Creator. Does a clay pot argue with its maker? Does the clay dispute with the one who shapes it, saying, 'Stop, you're doing it wrong!' Does the pot exclaim, 'How clumsy can you be?'"*

There are times I feel as though the pain of life is so great that God must be crushing me back into a lump of clay to begin again. It is at these times that I realize with great joy that He is lovingly and carefully fashioning me into exactly who He wants me to be.

Philippians 1:6 promises us, *"And I am certain that God, who began the good work within you, will continue his work until it is finally finished on the day when Christ Jesus returns."*

Do you feel as though you are being crushed back into a lump of clay?

Be encouraged.

God isn't finished with you yet.

DECEMBER 15

Preparing For Winter

"She has no fear of winter for her household, for everyone has warm clothes." —Proverbs 31:21

Have you ever noticed how God has programmed all of nature to prepare for the changing of the seasons?

The bears begin to eat ravenously in autumn to prepare for their winter hibernation. Their coat of fur grows long and thick.

Then there are the ants. Proverbs 30:25 says, *"Ants—they aren't strong, but they store up food all summer."*

But, there is more to preparing for the winters in our lives than just having enough food and warm clothing.

Our spiritual winters require a steady diet of God's Word in preparation for the difficulties and spiritual famines that come. We must meditate on His Word day and night to combat the forces of evil when they come against us.

There is a day of battle coming, and we must be prepared for it. Yet, our preparation is not enough. The final victory belongs to God, and we must have faith enough to trust Him to be the victor.

Proverbs 21:31 tells us, *"The horse is prepared for the day of battle, but the victory belongs to the LORD."*

May you meditate on God's Word so that you will be prepared when winter comes.

DECEMBER 16

A Grand Entrance

"Then God will give you a grand entrance into the eternal Kingdom of our Lord and Savior Jesus Christ." —2 Peter 1:11

Can you imagine it?

A grand entrance into the eternal Kingdom of Jesus Christ? I can only imagine.

What must we do to receive this grand entrance into Christ's eternal Kingdom?

2 Peter 1 tells us that God has given us everything we need to live a godly life, that we should work hard to prove that we are among those God has called and chosen, and that when we grow in godliness, our lives become more productive and useful for Christ.

2 Peter 1:9 tells us, *"But those who fail to develop in this way are shortsighted or blind, forgetting that they have been cleansed from their old sins."*

Yet, 2 Peter 1:10 promises, *"So, dear brothers and sisters, work hard to prove that you really are among those God has called and chosen. Do these things, and you will never fall away."*

What a glorious promise. God's Word is full of amazing promises.

The Christian life requires effort. It is not a mindless pursuit. A great deal of work is required.

But, the reward . . . is a grand entrance into God's eternal Kingdom.

DECEMBER 17

Clear Channel Communication

"My words are plain to anyone with understanding, clear to those with knowledge." — Proverbs 8:9

Do you ever have difficulty hearing the voice of wisdom in the mix of all the other voices screaming in the world?

This passage of Scripture tells us that the voice of wisdom is plain to anyone with understanding, and clear to those with knowledge.

But, how do you get knowledge and understanding?

The *Holy Bible* tells us clearly that knowledge and understanding come from the teaching of God.

Matthew 13:12 says, *"To those who listen to my teaching, more understanding will be given, and they will have an abundance of knowledge. But for those who are not listening, even what little understanding they have will be taken away from them."*

When we listen to the teaching of Christ, He opens a clear channel of communication for us into His wisdom. This wisdom will guide us every step of our lives as we follow God's perfect will.

James 3:13 tells us, *"If you are wise and understand God's ways, prove it by living an honorable life, doing good works with the humility that comes from wisdom."*

May you listen to the teachings of Christ, that you may hear Him communicating clearly to you right now.

DECEMBER 18

Wonderful, Merciful Savior

"The faithful love of the Lord never ends! His mercies never cease. Great is his faithfulness; his mercies begin afresh each morning." —Lamentations 3:22-23

The beautiful promise of this verse brings me to tears as I recount, with gratitude, the many sins my precious Savior has forgiven me.

What about you?

He has removed my sins as far from me as the east is from the west (Psalm 103:12). I cannot help but be overwhelmed with thanksgiving and praise for the richness of His mercy, His forgiveness, and His faithfulness.

Even when I am unfaithful, God is faithful.

When I am unlovable, God loves me.

When I don't deserve mercy, God is merciful.

Have you praised Him for having a fresh supply of mercy for you this morning?

Is your heart full of thanksgiving for all that Christ is doing in and through your life, regardless of your circumstance?

Psalm 103:2 says masterfully, *"Let all that I am praise the Lord; may I never forget the good things he does for me."*

May His deep, abiding love spur us on to acts of obedience, faithfulness, love, and bearing much good fruit.

DECEMBER 19

All That Glitters

"Your instructions are more valuable to me than millions in gold and silver." —Psalm 119:72

It starts at an early age . . . that pursuit of money and material things. It doesn't take us long to figure out how the world works.

Money makes the world go 'round.

But, that's the *world's* way.

What about God's way?

In Matthew 6:24, Jesus tells us, *"No one can serve two masters. For you will hate one and love the other; you will be devoted to one and despise the other. You cannot serve both God and money."*

Proverbs 11:28 says, *"Trust in your money and down you go! But the godly flourish like leaves in spring."*

And, I Timothy 6:17 reminds us, *"Teach those who are rich in this world not to be proud and not to trust in their money, which is so unreliable. Their trust should be in God, who richly gives us all we need for our enjoyment."*

All that glitters in God's world are the streets of gold. Seek His kingdom above all else, and live righteously, knowing that He will give you everything you need (Matthew 6:33).

DECEMBER 20

Revelation

"Remember, the sins of some people are obvious, leading them to certain judgment. But there are others whose sins will not be revealed until later. In the same way, the good deeds of some people are obvious. And the good deeds done in secret will someday come to light. "
—I Timothy 5:24-25

There is a judgment day coming one day for all of us.

Hebrews 9:27 tells us, *"And just as each person is destined to die once and after that comes judgment, so also Christ died once for all time as a sacrifice to take away the sins of many people. He will come again, not to deal with our sins, but to bring salvation to all who are eagerly waiting for him."*

One day, there will be a great revelation of all things that were once kept secret. Everything hidden will be brought out into the light for all the world to know and to see.

Luke 8:17 tells us, *"For all that is secret will eventually be brought into the open, and everything that is concealed will be brought to light and made known to all."*

But, these things are not for us to judge before God's appointed time.

As I Corinthians 4:5 says, *"So don't make judgments about anyone ahead of time—before the Lord returns. For he will bring our darkest secrets to light and will reveal our private motives. Then God will give to each one whatever praise is due."*

May we all live in such a way as to be ready for the day of God's revelation.

DECEMBER 21

Stealing The Limelight

"When you give to someone in need, don't do as the hypocrites do—blowing trumpets in the synagogues and streets to call attention to their acts of charity! I tell you the truth, they have received all the reward they will ever get." —Matthew 6:2

In our self-centered world of reality television in which we encourage everyone to be a star, we have clearly lost our proper focus on God.

It's not about me.

It's not about you.

It's all about Him.

That's what life is all about . . . Him.

It is sad that even our churches are filled with people longing to be seen, noticed, and recognized for all they are doing for God. Jealousy runs rampant because so-and-so was selected for a specific task, committee, or teaching assignment instead of us. And, rather than rejoicing at the advancement of God's Kingdom, we eagerly set a course toward building a *pseudo-Christian* kingdom of our own.

James 3:16 tells us, *"For wherever there is jealousy and selfish ambition, there you will find disorder and evil of every kind."*

Are you busy trying to steal God's limelight?

Remember, it's not about us.

It's all about God.

DECEMBER 22

His Story

"For a child is born to us, a son is given to us. The government will rest on his shoulders. And he will be called: Wonderful Counselor, Mighty God, Everlasting Father, Prince of Peace."
—Isaiah 9:6

Once upon a time, there was a baby born unlike any other had been or ever would be. This baby was God in human form.

He was the best teacher that ever lived, and the best storyteller, too.

He healed people of sickness, disease, and infirmities.

He brought people back to life after being dead for days!

And, the love He had . . . It was like nothing anyone had ever seen or imagined.

He loved us all—even those of us not yet born—so much that He died for all our sins.

But, He didn't stop there.

He came back from the dead, showing us that not even death could keep Him from loving us.

He was perfect in every way.

He never sinned—not even once.

O, come let us adore Him, our Wonderful Counselor, Mighty God, Everlasting Father, our Prince of Peace.

DECEMBER 23

Long-Expected Joy

"You also must be ready all the time, for the Son of Man will come when least expected."
—Luke 12:40

My firstborn child was a blessing that seemed to take forever. There had been seven long years of waiting before God's perfect timing brought her to be. Yet, joy doesn't come close to encompassing the feelings upon looking into her perfect little newborn face. She was, and is, a long-awaited blessing.

The baby, Jesus, was a long-expected blessing. Can you imagine how Simeon and Anna felt in Luke 2, as they beheld the long-awaited Savior of the world as a baby?

The *Holy Bible* gives us a glimpse of Simeon's reaction in Luke 2:30-35, *"I have seen your salvation, which you have prepared for all people. He is a light to reveal God to the nations, and he is the glory of your people Israel!"* Jesus' parents were amazed at what was being said about him. Then Simeon blessed them, and he said to Mary, the baby's mother, *"This child is destined to cause many in Israel to fall, but he will be a joy to many others. He has been sent as a sign from God, but many will oppose him. As a result, the deepest thoughts of many hearts will be revealed. And a sword will pierce your very soul."*

The world had waited so long for this miraculous birth.

I don't know about you, but I'm terrible at waiting--especially for something really good that I know is coming. True confessions: I always peeked in the present stack as a child at Christmas time.

Simeon and Anna got to peek in the present stack and see the very best gift anyone has ever seen—Jesus. They blabbed this tremendously juicy secret with great joy to all who would listen.

The wonderful hymn, entitled, "Come Thou Long-Expected Jesus" by Charles Wesley, says this: "Come, thou long-expected Jesus, born to set thy people free; from our fears and sins release us, let us find our rest in thee. Israel's strength and consolation, hope of all the earth thou art; dear desire of every nation, joy of every longing heart."

May Jesus fulfill your heart's every longing this Christmas. May you blab joyfully of His goodness at every opportunity. And, may you be ready whenever He chooses to return again.

DECEMBER 24

Jingle Bells

"Aaron will wear this robe whenever he ministers before the Lord, and the bells will tinkle as he goes in and out of the Lord's presence in the Holy Place. If he wears it, he will not die."
—Exodus 28:35

It is a beautiful picture.

The bells on Aaron's robe jingle, tinkle as he goes in and out of the Lord's presence in the Holy Place.

The robe was a protection for Aaron—given to him by God. It was a symbol of God's loving shield, honor, and favor.

This passage of Scripture gives a whole new meaning to the familiar Christmas carol.

Each time I pray at this time of year, I think of this traditional song, and quietly hum it in my heart as I enter the Lord's presence. Yet, I change the words a bit, to go something very simple like this:

> *Jingle bells, jingle bells*
> *Jingle all the way.*
> *Oh, what joy to enter into*
> *The Lord's presence today*

May you experience God's loving protection, His honor, favor, and joy as you humbly and reverently jingle into His presence this Christmas.

DECEMBER 25

Happy Birthday

"And you will have joy and gladness, and many will rejoice at his birth." —Luke 1:14

Don't you love a birthday party?

As we age, birthdays become all the more precious.

But, once upon a time, there was a birthday most precious.

It was the birthday of Jesus.

His was a spectacular party, complete with angels, amazing gifts, special party guests, and even a super bright star to tell everyone where the birthday party would take place.

People came from many miles for this birthday party.

And, the guest of honor . . . not just a king . . .

The King.

The King of all kings and Lord of all lords (I Timothy 6:15).

The angels—the armies of heaven—all praised God for His birth (Luke 2:13).

Just imagine it.

"For a child is born to us, a son is given to us. The government will rest on his shoulders. And he will be called: Wonderful Counselor, Mighty God, Everlasting Father, Prince of Peace" (Isaiah 9:6).

As Simeon said in Luke 2:32, *"He is a light to reveal God to the nations, and he is the glory of your people Israel!"*

May the birthday candle of Jesus shine brightly in our lives today and every day, and may all His wishes come true for your life and mine.

DECEMBER 26

Special Attention

"Then Jesus told this story: A man planted a fig tree in his garden and came again and again to see if there was any fruit on it, but he was always disappointed. Finally, he said to his gardener, 'I've waited three years, and there hasn't been a single fig! Cut it down. It's just taking up space in the garden.' The gardener answered, 'Sir, give it one more chance. Leave it another year, and I'll give it special attention and plenty of fertilizer. If we get figs next year, fine. If not, then you can cut it down.'" —Luke 13:6-9

As fruit trees in God's garden, we are expected to produce a good harvest, rather than simply taking up space in His garden. I am awed at the fact that I am even allowed to exist in God's wondrous garden!

If that fact alone were not astonishing enough, when we fail to produce a bountiful harvest for Christ, He pays special attention to us, providing plenty of fertilizer, pruning, watering, and caring for us in every possible way with the hope of fashioning us into the finest trees imaginable.

Then, and only then, when we fail to produce a harvest of good fruit in God's garden, Luke 13 tells us that we will be cut down and removed from the garden.

Do you feel the loving hand of the Master gardener's pruning shears upon your limbs?

Do you sense the special attention, care, and fertilizer being applied to your life?

Pay attention and yield to His special attention and care, that you may be the most bountiful tree in God's good garden.

DECEMBER 27

Dying God's Way

"A wise person thinks a lot about death, while a fool thinks only about having a good time."
—Ecclesiastes 7:4

Do you give much thought to your mortality? Do you think about what will be left of your time spent on earth after you have passed on?

You should.

Psalm 90:12 says so aptly, *"Teach us to realize the brevity of life, so that we may grow in wisdom."*

There is a focus, and thought is required if we are to live in accordance with the purposes of God.

We must be . . . intentional.

2 Corinthians 5:9 reminds us, *"Therefore we make it our aim, whether present or absent, to be well pleasing to Him."*

But, what about those times when we fail to be intentional?

2 Samuel 14:14 says, *"All of us must die eventually. Our lives are like water spilled out on the ground, which cannot be gathered up again. But God does not just sweep life away; instead, he devises ways to bring us back when we have been separated from him."*

God loves us with an everlasting love.

May the knowledge of this goodness draw us always to repentance and living life intentionally committed to His loving purposes for our life.

"The Lord cares deeply when his loved ones die" (Psalm 116:15).

DECEMBER 28

The Journey Ahead

"Then the angel of the Lord came again and touched him and said, 'Get up and eat some more, or the journey ahead will be too much for you.'" —*I Kings 19:7*

God lovingly delights in preparing His servants for life's journey, just as He prepared Elijah for his upcoming journey.

In Exodus 19:20, God promised His faithful protection and guidance to the Israelites on their journey in the wilderness, when He said, *"See, I am sending an angel before you to protect you on your journey and lead you safely to the place I have prepared for you."*

This journey is not too difficult if we walk in accordance with God's righteousness, as His Word tells us in Isaiah 26:7, *"But for those who are righteous, the way is not steep and rough. You are a God who does what is right, and you smooth out the path ahead of them."*

How wonderful that we have a loving Heavenly Father who prepares us for any and all difficulties in the journey ahead of us.

In Isaiah 42:6, God promised Israel, *"I will lead blind Israel down a new path, guiding them along an unfamiliar way. I will brighten the darkness before them and smooth out the road ahead of them. Yes, I will indeed do these things; I will not forsake them."*

May our loving Savior do the same for you and for me as we travel life's journey today.

DECEMBER 29

His Tender Touch

"The Lord is like a father to his children, tender and compassionate to those who fear him."
—*Psalm 103:13*

Our loving Lord is the perfect balance of strength and tenderness. Consider Job and the compassion with which God restored Him after He had endured much suffering.

James 5:11 tells us, *"We give great honor to those who endure under suffering. For instance, you know about Job, a man of great endurance. You can see how the Lord was kind to him at the end, for the Lord is full of tenderness and mercy."*

In my own life, there have been so many times in which I have cried out to the Lord, feeling as though I could not take one more ounce of difficulty or struggle.

Have you ever been there?

Each time I have cried out, our tender and compassionate Savior has answered me by taking the load He was waiting to carry all along.

Matthew 11:29 tells us, *"Take my yoke upon you. Let me teach you, because I am humble and gentle at heart, and you will find rest for your souls."*

May you grasp a deeper understanding of our Heavenly Father's tender touch and His love for you today.

DECEMBER 30

How Great Thou Art

"Before the mountains were born, before you gave birth to the earth and the world, from beginning to end, you are God." —Psalm 90:2

From the time I was a very small child, I listened to my father sing the well-known hymn, "How Great Thou Art". It was so much more than a song to him. The words encompassed a heartfelt prayer of gratitude to his beloved Lord.

When Carl Boberg of Sweden first penned the words to his poem, "O Store Gud" on March 13, 1886, which later became this beloved hymn, it was much more than just a poem to him, too. It was his own personal paraphrase of Psalm 8.

The author, Carl Boberg, gives the following inspiration for his poem:

"It was that time of year when everything seemed to be in its richest colouring; the birds were singing in trees and everywhere. It was very warm; a thunderstorm appeared on the horizon and soon thunder and lightning. We had to hurry to shelter. But the storm was soon over and the clear sky appeared. When I came home I opened my window toward the sea. There evidently had been a funeral and the bells were playing the tune of 'When eternity's clock calling my saved soul to its Sabbath rest.' That evening, I wrote the song, 'O Store Gud.'"[6]

Each time I hear George Beverly Shea, Cliff Barrows, or my father sing the words, my soul feels the evening joy and exhilaration with which God penned the words upon Carl Boberg's heart and mind.

"Then sings my soul, my Savior, God, to Thee. How great Thou art, how great Thou art!

---

6 Carl Boberg, quoted in Michael Ireland, "Veleky Bog: How Great is Our God! The story behind how a thunderstorm in Sweden prompted the writing of How Great Thou Art, one of Christianity's greatest and much-loved hymns" ASSIST News Service (Sunday, October 7, 2007).

DECEMBER 31

Home Again

"Don't let your hearts be troubled. Trust in God, and trust also in me. There is more than enough room in my Father's home. If this were not so, would I have told you that I am going to prepare a place for you? When everything is ready, I will come and get you, so that you will always be with me where I am."—John 14:1-3

When I was a little girl, I became homesick very easily. I couldn't stand to be away from my home and family for very long. Even when we were together on vacations, it was music to my ears to hear my mother say, "Home again, home again, jiggity-jig," as we pulled into the driveway after a long trip. There was, and is, no place like home.

At the age of seven, my mother became ill and had to be hospitalized for almost a year. Before she left, Mother came to me and said, "Tomorrow I have to go away, and I will be gone for a long time. But, don't worry. I'll be back."

As a seven-year-old, I didn't understand, and my heart was deeply troubled. "Where are you going?" I asked. "Why can't I go, too? When will you be back?" There were so many questions, and I knew I would be terribly homesick for my mother.

The disciples were deeply troubled that Jesus was telling them He would be going away, too. They didn't understand where He was going, or why they couldn't go. They didn't understand that His entire plan revolved around His love for them. They didn't understand that one day they would be home again—with Him.

One day, if Christ is your Savior, He will come to take you home again, too. And, there is no place like it. One day we will no longer be homesick—we will be home again, home again (jiggity-jig).

About the Author

Author Priscilla Doremus accepted Christ at the age of five and has written books, poems, and stories from a very early age. She is the author of *Prayers for Times of Crisis* and has a passion for sharing Christ through the written word.

Priscilla attended Baylor University, and has worked in the field of Insurance and Risk Management for many years. She has two children, and her family currently makes their home in Sugar Land, Texas.

For more information, visit Priscilla's blog at:
priscilla-joy.blogspot.com

www.ingramcontent.com/pod-product-compliance
Lightning Source LLC
Chambersburg PA
CBHW030902080526
44589CB00010B/101